# DNA IN FORENSIC SCIENCE
## Theory, Techniques and Applications

**ELLIS HORWOOD SERIES IN FORENSIC SCIENCE**

*Series Editor:* JAMES ROBERTSON, Head of Forensic Services Division, Australian Federal Police, Canberra, Australian Capital Territory

# DNA IN FORENSIC SCIENCE
## Theory, Techniques and Applications

*Editors*

**J. ROBERTSON** B.Sc., Ph.D.
Head of Forensic Services Division
Australian Federal Police
Canberra, Australian Capital Territory

**A. M. ROSS** M.Ap.Sci.
Senior Forensic Scientist
Forensic Science Centre, Adelaide, South Australia

**L. A. BURGOYNE** Ph.D.
Reader in Biological Sciences
Flinders University, Adelaide, South Australia

**ELLIS HORWOOD**
NEW YORK   LONDON   TORONTO   SYDNEY   TOKYO   SINGAPORE

First published in 1990 by
**ELLIS HORWOOD LIMITED**
Market Cross House, Cooper Street,
Chichester, West Sussex, PO19 1EB, England

A division of
Simon & Schuster International Group

© Ellis Horwood Limited, 1990

Typeset in Times by Ellis Horwood Limited
Printed and bound in Great Britain
by Bookcraft (Bath) Limited, Midsomer Norton

---

British Library Cataloguing in Publication Data

DNA in forensic science.
1. Forensic medicine. Role of organisms. DNA
I. Robertson, James II. Ross, A. M. III. Burgoyne, L. A.
614′.1
ISBN 0–13–217506–1

---

Library of Congress Cataloging-in-Publication Data

DNA in forensic science: theory, techniques, and applications
/ editors, J. Robertson, A. M. Ross, L. A. Burgoyne.
p. cm. — (Ellis Horwood series in forensic science)
ISBN 0–13–217506–1
1. DNA fingerprints. I. Robertson, James, 1950– . II. Ross,
A. M. (Alistair M.), 1948– . III. Burgoyne, L. A. (Leigh A.),
1939– . IV. Series.
RA1057.55.D64   1990
614.1–dc20                                     89–24495
                                                    CIP

# Table of contents

**3  Experimental techniques for the isolation and analysis of DNA
    from forensic materials**

Ivan Balazs, Michael Baird, Keven McElfresh and Robert Shaler

# Introduction

This is both an amateur's book and a user's book about DNA with the focus being on the practically useful information that can be gained from DNA in the forensic context. However, as the basic biology of DNA is inextricably bound up with the technology of gaining that information and its interpretation, these fundamentals are also covered.

Here is a very considerable challenge, a place where the legal practitioner and the scientific expert *must* meet. There is no choice; neither alone suffices. We hope that these chapters will help in this meeting.

For the lawyer, the uninformative acronym 'DNA' is not an encouragement to read on, and worse, its full name, deoxyribonucleic acid, not only confirms this bad initial impression but also, dangerously, assures one that this is the very sort of substance that is best left to the ivory towers of academia. Nothing could be further from the truth; DNA is fast becoming one more of those familiar modern monsters, another of those bodies of irresistible new knowledge that inevitably savages our old ethical landscape, compensates us with novel solutions to old problems but then leaves us a whole set of new problems.

The intent of this book is to allow the reader to access this complex field as little or as much as they wish. Thus some chapters are clearly more for the expert than others whilst there are chapters which are squarely aimed at the legal practitioner.

The first two chapters deal with the basic structure and organization of DNA in the organism. This lays the foundation for an understanding of the basis for individualization within a population. DNA is a relatively simple structure but like many things legal and scientific the simplicity is often lost in a mixture of jargon and endless details. We hope that these chapters in conjunction with the glossary help to clear away any confusion.

Those of us who were biology students twenty years or more ago really appreciated the enormous bank of diversity within the human genome. Chapter 1 in particular leads the reader step by step into the structure of DNA revealing how this diversity is encompassed in such an apparently simple structure.

Molecular biology has undergone an explosive development phase in the last few years and, inevitably, in such a rapidly moving field, current knowledge will date. Indeed some details in this book will be superseded even before it reaches the shelf! However the basic material presented in the first two chapters should not alter beyond recognition in the foreseeable future.

In some ways this will be less true of the information presented in the middle of the book. Here, our authors have attempted to cover some of the currently useful protocols and approaches used for forensic applications. At present, there are three broad approaches in application or development. The earliest to be successful, exemplified by the so-called 'minisatellite' technology of Jeffries and co-workers, then the less sensitive, but simpler, 'local detail' approach using 'single loci' and now the highly sensitive PCR (polymerase chain amplification) approach which promises to have the interpretive simplicity of the second approach but with the ability to work with ultra-low amounts of evidential material.

The non-scientist may well wonder why one of these approaches would be selected over the others and what are the underlying principles behind the methods which will remain long after any particular recipe has been superseded.

The main lesson is that all the current technical options merely represent the different prices to be paid in accessing different aspects of the large store of information within the DNA of a human being and the paying of these prices, that is to say, the choosing of a technology, can only be done wisely when one has carefully weighed a number of practical factors. The body of available technology may change its details but the necessity of weighing these factors is most unlikely to change.

This problem of how much to pay for the information begins with the basic questions.

How much biological sample do you have access to?

How much has it been subjected to the random degradative processes of decay?

What amount of information are you prepared to pay for?

And what background of knowledge exists for the interpretation of the information that each method extracts?

How do these questions lead to a choice of technologies?

The current names of the technologies may be of little lasting interest as this is a field of fashion in names and acronyms like 'minisatellites', 'macrosatellites', RFLP, PCR and VNTR and these collections of letters will probably change as technical improvements accumulate and transform. However, it does seem that there are two broad categories within these technologies, there are the 'broad brush' technologies for extracting information from DNA and there are those that concentrate on local details. The 'broad brush' methods are those that have a quick look at some of the grosser features of the arrangement of the genetic information within DNA. These methods usually require high-quality DNA and large amounts of DNA and are thus only really well adapted to paternity studies and clinical usage. Their advantage is speed and convenience and, currently, in the accumulated experience of their interpretation. The broad brush approaches do differ individually from each other, some will tolerate a little more degradation of the DNA than others, some require less DNA than others, some give less 'gel bands' per track and thus less confusing results than others. Then again, these latter require more 'tracks' and this means even more tissue and more work-cost. The 'minisatellites', the VNTR, and the 'macrosatellites' are 'broad brush' methods perfectly *valid* for criminal studies but requiring so much high-quality DNA that they are not commonly applicable.

Alternatively, the methodology that concentrates on local detail, selects out a small section of the DNA information and interprets it in detail. Currently there are two technologies that fall into this category. Firstly there is the old technology of 'unique sequence RFLP' often only referred to as 'RFLP'. This requires much high-quality DNA and produces only a little information per unit effort. It is thus only highly suitable for clinical purposes and is of some value in paternity studies. Once again, it is valid for criminal detection but unlikely to be usable.

Then there is the PCR (polymerase chain reaction) technique and the allied processes. This technique amplifies even the most minute traces of DNA from tiny and degraded tissue samples. A combination of this technique with 'amplifer sequencing' promises to be highly applicable to criminal science. Its current disadvantage is its newness and the caution required in the interpretation of its results. However, there can be little doubt that this or derivatives of it, will be the main basis of criminal detection technology in the future.

To the scientist the choice of technology will depend on the type of material to be analysed. The broad-brush approaches are most suited to parentage testing where relatively unlimited, undegraded sample is available. For blood stains and other 'criminal' case-samples PCR is likely to be the method of choice in the future. Also, and regrettably, it is also becoming clear that the choice for any particular laboratory may be dictated less by scientific criteria than by commercial pressures.

Whatever the method applied there are now clear warning signs to the forensic community that the introduction of DNA into the courts will not be without challenge and problems. It is the responsibility of the scientist to proceed with caution and to make certain that exemplary standards of quality assurance are met. Recent evidence would suggest that in our haste to apply DNA technology these standards have not always been defined much less agreed by the forensic community at large!

Our final chapters present a lawyer's and scientist's perspective of the problems which DNA may encounter as it reaches the courts.

The challenge in assembling a volume like this together has been considerable. Chapters have been included on topics which were not even conceived of when the book was begun. The temptation to wait until the field has matured infects everyone but DNA is in use *now* and so the field must be examined now, and by all of those concerned. The scientist and the lawyer must both accept the challenge of the new technology and we hope that this volume will provide considerable help to both parties.

# 1

# Structure and function of DNA: an introduction

Rory M. Hope
Department of Genetics, University of Adelaide, GPO Box 498, Adelaide, South Australia, 5000

## 1.1 INTRODUCTION

We commence life as a single celled **zygote**, a fertilized egg about 0.1 mm in diameter and weighing less than 1 $\mu$g. Replication of this cell, and subsequent differentiation, give rise to a large diversity of specialized tissues, culminating in an incredibly complex yet exquisitely coordinated human adult consisting of more than $10^{14}$ cells and weighing about 70 kg. The bulk of the cells in such an organism (the **somatic cells**) are mortal and do not directly contribute to future generations. In a sense, immortality is achieved by transmission of genetic material to future generations *via* successful reproduction. The reproductive cells (**gametes**) retain the potential, when combined with a gamete supplied by the opposite sex, for repeating the whole course of development from zygote to adult. The numerous biological 'instructions' that enable these developmental and functional processes to occur are encoded in the molecular configuration of the chemical of heredity, **deoxyribonucleic acid (DNA)** which, together with **protein**, constitute the 23 pairs of **chromosomes** in each somatic cell. Some DNA also occurs in the **mitochondria**, cellular organelles concerned with the production and chemical storage of energy. Thus it is to the chromosomal and mitochondrial DNA molecules that we must look for answers to what are probably amongst the most fascinating questions about life: how is biological information encoded in DNA, how is it transmitted from cell to cell and from generation to generation, and how is the expression of this information regulated in time and space? The more modest aims of forensic science, however, are concerned with developing reliable methods for establishing identity based on naturally occurring differences between individuals. Therefore, questions of direct relevance to forensic science are: what genetic differences exist between the DNA of an individual and between the individuals of a population, and how can these differences be utilized to advantage in forensic analyses?

The recent widespread application of the so called 'genetic engineering' techniques, which enable DNA to be manipulated and its structure explored with a high level of precision, have brought about a 'revolution' in the biological sciences which will, in the course of time, pervade many aspects of human endeavour. It will become desirable, and in many instances essential, particularly for those of us who completed our formal education before the advent of the DNA revolution, to gain a basic understanding of the structure and function of DNA and the principles and techniques involved in its manipulation. This is especially so in the field of forensic science where the pressures for applying new techniques are strong, and where application of the new DNA technology promises so much. Fortunately, despite the seemingly complex biological role of DNA, its structure and properties relevant to its use in forensic science can be appreciated without recourse to more than an elementary understanding of molecular genetics and biochemistry. The purpose of this chapter is to outline the general properties of DNA, with emphasis on its structure and function, in order to provide a framework against which the more specialized areas covered in the remainder of this book can be evaluated.

## 1.2 DNA AS THE CHEMICAL OF HEREDITY

In the early 1900s it became clear from studies on chromosome behaviour during cell division, and especially from studies of **meiosis** (the type of cell division that gives rise to gametes), that **genes**, the theoretical (and at the time somewhat mystical) units that obey Mendel's laws of inheritance, could be given a physical reality by supposing that they were an integral component of chromosomes. These are the thread-like structures that could be observed microscopically in the nucleus during cell division. The challenge then shifted towards giving genes a chemical reality. Chromosomes were known, at least since the early 1920s, to be composed of DNA (see 1.3) and protein (see 1.8) so these two substances became the main contenders for the chemical constituent of heredity. For many years, in fact up until at least 1950, protein was the front runner, partly because it was known to occur in a wide variety of forms suggesting a potential complexity capable of information storage. DNA, on the other hand, was thought at this time to have a simple homogeneous structure quite incapable of carrying information encoded in its molecular configuration. Chargaff (1950) showed that the earlier ideas of DNA homogeneity were incorrect, and that DNA existed in a wide variety of chemical configurations. His findings, when coupled with some earlier and very elegant genetic experiments using microorganisms (see Hershey & Chase 1952) convinced biologists that DNA was indeed the genetic material. This conclusion was ultimately consolidated by the exciting discovery in 1953 of the structure of DNA by James Watson and Francis Crick (Watson & Crick 1953), an event which marks the birth of modern molecular genetics. The Watson and Crick structure of DNA, based on X-ray diffraction studies and molecular model building, explained for the first time not only how this molecule could encode biological information, but also how the information could be precisely replicated during cell division.

A convenient feature of DNA particularly when compared with many other biochemical macromolecules, including proteins and **carbohydrates**, is the basic simplicity of its assembly.

## 1.3   THE STRUCTURE OF DNA

The structural units of DNA are deoxyribonucleotides, **nucleotides** for short. Nucleotides consist of three components:

(1) a 5 carbon sugar, deoxyribose;
(2) one or more phosphate groups (the nucleotide residues in DNA have a single phosphate group but the precursor molecules for DNA synthesis are nucleotide triphosphates), and
(3) a nitrogenous **base**.

The four different DNA nucleotides (listed below) possess identical sugar and phosphate groups but different bases.

| *Nucleotide* | *Corresponding base* | |
|---|---|---|
| deoxyadenosine monophosphate (dAMP) | adenine | (A) |
| deoxyguanosine monophosphate (dGMP) | guanine | (G) |
| deoxycytidine monophosphate (dCMP) | cytosine | (C) |
| deoxythymidine monophosphate (dTMP) | thymine | (T) |

The structure of the four bases, and the structure of a DNA nucleotide, are shown in Fig. 1.1.

A molecule of DNA is composed of the four nucleotide sub-units linked to form a long unbranched polynucleotide chain (Fig. 1.2). The nucleotides are linked by covalent phospho–diester bonds joining the 5′ C atom of one sugar to the 3′ C of the adjacent sugar *via* a phosphate group. Hence the 'backbone' of the DNA molecule is an invariant alternating series of sugar and phosphate residues. The specificity of DNA resides in its **base sequence**. (The terms 'base sequence', 'DNA sequence', and 'nucleotide sequence' are often used interchangeably). Note that the terminal nucleotides of single stranded DNA molecules have either a free 5′ phosphate or a free 3′ hydroxyl group (Fig. 1.2). This feature is used to orient DNA molecules. Cellular DNA occurs predominantly in a double stranded (duplex) form, the two polynucleotide strands being coiled around a common imaginary axis to form a double helix with bases projecting into the 'inside' of the helix, their planes being perpendicular to the helical axis. The two strands are linked by **hydrogen bonds** between pairs of bases, so called **complementary base pairs** (Fig. 1.1). Because of steric constraints imposed by the dimensions of the helix and atomic structure of the bases, adenine on one strand always pairs with thymine on the other *via* two hydrogen bonds, and guanine pairs with cytosine via three hydrogen bonds. These base pairing rules (A-T; G-C) are absolutely fundamental not only to the structure and function of DNA and **ribonucleic acid (RNA)** (see 1.4), but to many other biological processes not dealt with in this book.

The two strands of a duplex DNA molecule have opposite polarity and are said to be 'anti-parallel'; they are not identical in sequence. However, the base pairing constraints referred to above ensure that the sequence in one strand is the complement of the other. Therefore to specify the information content of a given duplex DNA molecule, it is necessary to record the base sequence of only one strand. By

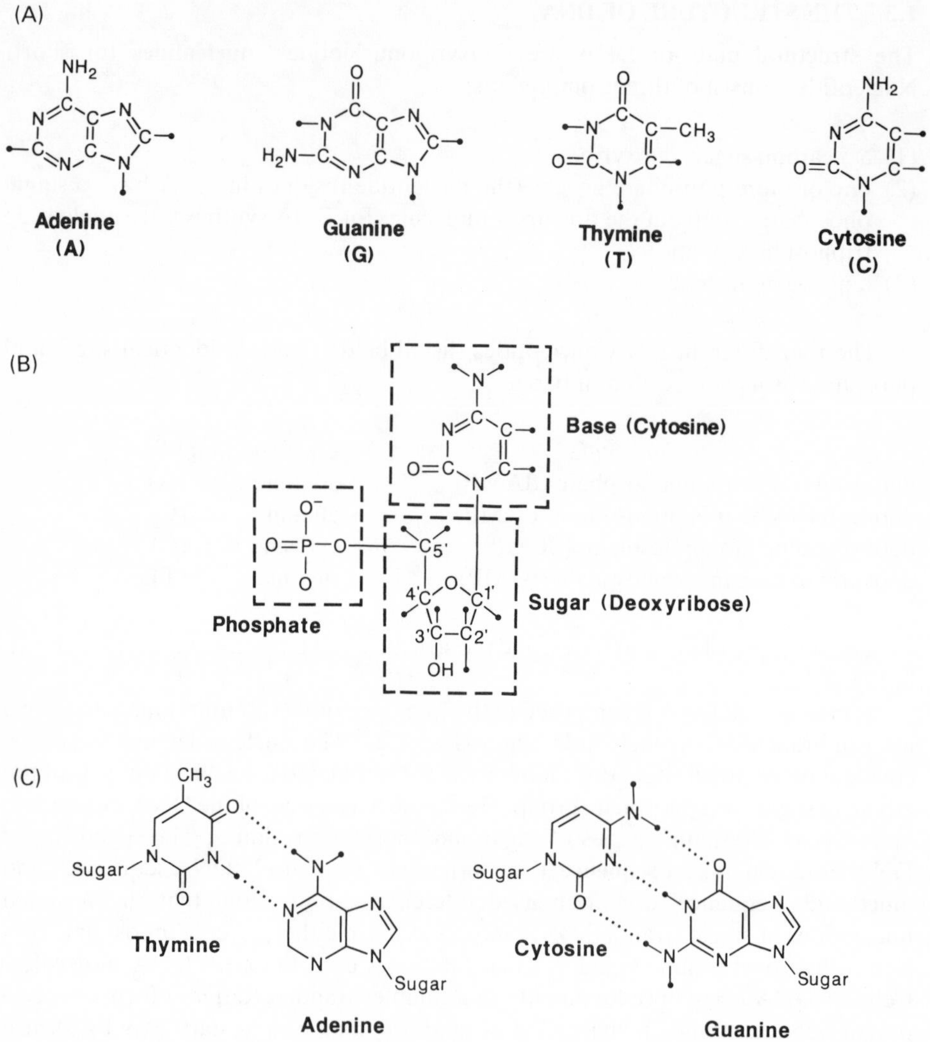

(A)

(B)

(C)

Fig. 1.1 — The structural components of DNA. (Some hydrogen atoms are indicated by dots). (A) Structure of the 4 DNA bases. (B) Structure of dCTP as an example of a nucleotide. The carbon atoms on the deoxyribose are conventionally numbered from 1′ to 5′. (C) Hydrogen bonds (repesented by dotted lines) between complementary pairs of DNA bases.

convention base sequences are recorded in a 5′ to 3′ orientation. For example, the small duplex molecule:

5′ ATGACCA 3′
3′ TACTGGT 5′

could be recorded simply as:

ATGACCA

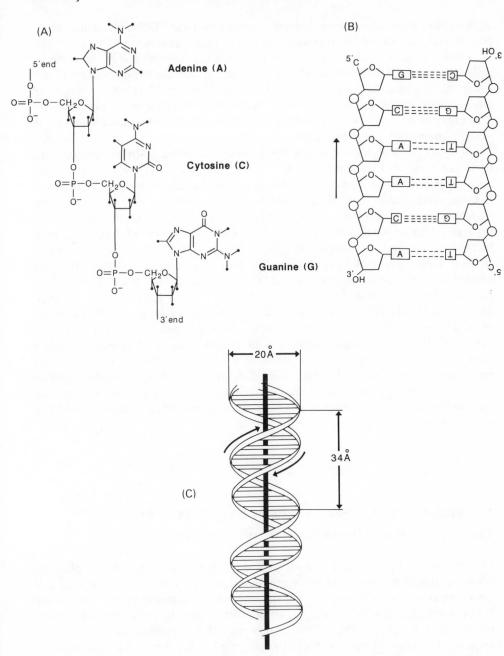

Fig. 1.2 — The structure of the DNA molecule. (Some hydrogen atoms are indicated by dots). (A) The structure of part of a single strand of DNA. (B) Schematic representation of DNA showing the antiparallel nature of the two strands and the hydrogen bonds linking base pairs. (C) Schematic representation of the DNA double helix as proposed by Watson and Crick (1953). The two strands of the helix represent the sugar-phosphate "backbones" of the molecule and the horizontal lines represent hydrogen-bonded base pairs. Distances are in Angstrom units (1 Å$=10^{-10}$ m).

without any loss of information. Indeed, for many purposes, DNA molecules can be conveniently, if incorrectly, considered as single linear sequences of bases.

The predominant helical form of DNA under normal cellular conditions is the so-called Watson and Crick right handed 'B form' which contains 10 nucleotide pairs for every 360 deg. revolution of the helix (Fig. 1.2). However, DNA has a degree of environmentally associated conformational flexibility. For example, a proportion of DNA may occur in a 'Z form' (see Rich *et al*. 1984) which is a left handed helix with about 12 nucleotides per revolution.

In comparison with the **covalent bonds** linking adjacent DNA nucleotides, the hydrogen bonds linking complementary bases in duplex DNA are relatively weak and may be broken by heat or by treatment with acid or alkali. Because of the extra hydrogen bond linking G-C compared with A-T base pairs, the melting temperature of DNA (i.e. the mid-point of the temperature range over which duplex DNA separates into its single strands) increases as the proportion of G-C base pairs increases. Melting temperature can thus be used to indicate the base pair composition of DNA. The molar ratio of (A+T) to (G+C) varies considerably between species and between different regions of DNA within a species. In contrast the base pairing rules ensure that the molar ratio of A to T is unity, and G to C is unity. Overall, human DNA contains about 40% (G+C) and melts at about 88°C under physiological conditions. As the temperature is lowered, melted duplex DNA will re-nature, the base pairs will re-form, and the strands take up their original helical conformation. Random molecular movement brings regions of complementary bases into juxtaposition and a zipper-like effect linking hydrogen bonds completes the duplex. This property of molecular recognition between DNA strands that contain complementary base sequences is utilized in a number laboratory techniques referred to in later chapters.

## 1.4   BIOLOGICAL CONSEQUENCES OF DNA STRUCTURE

There are three main consequences of the structure of DNA:

(1) The two complementary strands provide a mechanism for DNA replication whereby, during the so-called 'S' (synthesis) phase of the cell cycle, the hydrogen bonds break, the two strands separate, and each acts as a **template** (molecular mould) for the formation of a 'new' daughter strand with complementary base sequence to the parental strand (Kornberg 1980). An enzyme (DNA polymerase) catalyses the sequential addition of nucleotides to the growing DNA strands. As a consequence one DNA molecule becomes two by a process called 'semi-conservative replication'. Subsequently one cell becomes two by the process of **mitosis**.

(2) The base sequence provides a code for the storage and transmission of genetic information. A molecule of DNA only three base pairs long can potentially exist with $4^3 = 64$ different base sequences (AAA, AAT, AAG, AAC, ATA, etc.) A molecule 100 base pairs in length can exist with $4^{100}$ different sequences. DNA molecules are typically very long, their length being commonly measured in **kilobases (kb)**, 1 kb

being equivalent to a molecular length equal to 1000 base pairs of double stranded DNA or 1000 bases of single stranded DNA. As an example, the human X chromosome contains in excess of 150 million base pairs (150 000 kb) of DNA. A vast number ($4^{150\,000\,000}$) of different base sequences are possible in such a molecule. Only a minute fraction of all such sequences could ever have existed.

(3) DNA can act as a template for the formation of RNA (ribonucleic acid), the first step in protein synthesis. Like DNA, RNA is a polynucleotide, but the component nucleotides differ from DNA in the following ways: the sugar molecule is ribose instead of deoxyribose, and the base uracil replaces thymine. In addition, RNA is a single stranded molecule that cannot self-replicate but is synthesized on a DNA template in much the same general manner as daughter DNA strands are synthesized from parental templates during DNA replication. The RNA-DNA base pairing rules are: A-T; U-A; G-C; C-G. (The RNA base is shown first for each pair).

## 1.5   DNA IN CELLS

The total DNA content of a single human somatic cell is approx. $6 \times 10^6$ kb, weighs some 6 picograms, and has a **contour length** (i.e. molecular length when extended) of about 2 metres (Watson *et al.* 1987, Kornberg 1980). This constitutes nearly 1000 times the DNA content of a typical bacterial cell such as *E. coli*. The quantities of nuclear DNA in some different organisms are shown in Table 1.1.

**Table 1.1** — The quantities of nuclear DNA in some different organisms. Quantities are per haploid genome, i.e. the DNA content of only one set of chromosomes is given for organisms such as humans that possess two such sets. (Adapted from Fincham (1983) p. 4)

| Organism | Haploid DNA content per cell (approximate, in kb) |
|---|---|
| 0X174 (bacteriophage) | 5.5 |
| Adenovirus (virus) | 30.0 |
| *E. coli* (bacterium) | $4.5 \times 10^3$ |
| *S. cerevisae* (yeast) | $1.8 \times 10^4$ |
| *G. domestica* (fowl) | $1.3 \times 10^6$ |
| *X. laevis* (frog) | $3.0 \times 10^6$ |
| *M. musculus* (mouse) | $3.0 \times 10^6$ |
| *H. sapiens* (human) | $3.0 \times 10^6$ |
| *V. faba* (broad bean) | $1.2 \times 10^7$ |

Before DNA replication occurs, each of the 46 human chromosomes (23 homologous pairs) contains a single long duplex DNA molecule associated with proteins. The DNA/protein complex of chromosomes is called **chromatin**. After

DNA replication has finished but before mitotic cell division, each chromosome contains two **chromatids** joined at the **centromere**, each chromatid containing a single long duplex DNA molecule. The two chromatids of a chromosome have DNA molecules with identical base sequence. Subsequently, during mitosis, the centromere of each chromosome divides and the two chromatids segregate to the resultant daughter cells. The latter will then contain 46 chromosomes, each consisting of a single duplex DNA molecule. For a detailed account of the mechanical and genetical aspects of cell division, the reader is referred to Lewis & John (1964).

Human chromosomes vary considerably in DNA content. The largest, #1, contains about 250 000 kb corresponding to a contour length of about 8.5 cm. Apart from the mitochondrial 'chromosome' (16.5 kb), the smallest chromosomes (#21, #22, and Y) each contain about 50 000 kb corresponding to a contour length of about 1.4 cm. It is difficult to conceptualize the incredible amount of DNA in a single cell. If the entire base sequence of chromosome #11 (a typical-sized chromosome containing 137 000 kb DNA) was recorded thus:

...ATTACGTGTCACACCGTCAGGTVTAATGGCTTATTTAACACGCGTAGCACGTGGC...

over 2.2 million lines of print or about 47 000 pages would be required. Using the same scale, the DNA sequence of a single set of 23 chromosomes would require over 1 million pages of print.

This chromosomal DNA is packaged in a cell nucleus some 5 $\mu$m in diameter. It can be appreciated that a systematic and efficient form of DNA compaction is required. The packaging system must be sufficiently flexible to accommodate the changes in chromosome length that accompany the various stages of cell division. The total chromosomal length at maximum compaction (metaphase) is about 200 $\mu$m, requiring a packaging ratio (i.e. the ratio of DNA contour length to total chromosomal length) of up to 10 000. In non-dividing cells, chromosomes are far less compacted and individual chromosomes are not discernible, although, of course, they are still present.

Studies on the structure of chromatin have yet to unravel all the various levels of its structural organization. However, the basic sub-units of chromatin are **nucleosomes** (see Kornberg & Klug 1981) which form a series of linked repeating units, each being composed of a core group of proteins called histones, surrounded by two coiled loops of DNA containing about 140 base pairs (Fig. 1.3). Adjacent nucleosomes are connected by short stretches of linker DNA about 60 nucleotides long. Nucleosomes give DNA a packaging ratio of about six. The way in which the required higher order packaging organization is achieved is not fully understood. This packaging of DNA in cells is dealt with in more detail in Chapter 2 of this book.

## 1.6   DNA SEQUENCING

In the ten years that have elapsed since methods first became widely available for determining the order of the four bases A,G,C,T, along a given segment of DNA (Sanger & Coulson 1975, Maxam & Gilbert 1977), spectacular progress has been made in applying these techniques to explore many fundamental genetic problems. Coupled with the ability to be able to artificially synthesize DNA molecules with a

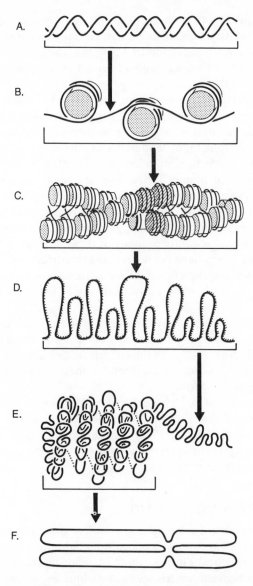

Fig. 1.3 — Schematic diagram showing different levels of chromatin packaging postulated to give rise to a highly condensed metaphase chromosome. (Adapted from Alberts *et al.*, 1983, p. 399). A, Duplex DNA molecule. B, Nucleosomes linked by short stretches of DNA. C, Higher order packaging of nucleosomes to form a chromatin fibre. D, An extended section of chromosome. E, Condensed section of chromatin. F, Highly condensed chromosome as seen during mitotic cell division.

predetermined sequence using so called 'gene machines', it is now possible to synthesize known genes; indeed several such artificial genes have been shown to function inside living organisms (Edge *et al.* 1981). Some simple organisms including the bacteriophage lambda (48.5 kb of DNA) have had their entire hereditary material sequenced, but as yet no single human chromosome has been sequenced. However, the 16.5 kb human mitochondrial genome was completely sequenced in 1981 (Anderson *et al*. 1981). Chromosome #11 contains the equivalent of over 8000 copies of mitochondrial DNA!

Despite these daunting statistics, specific regions of the human chromosomes, particularly regions that have been targeted for genetic analysis because of their special genetical/medical interest, are being sequenced, and it is expected that sequencing will spread from these landmarks much as in the time of the great explorers, maps of the world became filled in from the well known patches. The largest contiguous piece of human DNA that has been sequenced is 74 kb on chromosome #11. However, this only constitutes about 0.05% of the DNA of this chromosome. **Mutations** in this region of the chromosome result in serious genetic diseases, including thalassemia and sickle cell anaemia. DNA sequencing has enabled the precise molecular nature of many of these mutations to be determined (Weatherall 1985), and plans have been devised for 'correcting' genetic defects in this region by incorporating functional DNA sequences into the DNA of bone marrow precursor cells, with some early trials giving hope of eventual success (Thomas 1986).

An international effort is underway to sequence the entire human genome, and it has been persuasively argued that the benefits of such a molecular map would far outweigh the costs (Bodmer 1986). Technical advances including the use of automated DNA sequencing procedures may render these cost estimates ($US 2.25 thousand million) highly inaccurate.

The rapid accumulation of DNA sequence data from a wide variety of organisms has necessitated the use of powerful computers for storage, retrieval, and manipulation of such data (Soll & Roberts 1984). Accordingly, access *via* computers to international DNA and protein sequence data bases (e.g. 'Genbank' 1988) is now commonplace in molecular genetics laboratories.

## 1.7   GENE DEFINITION AND FUNCTION

Before the molecular structure and *modus operandi* of genes became understood, at least in part, it was necessary to use a conceptual definition of genes. They were considered to be hypothetical entities, units of inheritance that determined the development of particular characteristics such as blue eyes, and that obeyed the fundamental laws of genetic segregation and assortment proposed by Mendel in 1866 (see Whitehouse 1972). An important but often overlooked aspect of Mendel's theory of inheritance was the notion that genes were not themselves influenced by the phenotype they determined; they could be transmitted from one generation to another unmodified by their presence in an organism. A clear distinction was thus made between the genetic determinants and their expressed products. (In modern parlance this separatism finds expression in the so called central dogma which proposes a unidirectional flow of information from gene (DNA) to gene product (protein) *via* RNA intermediaries (Crick 1958).) Genes took on a physical reality of sorts with the discovery in the early 1900s that they were associated with chromosomes. Genes were envisaged as 'beads' located at fixed positions on strings (chromosomes). As early as 1908, Garrod proposed a link between genes and proteins (Garrod 1908). He suggested that a defective (mutant) gene could give rise to a nonfunctional product which in turn caused a block in metabolism resulting in an inherited disease, a so called 'inborn error of metabolism.' These ideas led eventually to the proposal of a 'one gene–one enzyme relationship' (Beadle 1945).

We now know that genes are segments of DNA which encode in their base sequence the information necessary for specifying the primary molecular structure of a specific nucleic acid and/or polypeptide product. In general, a 'one gene–one functional product' relationship holds true, although, as for most biological generalizations, exceptions exist. Differences between genes reside not in any gross structural or chemical alterations to DNA, but in differences in base sequence. Each chromosomal DNA molecule contains genes whose boundaries cannot be defined microscopically; they can be defined only in terms of DNA sequence and function. Therefore, before considering further the nature of genes *per se* it is necessary to give a brief overview of their function.

Some genes, referred to as 'housekeeping genes', are active in most cells as their products are continually required for normal basal cellular function. The genes that encode the different types of **transfer RNA (tRNA)** (see 1.9) are examples of housekeeping genes. Other genes have specialized functions and are active only in certain cell types. The haemoglobin genes (see 1.11) are inactive in connective tissue but are active in the red blood cell precursors. Temporal as well as spatial variation in gene activity also occur. Histone gene expression, for example, is cell cycle dependent, the genes being exclusively active during the DNA replication phase of the cell cycle (Heintz & Roeder 1984). Probably less than 5% of all genes are active in any single cell at any one time. Most genes exist in a 'switched off' state. In addition to the on/off states of gene activity, subtle modulation of active gene expression occurs. The nature of these various genetic regulatory processes, which are fundamental to the differentiation and function of organisms, is only partly understood.

## 1.8  PROTEIN STRUCTURE AND FUNCTION

Proteins, the primary products of genes, are composed of structural units called **amino acids**. There are 20 different amino acids encoded by genes, each consisting of an animo group, a carboxyl group, a hydrogen atom, and a distinctive side chain (or 'R group') covalently bonded to a central carbon atom (Fig. 1.4).

The side chain may vary from a hydrogen atom (in the simplest of all amino acids, glycine) to more complex groups. The 20 different amino acids and their commonly used three letter abbreviations are shown in Table 1.2. The properties of an amino acid (e.g. its electrostatic charge, chemical reactivity, etc.) depend on the composition of its side chain.

Proteins contain one or more polypeptides, each polypeptide consisting of a sequence of amino acids covalently linked by **peptide bonds** (Fig. 1.4). These bonds, which form during the part of protein synthesis termed **translation** (see 1.9), link the amino group of one amino acid with the carboxyl group of the adjacent amino acid. A typical polypeptide may contain hundreds of amino acids so linked in a linear sequence. Polypeptides have a free amino group at one end, and a free carboxyl group at the other, and, by convention, the amino acid sequence of a polypeptide

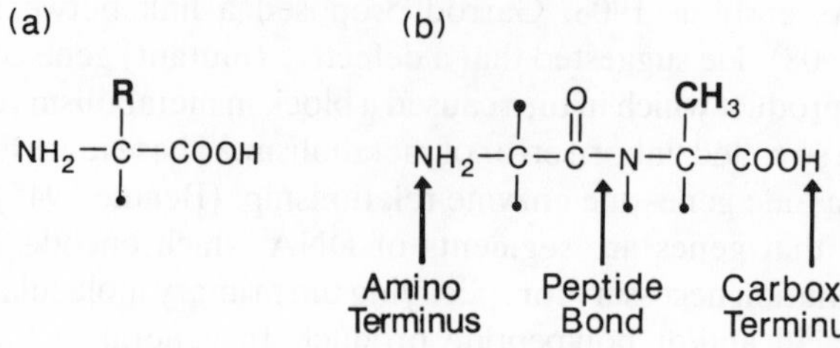

(a)                          (b)

$$\begin{array}{c} R \\ | \\ NH_2-C-COOH \\ | \end{array}$$

$$\begin{array}{ccc} & O & CH_3 \\ & || & | \\ NH_2-C-C-N-C-COOH \\ & | & | & | \end{array}$$

Amino        Peptide      Carboxyl
Terminus       Bond       Terminus

Fig. 1.4 — Amino acid and protein structure. (a) The general structure of an amino acid. Different side groups 'R' distinguish the 20 different amino acids (listed in Table 1.2). (b) A dipeptide composed of glycine (R=H) and alanine (R=CH3) amino acid residues linked by a peptide bond.

(often referred to as its primary structure) is recorded in sequence from the amino to the carboxyl end. The primary structure of the beta polypeptide of human haemoglobin, for example, would be recorded as:

Val His Leu Thr Pro Glu Glu Lys . . . etc.

Efficient and semi-automated methods now exist for determining the primary structures of polypeptides, and these protein sequences are stored in computer data bases for ready access and manipulation.

Many proteins are composed of more than one polypeptide, and these polypeptides may have identical or quite different primary structures. Molecules of adult human haemoglobin contain two identical alpha polypeptides each 141 amino acids in length, and two identical beta polypeptides, each of 146 amino acids.

In some proteins, covalent cross-links occur between the sulphur-containing R groups of two cysteine amino acid residues. These **disulphide bonds**, which may link different parts of the same polypeptide, or different polypeptides, strongly influence the molecular stability and three-dimensional configuration (and hence biological properties) of proteins. The three-dimensional structure of a protein is ultimately dependent on the primary structure of its constituent polypeptides, and such primary structures are, in turn, dependent on the DNA sequence/s of the appropriate gene/s.

Proteins play fundamental roles in virtually all biological processes. For example, proteins are involved in

(1) transport (e.g. haemoglobin transports oxygen, transferrin transports iron);
(2) the maintenance of structural integrity (e.g. collagen is largely responsible for the high tensile strength of skin and bone);
(3) the immune system (e.g. the various immunoglobulin molecules); and
(4) catalysis (e.g. the array of enzymes which catalyse biochemical reactions).

Proteins also play a role in packaging DNA into chromosomes (see 1.5) and in regulating gene activity. Some comparative properties of DNA and protein are summarized below:

| | *DNA* | *Protein* |
|---|---|---|
| Structural Units: | nucleotides | amino acids |
| No of different types of structural unit: | 4 | 20 |
| Nature of linkage between adjacent structural units: | phospho di-ester bonds | peptide bonds |
| Conventional orientation for recording sequence group: | 5'–3' | amino–carboxyl |

## 1.9   FROM GENE TO GENE PRODUCT

DNA does not itself act directly in protein synthesis; it acts as a master copy of information and a number of intermediary RNA molecules are involved in transporting and processing this information in the cell. Thus protein synthesis occurs in three stages: **transcription**, **processing** and **translation**, which are briefly described below and are summarized diagramatically in Fig. 1.5.

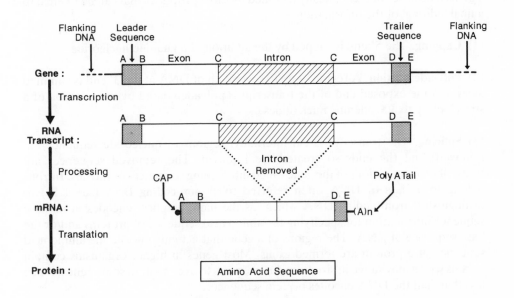

Fig. 1.5 — Representation of the various steps in transcription, processing, and translation for a hypothetical gene. The following signals are encoded in the DNA sequence: A=start of transcription (cap site); B=start of translation (AUG start codon); C=exon/intron boundary; D=end of translation (one of the three stop codons); E=end of transcription.

(1) An enzyme **RNA polymerase** recognizes and binds to a particular region of DNA 'upstream' (i.e. on the 5′ side) of the gene to be transcribed (i.e. read). This region of DNA is called the **promoter**.

(2) Hydrogen bonds linking the two DNA strands in the region of the gene are disrupted so that the strands separate and one strand acts as a template for the assembly, by RNA polymerase, of a single stranded RNA **transcript** (i.e. copy) whose base sequence is complementary to the transcribed DNA strand.

(3) The RNA transcript falls away from the DNA template, the latter re-adopting its helical conformation.

Signals in the form of particular base sequences mark the region of the DNA molecule for commencement and termination of transcription. By convention the base sequence of the non-transcribed strand of a gene is recorded. Because of the base pairing rules, the RNA transcript will have identical base sequence to this non-transcribed DNA strand except that the base U (in RNA) will replace T (in DNA).

*Processing:*
The RNA transcript is chemically modified by three processes that can be likened to a final 'editing' of the information:

(1) **Capping**. The 5′ end is capped by the addition of a guanine nucleotide.

(2) **Poly-adenylation**. A region of up to several kb of DNA at the 3′ end is trimmed away and the exposed end of the transcript is polyadenylated by the addition of a stretch of up to 300 adenine nucleotides.

(3) **Splicing**. The transcript is cut internally, regions of nucleotide sequence are removed, and the ends so created are rejoined. The removed sequences are transcribed from regions of the gene called intervening sequences or **introns**. Introns belong to a class of DNA often referred to as **non-coding DNA** (see 1.13) to distinguish it from coding DNA which, as the name implies, encodes in its base sequence information for specifying the amino acid sequence of proteins and/or the base sequence of RNA. The regions of a gene that actually encode the amino acid sequence of a protein are termed **exons**. Most genes in higher organisms contain introns which may range in size from 40 base pairs to over 1 kb. In some genes, much less than half the DNA encodes protein sequence.

The biological significance of capping, poly-adenylation, and splicing is not fully known. The reason for the existence of introns, if indeed there is one, is also not understood despite much speculation. Not all genes have introns (e.g. the mitochondrial genes are intron-free (Anderson *et al.* 1981)) and not all RNA transcripts are poly-adenylated (e.g. transcripts from most of the histone genes (Hentschel &

Birnstiel 1981)). Signals encoded in the base sequence of the RNA transcript (and hence in the transcribed DNA) indicate the locations at which these three processing events are to be carried out by various cellular mechanisms.

*Translation:*
The processed RNA, now called messenger RNA (mRNA), moves to the cell cytoplasm where, in combination with a ribosome which provides the appropriate molecular architecture and environment, its base sequence is translated into the amino acid sequence of a polypeptide.

(1) The ribosome recognizes and binds to a specific base sequence at the 5′ end of the mRNA molecule to form a ribosome/mRNA complex. The ribosome then moves along the mRNA in 'jumps' of three bases in a 5′ to 3′ direction.

(2) Individual amino acids are covalently (but reversibly) bound to transfer RNA (tRNA) molecules by specific enzymes. The type of amino acid attached to a given tRNA molecule is dependent on the latter's base sequence. In addition to an amino acid attachment site, tRNA molecules, which are about 75 bases long, contain an unpaired sequence of 3 bases called an **anticodon**. A tRNA molecule with a given anticodon (e.g. 5′ ACG 3′) will be receptive only to a particular type of amino acid, in this example cystein.

(3) In association with the moving ribosome, tRNA molecules hydrogen bond *via* their anti-codons to complementary, non-overlapping triplets of bases (**codons**) along the mRNA molecule. This process has the effect of arranging amino acids into a linear sequence that is entirely determined by the base sequence of mRNA and hence by the base sequence of the gene exons. Peptide bonds form between adjacent amino acids which then detach from their tRNA leaving it free to be loaded with another identical amino acid.

Information is encoded in the mRNA base sequence to signal the locations for the initiation and termination of translation. Regions at each end of the mRNA molecule called the **leader sequence** (5′ end) and **trailer sequence** (3′ end) are not translated into amino acids but have other largely unknown functions.

Transcription, processing, and translation are dynamic processes. An active (i.e. 'switched on') gene is continually serving as a template for transcription, and the processed transcripts are continually being translated and re-translated to form an output of polypeptide molecules with identical amino acid sequences. There is a direct, linear and non-overlapping relationship between the amino acid sequence of a polypeptide and the DNA base sequence of the coding region of a gene (Fig. 1.6).

## 1.10　THE GENETIC CODE

The idea that a sequence of nucleotides in DNA could determine the sequence of amino acids in a polypeptide was first proposed by Dounce (1952). The genetic code (Table 1.2), which was deciphered in the 1960s (see Whitehouse 1972), long before it became possible to directly determine DNA and RNA sequences, gives the relation-

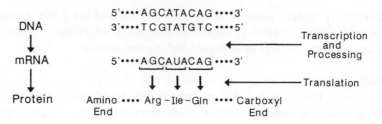

Fig. 1.6 — Relationship between DNA and mRNA base sequence and amino acid sequence for an hypothetical coding region of DNA.

ship between mRNA bases and amino acids. It is a **triplet code** (i.e. the code signal for each amino acid is a set of three sequential nucleotides). The code is non-overlapping and, with minor exceptions, is universal throughout the plant and animal kingdoms.

Given all permutations of four different bases, 64 possible base triplets are possible in DNA (see 1.4) and RNA; 61 of the mRNA triplets code for amino acids, and as there are only 20 amino acids the code is said to be degenerate, most amino acids having more than one codon. Only the amino acids tryptophan and methionine have a single codon. One consequence of code degeneracy is that a proportion of base substitutions that may occur in a gene as a result of mutation do not result in alteration to the amino acid sequence of the encoded protein. The remaining three codons (stop codons) are not read by tRNA anti-codons, but signal the end of polypeptide chain synthesis when encountered during translation. The codon AUG codes for the amino acid methionine, but also acts as a start codon marking the point on mRNA for the commencement of translation.

Despite the major function of DNA as a carrier of encoded information for determining protein sequence, it is likely that well over 90% of human DNA does not encode RNA or protein products. For example human chromosome #11 probably contains between 500 and 1000 genes sparsely distributed amongst long tracts of non-coding DNA. Non-coding DNA is further discussed in 1.13.

Even without prior knowledge of the function of a region of DNA, its base sequence can provide evidence of its possible protein coding potential. Coding DNA should contain an AUG start codon followed by an **open reading frame** of 100 or so codons, i.e. a stretch of base triplets free of the three stop codons UAA, UAG, and UGA. Fincham (1983) describes this succinctly as follows:

'The chance that a random sequence of $3n$ bases read off in threes from a (start) codon will not include a (stop) codon will be $(61/64)^n$ assuming 50% (G+C). This chance is about 0.6% for $n=100$. So a long sequence of a few hundred amino acid codons suggests strongly that the DNA has been selected for a protein coding function.'

The hypothetical sequence shown in Fig. 1.7 would be unlikely to be part of a coding region of DNA, as conceptual translation (based on the genetic code, Table 1.2) reveals the presence of stop codons in all 6 possible reading frames.

**Table 1.2** — The genetic code showing the 64 possible base triplets (codons) which may occur in mRNA and the amino acids that each codon specifies during protein synthesis. The three *stop* codons UAA, UAG and UGA act as termination signals during translation of the code. AUG codes for Met but may also act as an initiation (*start*) codon. The first position of each codon (5′ end) is given the left hand column, etc. The amino acids and their abbreviations are shown below the genetic code.

Second position

| | U | C | A | G | |
|---|---|---|---|---|---|
| **U** | UUU ⎫ Phe<br>UUC ⎭<br>UUA ⎫ Leu<br>UUG ⎭ | UCU<br>UCC<br>UCA ⎬ Ser<br>UCG | UAU ⎫ Tyr<br>UAC ⎭<br>UAA *STOP*<br>UAG *STOP* | UGU ⎫ Cys<br>UGC ⎭<br>UGA *STOP*<br>UGG Trp | U<br>C<br>A<br>G |
| **C** | CUU ⎫<br>CUC ⎬ Ile<br>CUA ⎭<br>CUG Met | CCU<br>CCC<br>CCA ⎬ Pro<br>CCG | CAU ⎫ His<br>CAC ⎭<br>CAA ⎫ Gln<br>CAG ⎭ | CGU<br>CGC<br>CGA ⎬ Arg<br>CGG | U<br>C<br>A<br>G |
| **A** | AUU ⎫<br>AUC ⎬ Val<br>AUA ⎭<br>AUG | ACU<br>ACC<br>ACA ⎬ Thr<br>ACG | AAU ⎫ Asn<br>AAC ⎭<br>AAA ⎫ Lys<br>AAG ⎭ | AGU ⎫ Ser<br>AGC ⎭<br>AGA ⎫ Arg<br>AGG ⎭ | U<br>C<br>A<br>G |
| **G** | GUU<br>GUC<br>GUA ⎬ Val<br>GUG | GCU<br>GCC<br>GCA ⎬ Ala<br>GCG | GAU ⎫ Asp<br>GAC ⎭<br>GAA ⎫ Glu<br>GAG ⎭ | GGU<br>GGC<br>GGA ⎬ Gly<br>GGG | U<br>C<br>A<br>G |

| | | | |
|---|---|---|---|
| Ala: | alanine | Gly: glycine | Pro: proline |
| Arg: | arginine | His: histidine | Ser: serine |
| Asn: | asparigine | Ile: isoleucine | Thr: threonine |
| Asp: | aspartic acid | Leu: leucine | Trp: tryptophan |
| Cys: | cysteine | Lys: lysine | Tyr: tyrosine |
| Gln: | glutamine | Met: methionine | Val: valine |
| Glu: | glutamic acid | Phe: phenylalanine | |

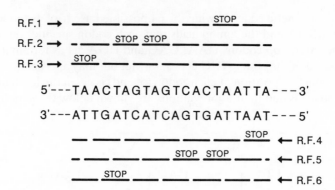

Fig. 1.7 — Conceptual translation (using the genetic code (Table 1.2) in all 6 possible reading frames (R.F.) of a probable non-coding region of duplex DNA. Only stop codons are indicated; all other base triplets encode amino acids. Reading directions are indicated by arrows.

How do we define the start and finish of a gene, and how can our definition cope with internal non-coding sequences such as introns? Do we include as part of a gene, the flanking non-transcribed sequences whose presence is essential for the initiation of transcription? How do we cope with the known cases where different transcripts are made from the same region of DNA? Paradoxically, it has become more difficult to define genes as more becomes known about their structure and function. That there is no totally satisfactory, all-embracing definition of a gene can be readily gauged from the glossaries of modern texts on genetics. As a reasonable definition that covers most situations, we will define a gene as 'a transcriptional unit, a contiguous sequence of DNA nucleotides that is transcribed into an RNA molecule'. This definition excludes from genes non-transcribed regulatory elements such as **enhancers** (see 1.13) and promoters, but includes introns, leader and trailer sequences.

## 1.11  SOME GENES OF INTEREST

There are many examples of different genes that encode proteins with similar but non-identical structure and function. Such genes, which are thought to be the evolutionary descendants of a common ancestral DNA sequence, can be thought of as members of a **gene family**. The member genes may be subject to differential regulation giving rise to a different spectrum of expressed products in different cells at different times. Gene families may be dispersed (e.g. the genes that encode the protein actin are found on chromosomes #1, #7, and #15), or may be clustered in close proximity on a single chromosome, examples being the histocompatibility genes on chromosome #6, histone A genes (#7), leukocyte interferon genes (#11), and immunoglobulin heavy chain genes (#14) (McKusick 1986).

In much of the remainder of this section, it is proposed to single out for illustrative purposes and describe in some detail, particular regions of the human genome. No attempt will be made to give a general balanced coverage. A region on the short arm of chromosome #11 will be frequently referred to (Fig. 1.8). This region contains the

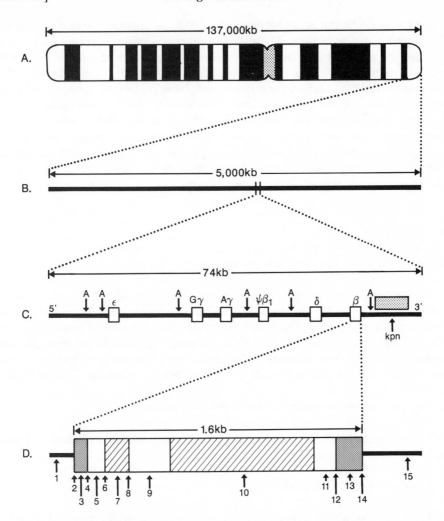

Fig. 1.8 — The beta-globin gene family on chromosome #11. (drawn approximately to scale).
(A) Diagram of chromosome #11 stained to reveal G bands. The beta-globin family of genes is
located in the terminal G band on the short arm at position 11p15.5. (B) An expanded
representation of the DNA in band 11p15.5. (C) An expanded representation of the beta-
globin gene family showing 5 protein-genes ($\epsilon$, G$\gamma$, A$\gamma$, $\delta$, $\beta$) and one non-functional
pseudogene ($\psi\beta_1$). The locations of 6 *Alu* sequences and a *Kpn* sequence are shown. (D) An
expanded representation of the beta-globin gene. Different regions of the gene are indicated by
different shadings. (Stippled=leader and trailer sequences, cross hatching=introns, unshaded
=exons). Description of the gene including its various features (indicated numerically) is given
in the text.

beta-globin gene cluster (Weatherall 1985) which is composed of a family of five
related globin genes ($\epsilon$, G$\gamma$, A$\gamma$, $\delta$ and $\beta$) and one non-functional pseudogene, spaced
over a region of about 74 kb that has been completely sequenced. It also contains the
*H-ras* proto-oncogene and genes for the hormone insulin and the enzyme tyrosine
hydroxylase as well as a number of non-coding sequences that will be referred to later
(Human Gene Mapping 9 1987).

The five genes in the beta-globin family encode polypeptides with different but related amino acid sequences. These 'beta-like' polypeptides combine with alpha-globin polypeptides encoded by members of another globin gene family on chromosome #16, to form the globin component of haemoglobin, the oxygen transporting protein of the red blood cells. Functional haemoglobin is a tetramer composed of two alpha-like chains and two beta-like chains. Significantly, the different member genes of the two gene families are expressed in different tissues and at different times during the development, giving rise to a coordinated and changing spectrum of haemoglobin molecules with various sub-unit compositions. Each of the five beta-globin genes contains two introns which, although of slightly different lengths, interrupt the coding regions at the same positions.

**Beta-globin gene**
There is, of course, no such thing as a 'typical' gene, but many common features of protein coding genes are illustrated by the beta-globin gene (Fig. 1.8).

(1) The promoter region contains sequences involved in the initiation and regulation of transcription. The **TATA box** and **CAT box** are highly conserved in sequence between genes and species. The TATA box is commonly centred around 28 bases 5′ of the cap site. The location of the CAT box is more variable. These sequences are essential for the initiation of transcription and for accurate positioning of the start of transcription by RNA polymerase (Myers *et al.* 1985, Watson *et al.* 1987, p. 704).

(2) Cap site, the site of commencement of transcription.

(3) 5′ untranslated **leader region** contains sequences involved in ribosome binding and initiation of translation.

(4) The first codon (AUG) to be translated.

(5) The first exon, a protein coding region containing the AUG start codon and 29 additional codons, plus two bases which form a complete codon when linked to the next exon after splicing.

(6, 8) Exon/intron/exon junctions containing conserved boundary sequences involved in splicing recognition. The sequence GU at the 5′ end and AG at the 3′ end of the introns appear to be invariant amongst the introns of higher organisms (Mount 1982).

(7) The first intron, a non-coding region that is removed from the RNA transcript before translation.

(9, 11) The second and third exons. The three exons together encode the 146 amino acids of the beta-globin polypeptide.

(10) The second and larger of the two introns.

(12)  UAA stop codon signals the end of translation.

(13)  3′ untranslated **trailer sequence** contains signals for mRNA end formation and poly-adenylation.

(14)  Poly-adenylation site. (The end point of transcription resides to the 3′ side of this point.)

(15)  3′ flanking region contains sequences concerned with the regulation and termination of transcription. An enhancer sequence (see 1.13) resides within a region 520 base pairs on the 3′ side of the poly A attachment site (Behringer *et al.* 1987). The 5′ and 3′ limits of the enhancer have not yet been delineated.

**Insulin gene**
The insulin gene (Fig. 1.9) consists of two exons that encode a polypeptide that is

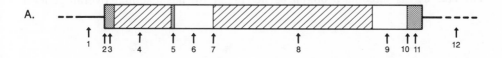

Fig. 1.9 — The insulin gene. (A) Regions of the gene (total length=1.53 kb) are drawn to approximate scale. A description of the gene including its various features (indicated numerically) is given in the text. (Shading is as indicated in Fig. 1.8(D)). (B) Short tandem repeat that commences 362 bases upstream of the insulin gene cap site. Each box represents one copy of the consensus sequence. Numbered boxes vary from the consensus sequence as indicated below. The bases in brackets are *additions* to the sequence:

|  | Consensus sequence: | ACAGGGGTGTGGGG |  |
|---|---|---|---|
|  | Variant 1: |  | CC |
|  | 2: |  | TCC |
|  | 3: |  | C |
|  | 4: |  | CC(T) |
|  | 5: | T |  |
|  | 6: |  | CC(C) |
|  | 7: |  | C   A |
|  | 8: |  |  | C |

subsequently modified to form the active insulin hormone. There are two introns, the first of which interrupts the leader sequence; only the second interrupts the coding sequence (Bell *et al.* 1980).

(1)  5′ flanking region. A short tandemly repeated DNA sequence residing about 1 kb upstream of the cap site is referred to later (1.13).

(2) Cap site.

(3, 5) Leader sequence interrupted by the first intron. (4).

(6) AUG start codon.

(7, 9) Two exons that encode the insulin polypeptide precursor, interrupted by the second intron. (8).

(10) Stop codon (UAG).

(11) Trailer sequence.

(12) 3′ flanking sequence.

**c-Ha-ras1 proto-oncogene**
The Harvey ras sarcoma **proto-oncogene** (Fig. 1.10) has a similar overall general

Fig. 1.10 — The *c-Ha-ras1* proto-oncogene (2.46 kb) drawn approximately to scale. Different regions of the gene are indicated as in Fig. 1.8 (D).

structure to the beta-globin gene, except that it is slightly longer (2.5 kb cf. 1.6 kb), it encodes a larger polypeptide (189 amino acids cf. 146 amino acids), and it has three introns instead of two (Capon *et al*. 1983).

This gene is one of over 60 known human proto-oncogenes (sometimes called cellular oncogenes). These genes have a normal cellular function, often encoding products that affect growth, cell division, and differentiation; they may, however, become hyper-activated to form **oncogenes**. Oncogenes can transform cultured animal cells to a malignant state and can cause tumour formation in animals. The presence of oncogenes is associated, in a way that is not fully understood, with the development of human cancers. Activation of proto-oncogenes leading to abnormal cell growth and division can result from a number of factors. Chromosomal translocation, for example, may place such a gene under the abnormal influence of an active promoter (Adams 1985). Simple mutational events, including single DNA base pair substitutions, can also activate proto-oncogenes (Reddy *et al*. 1982). **Retroviruses** (see 1.13) have the capacity to incorporate cellular oncogenes into their genome, activate them into oncogenes (so called viral oncogenes), and reinsert them into the genome of an animal cell resulting in **neoplastic transformation**. For additional information on oncogenes and their association with cancer see Watson *et al.* (1987 Chapts. 26 and 27) and Bishop (1985).

   *c-Ha-ras1* is located on chromosome #11 near the beta-globin gene family (Human Gen Mapping 9 1987). The gene encodes a 189 amino acid protein (the p21 protein) localized in the cell membrane, whose normal function is unknown. Activation of the gene to the oncogene found in cell lines derived from certain bladder and lung cancers results from a single base substitution (G-T) which alters the 12th amino acid of the p21 protein from valine to glycine (Reddy *et al.* 1982). The activated oncogene found in human bladder cancer is capable of transforming mouse cells *in vitro*. However, it will not transform normal human cells, so additional events must occur to give rise to these cancers.

**Ribosomal RNA (rRNA) gene**
Another type of gene family is represented by the genes that encode three sub-units of rRNA: 5.8S (0.16 kb), 18S (2.3 kb) and 28S (4.2 kb) (Fig. 1.11). (S denotes

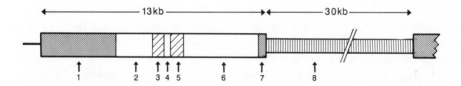

Fig. 1.11 — The repeating unit of a ribosomal RNA (rRNA) gene cluster (Adapted from Watson *et al.*, 1987, p. 699). Features of the gene are indicated numerically and are discussed in the text.

Svedberg units which are measures of sedimentation properties after ultracentrifugation). Unlike most genes (including the beta-globin gene) which occur in only a single copy in each set of human chromosomes, these genes for rRNA occur as clusters of tandemly repeated, near-identical sequences (Planta & Meyerink 1980). Their physical amplification is thought to be an evolutionary response to the large amount of rRNA required for normal cell function. There are about 300 copies of the basic repeating unit, forming clusters on chromosomes #13, #14, #15, #21 and #22. Single precursor RNA molecules are transcribed from each repeating unit. These are subsequently cleaved and about half the RNA is degraded, leaving the three mature ribosomal sub-units.

(1) Leader sequence (external transcribed spacer), removed and degraded during maturation.

(2) Coding sequence for 18S rRNA sub-unit.

(3, 5) Internal transcribed spacers, removed and degraded during maturation.

(4)  Coding sequence for 5.8S sub-unit.

(6)  Trailer sequence (external transcribed spacer), removed during maturation.

(7)  Non-transcribed spacer which separates adjacent repeated transcriptional units in the cluster and contains promoter elements. Its sequence is highly conserved between repeats.

## 1.12   THE NUMBER AND DISTRIBUTION OF GENES

Genes vary enormously in size, ranging from as small as 0.1 kb (small nuclear RNA genes (Busch *et al.* 1982)) to 2000 kb (a gene on the X chromosome, mutations in which cause the disease Duchenne muscular dystrophy (Koenig *et al.* 1987)). As a very crude approximation an average gene may be about 5 kb in length, and an average polypeptide product may consist of about 300 amino acids.

We can obtain some idea of the coding ratio of DNA (i.e. the proportion of nucleotides in a region of DNA that encodes a protein product) from the beta-globin gene family. The 70 kb (approx.) of DNA in this region encodes five protein products each of 146 amino acids giving a coding ratio of $5\times146\times3/70\,000$ or approximately 3%. In other words, 97% of the DNA in the region of the beta-globin gene family is non-coding. We cannot directly extrapolate from estimates such as this to the entire human genome because there are no accurate data on the average spacing between clustered gene families. The distances between genes that occur as non-clustered single functional units are not known. Another difficulty concerns the occurrence of non-coding repetitious DNA (see 1.13).

Making a number of assumptions, Bodmer (1986) has estimated that the number of genes in the human genome is likely to be no more than 10000, about 7000 of which occur as members of clustered gene families. (In contrast, McKusick (1986) has estimated an upper limit of 50000 genes.) Given the $3\times10^6$ kb in one set of 23 chromosomes, and supposing a typical gene involves about 5 kb, we can conclude very tentatively that 1.5% of cellular DNA is actually part of a transcriptional unit. The remaining 98.5% is flanking DNA and repetitious DNA of largely unknown function.

To obtain some idea of scale and distribution of genes consider human chromosome #11, which contains about 5% of the total DNA (i.e. $1.5\times10^5$ kb), and can be stained cytologically to reveal 30 microscopically distinct and characteristic regions called **G-bands** (Fig. 1.8). Each of these chromosomal bands contains about $5\times10^3$ kb of DNA. Assuming 1.5% of all DNA is part of a gene and an average gene is 5 kb in length, then each of these bands is expected to contain about 15 genes. The G band identified as 11p15.5 is already known to contain eight genes, so we may guess that another half dozen or so genes remain to be discovered in this region of the chromosome.

The advance in our knowledge of the human gene map has been spectacular (Fig. 1.12). In the 34 years since 1956 we have progressed from establishing the correct

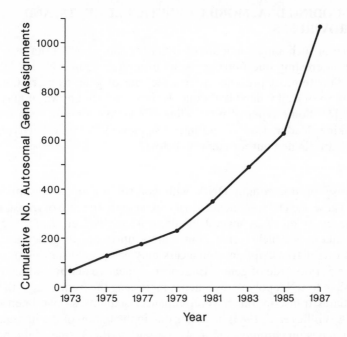

Fig. 1.12 — Increase in our knowledge of the human gene map since 1973. (Data from Human
Gene Mapping 9 (1987) and references cited therein).

human chromosome number, to knowing the chromosomal location of over 1000
genes, representing perhaps 10% of all genes. These advances have been made
possible by exploiting certain peculiar properties of somatic cell hybrids made by
fusing human and rodent cells, and more recently by applying **recombinant DNA**
techniques.

In addition to genes, a large number of 'anonymous' DNA sequences have been
mapped. These mainly non-coding sequences provide useful genetic markers.
Perhaps the ultimate genetic map is a complete nucleotide sequence of the human
genome.

The availability of a detailed gene map has a number of basic scientific implications as well as practical applications. Comparisons between the gene maps of
different species will enable questions about the nature of evolutionary constraints
on gene arrangement and organization to be answered (O'Brien et al. 1985). In the
field of medical genetics, a knowledge of the location of a disease gene can be used
for diagnosis (Caskey 1987). It can also be used to identify the gene itself, to
determine the nature of the causal mutation, and the structure, cellular location, and
even function of the gene product, opening the way for developing methods of
treatment. This so-called 'reverse genetics' approach (Orkin 1986) has been used to
study the molecular pathology of a number of inherited diseases including cystic
fibrosis (Estivill et al. 1987, Farrall et al. 1988) and Duchenne muscular dystrophy
(Hoffman et al. 1987, Monaco & Kunkel 1987).

## 1.13   NON-CODING DNA, MOBILE GENETIC ELEMENTS, AND RETROVIRUSES

The existence of such a huge amount of DNA (i.e. about 99%) that is non-coding DNA raises interesting questions about its properties. Some of this DNA has a control function (e.g. its presence affects the rate of gene transcription) but the function of most of it, if indeed it has one, is completely unknown; it may be **selfish DNA** (see 1.14). Some types of non-coding DNA have already been referred to, namely flanking, leader, trailer, and intron sequences. Some other types of non-coding DNA are singled out for mention below.

### Enhancers

A classic case of non-coding DNA with control functions is represented by enhancers. These are DNA sequences that can increase the rate of transcription of a nearby gene by as much as several hundredfold (Schaffner *et al*. 1985). Unlike promoter sequences which reside immediately upstream of genes and serve to initiate and orient transcription, enhancers may act over distances of several kb either on the 5' or 3' side of genes. Enhancers appear to act by making promoters more accessible to RNA polymerase, hence increasing the frequency with which this enzyme initiates transcription. Several enhancer sequences have been located in human DNA (Gillies *et al*. 1983) including one in the region of the immunoglobulin heavy chain genes on chromosome #14, and one on the 3' side of the beta-globin gene (Behringer *et al*. 1987).

### Pseudogenes

These are duplicates of functional genes that have been rendered inactive by mutation (Little 1982). They show close homology in base sequence to their normal functional counterpart/s, but base substitutions, additions, and deletions have altered, for example, the translation start codon (AUG) or the translation reading frame resulting in premature stop codons. Some pseudogenes are not transcribed, owing to incorrect promoters. It is doubtful whether pseudogenes, which can be considered as evolutionary debris, serve any useful purpose, although it is conceivable that they could evolve into functional genes with new properties. Because they are removed from the normal pressures of natural selection, they rapidly accumulate mutations.

Pseudogenes are commonly found amongst gene families. Both the alpha- and beta-globin gene families contain at least one such identified gene (Chang & Slightom 1984). When compared with the normal functional beta-globin gene (see 1.11 and Fig. 1.8), the beta-globin pseudogene has (i) altered TATA and CAT boxes; (ii) base insertions in the leader sequence (3 bases), second intron (4 bases) and trailer sequence (136 bases); (iii) base deletions in the first exon (1 base), third exon (1 base), and first intron (9 bases); and (iv) a number of base substitutions including a change of the start codon from AUG to GUA. All these alterations render the gene quite incapable of normal function.

Some pseudogenes differ from their functional counterparts in a strikingly suggestive way. They lack promoters, they have their introns precisely removed, and they possess short 3' poly A sequences typical of mRNA molecules. Additionally, they are flanked by short direct repeats of DNA sequence (Lee *et al*. 1983). The latter is a typical characteristic of **transposons** and endogenous retroviruses (see later). It has been suggested that these so-called 'processed pseudogenes' arose by the synthesis of a DNA molecule from an RNA template, and subsequent back-insertion of the DNA into a chromosome. Indeed, certain RNA viruses (retro-viruses) possess enzymes capable of such reverse transcription and insertion.

A remarkable observation is the large number of **small nuclear RNA (snRNA)** pseudogenes. snRNA molecules are several hundred nucleotides long and are thought to assist with the RNA splicing mechanism referred to in 1.9. Like rRNA, the snRNA molecules are encoded by multiples copies of identical genes in tandem arrays. About 30 copies of the U1 snRNA gene occur in chromosome #1, as do over 500 snRNA pseudogenes (Bernstein *et al*. 1985)!

**Repetitious DNA**

As much of 30% of human DNA occurs as multiple copies of variable length non-coding DNA sequences (Marx *et al*. 1976, Singer 1982). Some of these sequences occur in more than 100 000 copies per cell. Variation in copy number, sequence, and location of this repetitive DNA provides a rich source of markers for individual identification. Repetitive DNA and its relevance to forensic biology have been the subject of a recent concise and excellent review (Fowler *et al*. 1988). Some examples of such repetitive DNA will be briefly described.

About half the repetitive DNA is called **satellite DNA**, and it occurs as localized, highly repeated units. The repeated units range in length from five to several hundred base pairs, and they are repeated many thousands of times in tandem arrays, often in localized regions such as near the centromeres of chromosomes. An example is satellite III, which is localized to the centromeric region of chromosome #1, and to the Y chromosome (Micklos 1985). The repeat unit of satellite III is a pentanucleotide with the **consensus sequence** TTCCA. (A consensus sequence is a conceptual DNA sequence in which each base is the most commonly found base at a given position when many DNA sequences of a certain type are compared.) Variations in sequence occur amongst the repeats that make up each sequence run (Fig. 1.13). Differences in sequence and number of repeats occur between chromo-

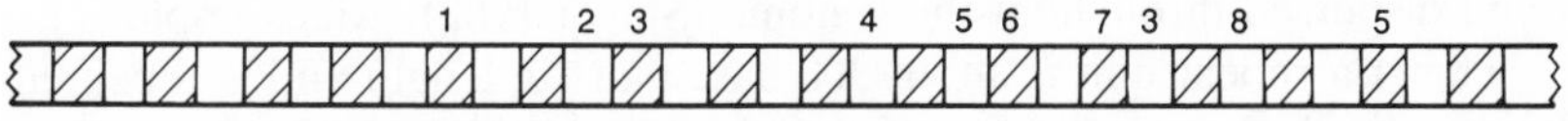

Fig. 1.13 — Variation in human Satellite III sequence. A sequenced stretch of satellite III made up of repeats of the consensus sequence TTCCA shown as blocks of alternating shaded and un-shaded regions. The chromosomal location of this particular satellite III sequence is unknown. (Data from Deininger *et al*., 1981). Numbered boxes represent repeats that differ from the consensus sequence as indicated below:

```
            Consensus:    TTCCA
            Variant 1            G
            Variant 2           GT
            Variant 3    G  TG
            Variant 4    C
            Variant 5    A
            Variant 6        A
            Variant 7    C   GG
            Variant 8            T
```

somes and between individuals. Analyses of long stretches of satellite III reveal higher order periodicities composed of simpler primordial 5 base repeats.

The human mind is frustrated by an unfulfilled desire to classify and seek *raisons d'être* for things biological and psychological. According to Micklos (1985) 'Despite attempts to force (satellite DNAs) into intellectually satisfying biological categories, these sequences are excellent candidates for genetic flotsam and jetsam.' This comment may well apply more widely to the human genome, especially to the non-coding fraction. To the forensic scientist, the flotsam and jetsam is just one more property that goes to make up an individual's unique molecular 'personality', and it can be used to great advantage in establishing individual identity.

Another form of repetitive DNA occurs as **short tandem repeats**. These consist of units of variable length, usually between 100 and 1000 base pairs, that are tandemly repeated usually fewer than 100 times at a given site in the genome (Wyman & White 1980). The blocks of repeated units at different sites tend to have unique overall sequence, but often share common 'core' sequences. A region of DNA about 1 kb 5' of the insulin gene cap site on chromosome #11 (Fig. 1.9) contains such a short tandem repeat (Bell *et al.* 1982) with the 13 base pair consensus sequence:

ACAGGGGTGTGGG

The number of repeats may differ between the two chromosome #11s of an individual and between individuals in a population. This site-specific repeat is not found elsewhere in the genome.

Techniques described in Chapter 3 can be used to detect variation in tandemly repeated DNA. These variants, which are of special relevance to forensic science because of their discriminating power, go by the names: **variable number tandem repeats (VNTR)** or mini-satellites (Jeffries *et al.* 1985, Jeffries 1987, Nakamura *et al.* 1987).

In addition to tandemly repeated DNA, a significant proportion of the genome is composed of **interspersed repetitive DNA**, i.e. sequences that are repeated not in tandem array but as individual units interspersed with longer tracts of single copy DNA and dispersed throughout the genome (Singer 1982). An example is the *Alu* family. The *Alu* repeat unit is about 300 base pairs in length and is repeated over 300 000 times in the human genome (Schmid & Shen 1985). *Alu* sequences therefore make up at least several percent of the total human DNA. Individual *Alu* repeats are closely related but not identical in sequence. They differ from a consensus sequence by about 14% on average (Jelinek & Schmid 1982). Most of these variants involve single base pair substitutions. An important feature of *Alu* units is that they are generally flanked at each end by short direct repeats of about 10 base pairs. The repeat flanking one of the eight *Alu* sequences that occur in the region of the beta-globin gene family (Fig. 1.8.) is:

————GAGAGTAGATTTT—Alu—GAGAGTAGATCTT————

With the exception of one base difference, this is a perfect direct repeat. Like some pseudogenes, *Alu* sequences have A-rich regions at their 3' ends. *Alu* is sometimes found within introns, leader, or trailer sequences of genes. *Alu* sequences are capable of being transcribed under artificial conditions, but the extent of their transcription in normal cells is unknown. Furthermore, it is unknown if they carry out any essential function. It is speculated that *Alu* sequences have been distributed around the genome by transposition-like events (see below).

Also found in this region is another example of an interspersed repetitive sequence called *Kpn*. There are about 50 000 copies of *Kpn*-like sequences making up several percent of the total human DNA (Jelinek & Schmid 1982). Members of the *Kpn* family vary considerably in length owing to 5′ truncation. The *Kpn* element found at the 3′ end of the beta-globin gene family (Fig. 1.8) has a length of 6.1 kb.

### Mobile genetic elements and retroviruses

Until recently it was assumed that any given DNA sequence would, in general, remain at a fixed site in the genome. Our ability to be able to construct detailed genetic maps that have reliable predictive properties was based on and gave credence to this assumption. Chromosome translocations, whereby relatively large pieces of chromatin (i.e. 2,000 kb or more) are broken away from their normal site and re-joined in an abnormal location, are known to occur with low frequency. However, these events are strongly selected against because of resultant mechanical difficulties during gamete formation and genetic imbalance of gametes. At a finer level of change, the immunoglobulin genes undergo developmental rearrangement associated with the generation of antibody diversity (Hozumi & Tonegawa 1976, Brack *et al.* 1978). However, these alterations, which probably represent a 'special case', are restricted to antibody producing somatic cells and are not transmitted through the germ line. Overall, however, the human genome was considered to be relatively static, subject only to slow evolutionary change resulting from chance effects (random drift) and the action of natural selection on variation generated by reciprocal recombination between homologous sequences, and by very rare mutational events involving base substitution, addition, or deletion. This view of localizational stability has been modified as a result of recent discoveries of mobile DNA sequences that can change location from one region of the genome to another, and that can be transmitted between generations through the germ line.

**Transposable elements** are pieces of DNA, up to 8 kb in length, that have the potential to move around the genome (Finnegan 1985). Insertion of a transposable element into a gene is likely to render the gene inactive, and several gene mutations in the vinegar fly *Drosophila* have been described which result from such insertions. Most research on these transposons has been carried out in bacteria where the mechanisms of transposition are becoming well understood (Shapiro 1983). Some bacterial transposons contain within their sequence genes that encode the proteins that aid their own transposition. Such transposons can be considered as parasitic DNA. Much less is known about transposition in higher organisms, although transposon-like mobile elements have been identified in yeast and *Drosophila* and will almost certainly be discovered in humans. Three notable features of transposons are:

(1) When inserted into a region of the genome, they may carry with them DNA sequences acquired from another region of the genome where they had previously resided.

(2) The process of transposition generates short (less than 20 base pairs) direct DNA sequence repeats, derived from pre-existing genomic sequences, at the target site. This results in the integrated transposon being flanked by a short repeated DNA sequence.
(3) Transposons have no independent life outside the cell. They never exist as free DNA molecules.

The existence of short direct repeats that flank some dispersed repetitive elements, such as *Alu*, suggests that these elements may have been incorporated into the genome by transposition-like events.

**Retroviruses** are RNA viruses which, in order to propagate, infect animal cells and reverse transcribe their genome into a DNA molecule which then integrates at random (and usually at more than one site) into the host genome to form a pro-virus. In this form, the pro-viral DNA may be transcribed and translated by the machinery of the host cell to produce new infectious virus particles. The mechanism of pro-viral integration like that of transposition results in the formation at the target site of short direct repeats.

Retroviruses may be infectious, in which case they occur only in somatic cells of affected individuals, and are transmitted horizontally within the species, usually with pathological consequences. The virus isolated from patients with acquired immune deficiency syndrome (AIDS) is an example of an infectious human retrovirus.

Some retroviral sequences are endogenous and non-infectious within the species, although they can sometimes replicate in cells of hererologous species. Endogenous retroviral (ERV) sequences are present in multiple copies of restricted sites in both somatic and germ line cells. Moreover, they are transmitted vertically from generation to generation, just as if they were 'normal' genes. Several ERV sequences have been identified in the human genome. About 12 repeats of the Type C retrovirus *ERV-I* are located near the tip of the long arm of chromosome #18, and there is evidence that these sequences have existed at this site since the divergence of the human and chimpanzee lineages. Another retrovirus, *ERV-III*, a full length but defective human pro-virus, is located on chromosome #7. For additional information on retroviruses see Watson *et al.* (1987, Chapters 24–27) and Benveniste (1985).

Retroviruses in animal cells can cause malignant transformation by altering the transcriptional regulation of a normal host cell gene by integration nearby. Retroviruses may contain viral oncogenes (the viral counterparts of an activated cellular oncogene) which, on insertion into the host genome, bring about malignant transformation. These viral oncogenes are derived from normal cellular genes and have been 'picked up' by the virus during the pro-viral part of its life cycle, and subsequently activated to fully fledged oncogene. The Harvey murine leukemia virus, for example, contains the *v-Ha-rasI* oncogene which, as the name suggests, is an RNA tumour virus that can cause leukemia in rodents.

## 1.14 SELFISH DNA

The existence of so much non-coding DNA in higher organisms, and in particular the existence of repetitious DNA which appears to serve no useful purpose, has prompted suggestions that at least some of this DNA is inherently 'selfish' (Orgel & Crick 1980, Doolittle & Sapienza 1980). It is proposed that such parasitic DNA tends to multiply, not because of any benefit it confers on its host, but simply as a result of the suitable environment the host cells provide.

The *Alu* sequence is a strong candidate for selfish DNA. It seems likely that the 300 000 or so copies of *Alu* arose and spread in parasitic fashion from a single primordial *Alu* sequence. Perhaps all the dispersed repetitious DNA arose in similar manner. The highly repeated satellite DNA sequences also appear to have the property of multiplication to form tandem arrays, but they lack the tell-tale signs of transposition such as direct flanking repeats. The spreading of these satellite sequences (which have been termed 'ignorant' as distinct from 'selfish' DNA by Dover (1980)) can be explained by recombinational events that occur as a consequence of the repetition *per se* rather than from an innate tendency to parasitize.

Fincham's comment (Fincham 1983) is relevant here:

'The selfish DNA concept is a valuable one insofar as it counteracts naive teleology (argument based on presumed 'purpose'). Its possible danger is that it may serve as a device for avoiding thought — once a particular class of DNA has been labelled 'selfish' we may excuse ourselves from worrying any more about possible function. A product of scepticism, it should itself be viewed sceptically.'

## 1.15 GENETICAL VARIATION

Having discussed the structure and function of DNA we now turn to a brief consideration of differences between individuals in their genetic constitution. While we are all recognizably human in nature and form, individual differences are clearly apparent, differences that are the outward manifestations of interactions between environmental factors (in the broadest sense) and genetic constitution (**genotype**). Less obvious but nevertheless measurable differences between individuals in, for example, their biochemical constitution are widespread. These also have both genetic and environmental causation. It is now clear that inherited differences between individuals in their DNA are so widespread that with the possible exception of monozygous twins, no two humans are identical genotypically (Jeffries *et al.* 1985, Jeffries 1987). Scientists believe that the existence of such genetic variation provides flexibility for evolution to proceed in a changing environment. A fixed inflexible mechanism for storing and retrieving genetic information would be likely to doom a species to eventual extinction. Less is known about the amount of genetic variation between the somatic cells within individuals, but the available evidence (for example, see, Hall 1988) suggests that such variation is limited, the process of mitotic cell division replicating cellular genotypes with incredibly high precision.

It is the existence of genetic variation between individuals that enables DNA to be used for identification in forensic science. Methods for detecting and identifying individual DNA differences are described in detail in later chapters. For a general discussion about the origins and biological significance of genetic variability in populations, readers are referred to Hartl (1980).

It is necessary to introduce some classical genetic terminology. For convenience this discussion is confined to genes (or DNA sequences) carried on the 22 pairs of human **autosomes** (i.e. the non-sex chromosomes), and it will be assumed that all the somatic cells of an individual are genotypically identical.

There are two copies of each gene in every somatic cell of an individual. These pairs of genes, called **alleles** because they behave as alternatives in inheritance, reside at specific sites or loci on pairs of **homologous chromosomes**. Each gamete produced by an individual contains only one member of each homologous pair of chromosomes, and hence only one of each allelic pair of genes.

Consider the beta-globin gene for example. Each of the two chromosomes #11 present in a somatic cell contains, at a specific site (Fig. 1.8), a DNA sequence that encodes the beta-globin polypeptide. Both of these allelic genes are transcriptionally active in haemoglobin-synthesizing red blood cell precursors although they are 'switched off' in skin and brain cells for example. The insulin locus resides further along the same chromosome. Again, each somatic cell has two allelic insulin genes at corresponding sites in each chromosome #11.

Individuals with two identical alleles are said to be **homozygous** at the relevant locus. An individual with two copies of the normal beta globin gene $Hb\beta^A$ would have the genotype $Hb\beta^A Hb\beta^A$. Individuals with sickle cell anaemia are homozygous for the mutant gene $Hb\beta^S$ and have the genotype $Hb\beta^S Hb\beta^S$. Each of these alleles differs from the normal allele by a single base substitution in the fifth codon of the first exon (see Fig. 1.8) and encodes a beta globin polypeptide differing from normal by a single amino acid substitution. Individuals may also be of the genotype $Hb\beta^A Hb\beta^S$, having inherited an $Hb\beta^A$-carrying chromosome from one parent and an $Hb\beta^S$-carrying chromosome #11 from the other. Such individuals are said to be **heterozygous** at the $Hb\beta$ locus. Considering only two alleles at a locus, it can be seen that there are three possible genotypes in a population. A large number of relatively rare $Hb$ alleles have been described, and therefore many genotypes at this locus may theoretically exist, and many have in fact been detected.

The concept of **genetic polymorphism** also needs introducing here. A genetic polymorphism is the occurrence, within a population, of two or more alternative and distinct phenotypes that result from allelic variation at a single genetic locus. Arbitrarily, a locus is said to be polymorphic if the commonest allele has a population frequency of less than 99%.

It should be noted that the terms 'allele', 'locus' 'homozygous'. 'heterozygous', and 'polymorphism' were originally used to describe the genetic constitution (genotype) of an individual, and, by necessity, differences in genotype were inferred from phenotypic differences. For example, a knowledge of the ABO blood group polymorphism and the mode of inheritance of the phenotypic differences involved, enabled individuals in a population to be genotypically classified. Not only was genotypic determination inferential but it was, by and large, confined to those regions of the genome (i.e. genes) that encoded functional gene products.

With the availability of the new methods in molecular biology that permit determination of DNA sequences, it has become possible to directly detect differences between individuals in DNA constitution, i.e. we can study genotypes directly. In a sense, the **phenotype** (i.e. the characteristics of an individual that can be observed and measured) has approached and eventually become the genotype! The inferential nature of much of genetic analysis is no longer essential, and terms such as 'heterozygous' and 'polymorphism' have taken on rather different meanings. For one thing, they need no longer be confined to describing differences in genes but can be applied to any identifiable stretch of DNA, coding or non-coding.

The classical view of population structure, widely held up until the 1950s, was that genetic differences between individuals were rare. Genes, it was supposed, could be classified as either 'wild type' (i.e. functionally 'normal' and commonly occurring) or 'mutant' (i.e. defective and uncommon). Nearly all individuals in a population were thought to be homozygous for wild type alleles at most genetic loci. Rare alleles occurred predominantly in combination with a wild type allele (i.e. in heterozygous form). Wild type alleles were usually dominant, that is to say their effect masked the effect of recessive mutants. The 'purifying' effect of natural selection kept deleterious recessive mutant alleles at low frequency. Examples of polymorphisms were known (e.g. the ABO blood groups) but these were thought to be uncommon. The prevailing view was one of population genetic homogeneity.

This view has now totally changed. The existence of genetically determined individual differences, whether in coding or non-coding parts of the genome, is known to be the rule rather than the exception, and the concept of common 'wild type' and rare 'mutant' alleles has been shown to be misleading.

The commonality of genetic polymorphism derives initially from studies of gene products (and in particular **isozymes**), using the technique of gel electrophoresis which is well known to forensic scientists. Two measurements of population variation were made: (i) the proportion of gene loci in a population that were polymorphic ($P$), and (ii), the proportion of individuals heterozygous at a locus, when averaged over all loci. This latter measurement, referred to as the **average heterozygosity** ($H$), is the more meaningful measure of population variation as it is not subject to the arbitrary definition of polymorphism. In addition, measurements of $H$ take into account the number and frequency of detectable alleles at a locus, whereas measurements of $P$ are concerned only with the presence or absence of polymorphism regardless of the degree to which variation at the locus can discriminate between individuals in the population.

Electrophoretic studies on 71 randomly chosen human enzyme-encoding gene loci in a random sample of Europeans gave estimates of $P=0.28$ and $H=0.07$ (Harris & Hopkinson 1972). In other words, nearly 30% of the loci studied were polymorphic and individuals were heterozygous at 7% of loci on average. Similar estimates of $P$ and $H$ were obtained when a wide variety of other sexually reproducing plant and animal populations were studied in this way (Ayala & Kiger 1984, p. 756).

The extent to which these estimates can be extrapolated to accurately reflect overall levels of genetic variation in naturally occurring populations is problematical. The estimates were based on studies of a very small and possibly biased sample of gene products. Furthermore, electrophoresis would detect only a proportion of the alleles at a locus, i.e. those that affect the electrostatic charge of the encoded protein. Many amino acid substitutions would therefore escape detection. In addition the degeneracy of the genetic code ensures that some DNA base substitutions do not result in detectably different gene products. Despite these and other reservations about the meaningfulness of these estimates of $P$ and $H$, there is clearly a high level of genetic variability within human and other populations. If we take a very conservative estimate of $H=0.04$, and if we assume that the number of human genes is about 10 000, then a randomly chosen individual would be heterozygous at about 400 loci and could potentially produce $2^{400}=10^{120}$ different genetic gametic types, an incredibly large number. This illustrates, albeit in a rather simplistic way, the tremendous amount of genetic diversity in human populations predicted by these studies.

Up until now we have been considering estimates of genetic variation based on the analyses of gene products. However, not all genetic variation gives rise to detectable differences in gene product. Recall that over 90% of human DNA is non-coding. How can estimates be made of the amount of DNA variation amongst individuals in human populations, regardless of whether or not such variation is expressed through gene product differences? Can we use $H$ to quantify directly, rather than inferentially, DNA sequence variation in human populations? One approach to these problems would be to determine the sequence of an identifiable region of DNA (or a random selection of such regions) in a random sample of individuals from a population. It may then be possible to estimate the average probability that any two individuals (or any two homologous chromosomes) differ at a single nucleotide site in their DNA sequence. Hence one could estimate heterozy-gosities per nucleotide ($H$ (nucleotide)) rather than per gene; i.e. the nucleotide site rather than the gene would become the locus in question. (Note that a given nucleotide site could have a maximum of four different 'alleles', A,G,T, and C in a population.) Up until very recently, the sequencing of a piece of human DNA required that it be first cloned, a technically demanding and time consuming procedure. As a consequence, no systematic survey aimed at quantifying levels of population variation using this direct DNA sequencing approach has been under-taken. Application of the recently devised polymerase chain reaction (PCR) tech-nique (see Chapter 7) promises to provide reliable data on overall levels of DNA variation between individuals in the near future.

However, direct DNA sequencing has provided some very limited data on levels of genetic variation in humans. For example, the two gamma-A globin alleles (each about 1.65 kb) from a single individual were shown by cloning and sequencing to differ at 13 sites by single nucleotide substitutions (Slightom *et al.* 1980). In addition three segments differed by deletions of between 4 and 18 nucleotides in one or other allele. Significantly none of the substitutions or deletions occurred in exons. If only the substitutions are considered, then $H$ (nucleotide) can be estimated to be 13/1650=0.8%. Futhermore, if each deletion is considered to be one additional nucleotide difference, then $H=16/1650=1$%. Ayala & Kiger (1984) cite data on heterozygosity for several other genes where two alleles have been sequenced, and concludes that 'the average nucleotide heterozygosity for structural genes and other single sequence DNA of eukaryotes is likely to be around 1 or 2%'. It follows from these estimates that the DNA sequences of the two allelic forms of a gene in an individual are expected to differ about once every 100 nucleotides, most of the variation residing in non-coding regions. Given that genes are commonly at least several kilobases long, it may be concluded that the probability of homozygosity (at the DNA sequence level) for any gene in any individual is extremely small.

Another method of quantifying population variation in DNA sequence is to screen randomly chosen DNA samples for **restriction fragment length polymor-**

**phisms (RFLP)**. These polymorphisms are detected, not by DNA sequencing *per se*, but by digesting DNA with restriction endonucleases (enzymes that recognize short specific duplex DNA sequences and 'cut' the DNA into correponding fragments) and then detecting different sized fragments by electrophoresis, Southern blotting, and molecular hybridization, using cloned DNA probes. (These techniques are described in Chapter 3). Using these approaches, Cooper and his colleagues (Cooper *et al.* 1985) have derived what they claim to be 'the first unbiased estimate of heterozygosity for the human genome'. Based on screening DNA from 10 to 15 individuals with 19 randomly selected molecular probes and 6 restriction endonucleases, $H$ (nucleotide) was estimated to be approximately 0.4%. Other studies have resulted in heterozygosity estimates of similar magnitude (e.g. Jeffries 1979). Nevertheless, all these estimates need substantiating by additional studies. The data at present available are limited by small sample sizes, and the probes used to detect variation are not strictly random in the sense that probes that detect repititious DNA were purposely omitted from the analyses for technical reasons.

Estimates of average nucleotide heterozygosity hide the marked differences in levels of variation that occur between different regions of the genome. **Non-synonymous nucleotide sites** (i.e. sites in exons that, if altered by nucleotide substitution, encode peptides with altered amino acid sequence) are highly conserved in DNA sequence, as might be expected from the functional constraints they presumably operate under. In contrast, synonymous sites in coding regions, as well as sites in introns, pseudogenes, and other non-coding regions of DNA, are in general much more variable (Li *et al.* 1985).

## 1.16  CONCLUSIONS

The chapter has emphasized the structure, function, and variability of DNA. It is contended that an understanding of at least these three features of DNA is fundamental to an appreciation of the experimental approaches, many of which are outlined in this book, that are used in DNA analyses. Some areas of importance that have not been covered are classical Mendelian genetics, mutation, linkage, and population genetics, all of which are of relevance to certain aspects of forensic science. Some texts covering these topics are listed under *General Reading*.

We are living in a particularly exciting period when the new and powerful techniques of molecular biology are rapidly penetrating the barriers to our understanding of life. The chances are that accounts such as this will be largely outdated within ten years! In fact our perception of the human genome has undergone marked changes recently. The old ideas that the genome could be likened to 'beads' (genes) on 'strings' (chromosomes), and that most individuals possessed identical sets of beads, has been shown to be misleadingly simplistic. We now know that the 10 000 or so genes in humans are interspersed unevenly amongst vast tracts of non-coding DNA, some of which is highly repititious, possibly having parasitic properties making it capable of movement and amplification. The definition of genes themselves is far from straightforward, many of them being interrupted by non-coding introns and some of them overlapping in sequence. In addition there is a considerable level of individual variability in DNA sequence among individuals and even between pairs of homologous chromosomes within individuals. This variability, most of which resides in non-coding DNA, provides raw material for the forensic scientist. However, it must be remembered that the existence of such variation poses important questions about its origins and biological significance. Indeed, a major challenge of modern biology is to understand the significance of the 90% or above of our DNA that has no known function. It is paradoxical that it is this non-coding (non-understood!) DNA that is of so much use in forensic science.

Not surprisingly, the science of molecular genetics, which is aimed at understanding the structure, function, transmission, and variation of DNA, has the potential to make an important contribution to forensic science. The DNA molecule has an essentially unlimited capacity for storing biological information; it has the capacity to accurately replicate this information during growth and development of the individual; it is transmitted from generation to generation in accord with well established and tested genetic principles; and it confers an individuality on essentially every human being. These properties make DNA an ideal, perhaps even the ultimate, source of biological material for use in forensic identification. In analyzing differences between individuals in their DNA, we are directly examining differences that lie at the very heart of biological diversity.

## ACKNOWLEDGEMENTS

I thank Professor Henry Bennett for constructive comments on an early draft of this article, and Dr Alan Wilton and Mr Clive Chesson for many helpful discussions.

## REFERENCES

Adams, J. (1985) Oncogene activation by fusion of chromosomes in leukemia. *Nature* **315** 542–543.

Alberts, B., Bray, D., Lewis, J., Raff, M., Roberts, K., & Watson, J. D. (1983) *Molecular biology of the cell.* Garland, New York.

Anderson, S., Bankier, A. T., Barrell, B. G., deBruijn, M. H. L., Coulson, A. R., Drouin, J., Eperon, I. C., Nierlich, D. P., Roe, B. A., Sanger, F., Schreier, P. H., Smith, A. J. H., Staden, R., & Young, I. G. (1981) Sequence and organization of the human mitochondrial genome. *Nature* **290** 457–465.

Ayala, F. J. & Kiger, J. A. (1984) *Modern genetics.* 2nd. ed. Benjamin/Cummings, California.

Beadle, G. W. (1945) Genetics and metabolism in *Neurospora. Physiol. Rev.* **25** 643–663.

Behringer, R. R., Hammer, R. E., Brinster, R. L., & Palmiter, R. D. (1987) Two 3' sequences direct adult erythroid-specific expression of human β-globin genes in transgenic mice. *Proc. Nat. Acad Sci.* **84** 7056–7060.

Bell, G. T., Selby, M. J., & Rutter, W. J. (1982) The highly polymorphic region near the human insulin gene is composed of single tandemly repeated sequences. *Nature* **295** 31–35.

Bell, G. T., Picket, R. I., Rutter, W. J., Cordell, B., Tischar, E., & Goodman, H. M. (1980) Sequence of the human insulin gene. *Nature* **284** 26–32.

Benveniste, R. E. (1985) The contribution of retroviruses to the study of mammalian evolution. In: MacIntyre, R. J. (ed.) *Molecular evolutionary genetics*. Plenum Press, New York, pp. 359–417.

Bernstein, L. B., Manser, T., & Weiner, A. M. (1985) Human U1 small nuclear RNA genes: extensive conservation of flanking sequences suggests cycles of gene amplification and transposition. *Mol. Cell. Biol.* **5** 2159–2171.

Bishop, J. M. (1985) Viral oncogenes. *Cell* **42** 23–38.

Bodmer, W. F. (1986) Human genetics: the molecular challenge. *Cold Spring Harbor Symp Quant. Biol.* **51** 1–13.

Brack, C., Hirama, M., Lenhard-Schuller, R., & Tonegawa, S. (1978) A complete immunoglobulin gene is created by somatic recombination. *Cell* **15** 1–14.

Busch, H., Reddy, R., & Rothblum, L. (1982) SnRNAs, SnRNPs, and RNA processing. *Ann. Rev. Biochem.* **51** 617–654.

Capon, D. J., Chen, E. Y., Levinson, A. D., Seeburg, P. H., & Goeddel, D. V. (1983) Complete nucleotide sequence of the T24 human bladder carcinoma oncogene and its normal homologue. *Nature* **302** 33–37.

Caskey, C. T. (1987) Disease diagnosis by recombinant DNA methods. *Science* **236** 1223–1229.

Chang, L.-Y. E. & Slightom, J. L. (1984) Isolation and nucleotide sequence analysis of the beta-type globin pseudogene from human, gorilla and chimpanzee. *J. Mol. Biol.* **180** 767–784.

Chargaff, E. (1950) Chemical specificity of nucleic acids and mechanisms of their enzymatic degradation. *Experimentia* **6** 201–209.

Cooper, D. N., Smith, B. A., Cooke, H. J., Niemann, S., & Schmidtke, J. (1985) An estimate of unique DNA sequence heterozygosity in the human genome. *Hum. Genet.* **69** 201–205.

Crick, F. H. C. (1958) On protein synthesis. *Symp. Soc. Exp. Biol.* **12** 548–555.

Deininger, P. L., Jolly, D. J., Rubin, C. M., Friedmann, T., & Schmid, C. W. (1981) Base sequence studies of 300 nucleotide renatured repeated human DNA clones. *J. Mol. Biol.* **151**, 17–33.

Doolittle, W. F. & Sapienza, C. (1980) Selfish genes, the phenotype paradigm and genome evolution. *Nature* **284** 601–603.

Dounce, A. L. (1952) Duplicating mechanism for peptide chain and nucleic acid synthesis. *Enzymologia* **15** 251–258.

Dover, G. A. (1980) Ignorant DNA? *Nature* **285** 618–620.

Edge, M. D., Greene, A. R., Heathcliffe, G. R., Meacock, P. A., Schuch, W., Scanlon, D. B., Atkinson, T. C., Newton, C. R., & Markham, A. F. (1981) Total synthesis of a human leukocyte interferon gene. *Nature* **292** 756–762.

Estivill, X., Farrall, M., Scambler, P. J., Bell, G. M., Hawley, K. M. F., Lench, N. J., Bates, G. P., Kruyer, H. C., Frederick, P. A., Stanier, P., Watson, E. K., Williamson, R., & Wainwright, B. J. (1987) A candidate gene for the cystic fibrosis locus isolated by selection for methylation-free islands. *Nature* **326** 840–845.

Farrall, M., Wainwright, B. J., Feldman, G. L., Beaudet, A., Sretenovic, Z., Halley, D., Simon, M., Dickerman, L., Devoto, M., Romeo, G., Kaplan, J.-C. Kitzis, A., & Williamson, R. (1988) Recombination between *IRP* and cystic fibrosis. *Am. J. Hum. Genet.* **43** 471–475.

Fincham, J. R. S. (1983) *Genetics*. John Wright, Bristol, U.K.

Finnegan, D. J. (1985) Transposable elements in eukaryotes. *Int. Rev. Cytol.* **93** 281–326.

Fowler, J. C. S., Burgoyne, L. A., Scott, A. C., & Harding, H. W. J. (1988) Repetitive DNA and human genome variation — a concise review relevant to forensic biology. *J. For. Sci.* **33**, 1111–1126.

Garrod, A. E. (1908) Inborn errors of metabolism. *Lancet* **2** 1–7, 73–79, 142–148, 214–220.

'*Genbank nucleic acids*' (1988) IntelliGenetics Inc., California, U.S.A.

Gillies, S. D., Morrison, S. L., Oi, V. T., & Tonegawa, S. (1983) A tissue-specific transcription enhancer element is located in the major intron of a rearranged immunoglobulin heavy chain gene. *Cell* **33** 717–728.

Hall, J. G. (1988) Somatic mosaicism: observations related to clinical genetics. *Am. J. Hum. Genet.* **43** 355–463.

Harris, H. & Hopkinson, D. A. (1972) Average heterozygosity per locus in man: an estimate of the incidence of enzyme polymorphisms. *Ann. Hum. Genet.* **36** 9–20.

Hartl, D. L. (1980) *Principles of population genetics*. Sunderland, Mass.

Heintz, N. & Roeder, R. G. (1984) Transcription of human histone genes in extracts from synchronized HeLa cells. *Proc. Nat. Acad. Sci.* **81** 2713–2717.

Hentschel, C. C. & Birnstiel, M. L. (1981) The organization and expression of histone gene families. *Cell* **25** 301–313.

Hershey, A. D. & Chase, M. (1952) Independent functions of viral protein and nucleic acid in growth of bacteriophage. *J. Gen. Physiol.* **36** 89–96.

Hoffman, E. P., Brown, R. H., & Kunkel, L. M. (1987) Dystropin: the protein product of the Duchenne muscular dystrophy locus. *Cell* **51** 919–928.

Hozumi, N. & Tonegawa, S. (1976) Evidence for somatic rearrangement of immunoglobulin genes coding for variable and constant regions. *Proc. Nat. Acad. Sci.* **73** 3628–3632.

Human Gene Mapping 9 (1987) *Ninth international workshop on human gene mapping. Cytogenet. Cell Genet.* **46** Nos. 1–4.

Jeffreys, A. J. (1979) DNA sequence variants in the Gγ, Aγ, δ and β globin genes of man. *Cell* **18** 1–10.

Jeffreys, A. J. (1987) Highly variable minisatellites and DNA fingerprints. *Biochem. Soc. Trans.* **15** 309–317.

Jeffreys, A. J., Wilson, V., & Thein, S. L. (1985) Hypervariable "minisatellite" regions in human DNA. *Nature* **314** 67–73.

Jelinek, W. R. & Schmid, C. W. (1982) Repetitive sequences in eukaryotic DNA and their expression. *Ann. Rev. Biochem.* **51** 813–844.

Koenig, G. M., Hoffman, E. P., Bartelson, S. J., Monaco, A. P., Feener, C., & Kunkel, L. M. (1987) Complete cloning of the Duchenne muscular dystrophy (DMD) cDNA and preliminary genomic organization of the DMD gene in normal and affected individuals. *Cell* **50** 509–517.

Kornberg, A. (1980) *DNA replication*. W. H. Freeman, San Fransisco.

Kornberg, R. D. & Klug, A. (1981) The nucleosome. *Sci. Amer.* **244** 52–64.

Lee, M. G.-S., Lewis, S. A., Wilde, C. D., & Cowan, N. J. (1983) Evolutionary history of a multigene family: an expressed human beta-tubulin gene and three processed pseudogenes. *Cell* **33** 477–487.

Lewis, K. R. & John, B. (1964) *The matter of Mendelian heredity*. J. A. Churchill, London.

Li, W-H., Luo, C-C., & Wu, C-I. (1985) Evolution of DNA sequences. In MacIntyre, R. J., (ed.) *Molecular evolutionary genetics*. Plenum Press, New York, pp. 1–94.

Little, P. F. R. (1982) Globin pseudogenes. *Cell* **28** 683–684.

Marx, K. A., Allan, J. R., & Hearts, J. E. (1976). Characterization of the repetitious human DNA families. *Biochem. Biophys. Acta* **425** 129–147.

Maxam, A. M. & Gilbert, W. (1977) A new method of sequencing DNA. *Proc. Nat. Acad. Sci.* **74** 560–564.

McKusick, V. A. (1986) The gene map of *Homo sapiens*: status and prospectus. *Cold Spring Harbor Symp. Quant. Biol.* **51** 15–27.

Micklos, G. L. G. (1985) Localized highly repetitive DNA sequences in vertebrate and invertebrate genomes. In: MacIntyre, R. J. (ed.) *Molecular evolutionary genetics*. Plenum Press, New York, 241–321.

Monaco, A. P. & Kunkel, L. M. (1987) A giant locus for the Duchenne and Becker muscular dystrophy gene. *Trends in Genetics* **3** 33–37.

Mount, S. M. (1982) A catalogue of splice junction sequences. *Nucleic Acid Res.* **10** 459–472.

Myers, R. M., Lerman, L. S., & Maniatis, T. (1985) A general method for saturation mutagenesis of cloned DNA fragments. *Science* **229** 242–247.

Nakamura, Y., Lepper, T. M., O'Connell, P., Wolff, R., Holm, T., Culver, M., Martin, C., Fujimoto, E., Hoff, M., Kumlin, E., & White, R. (1987) Variable number of tandem repeats (VNTR) markers for human gene mapping. *Science* **235** 1616–1622.

O'Brien, S. J., Seuanez, H. N., & Womack, J. E. (1985) On the evolution of genome organization in mammals. In: MacIntyre, R. J. (ed.) *Molecular evolutionary genetics*. Plenum Press, New York. 519–589.

Orgel, L. E. & Crick, F. H. C. (1980) Selfish DNA: the ultimate parasite. *Nature* **284** 604–607.

Orkin, S. H. (1986) Reverse genetics and human disease. *Cell* **47** 845–850.

Planta, R. J. & Meyerink, J. H. (1980) Organization of the ribosomal RNA genes in eukaryotes. In: Chambliss, G., Craven, G. R., Davies, J., Davis, K., Kahan, L., & Nomura, M. (eds.) *Ribosomes: structure, function and genes*. University Park Press, Baltimore, 871–887.

Reddy, E. P., Reynold, R. K., Santos, E., & Barbacid, M. (1982) A point mutation is responsible for the acquisition of transforming properties of the t24 human bladder carcinoma oncogene. *Nature* **300** 149–152.

Rich, A., Nordheim, A., & Wang, H. J. (1984) The chemistry and biology of left-handed Z DNA. *Ann. Rev. Biochem.* **53** 791–846.

Sanger, F. & Coulson, A. R. (1975) A rapid method for determining sequences in DNA by primed synthesis with DNA polymerase. *J. Mol. Biol.* **94** 444–448.

Schaffner, W., Serfling, E., & Jasin, M. (1985) Enhancers and eukaryotic gene transcription. *Trends in Genet.* **1** 224–230.

Schmid, C. W. & Shen, C-K. J. (1985) The evolution of interspersed repetitive DNA sequences in mammals and other vertebrates. In: MacIntyre, R. J. (ed.) *Molecular evolutionary genetics*. Plenum Press, New York. 519–589.

Shapiro, J. A. (1983) *Mobile genetic elements*. Academic Press, New York.

Singer, M. F. (1982) Highly repeated sequences in mammalian genomes. *Int. Rev. Cytol.* **76** 67–112.

Slightom, J. L., Blechland, A. E., & Smithies, O. (1980) Human fetal Gγ- and Aγ-globin genes: complete nucleotide sequences suggest that DNA can be exchanged between these duplicated genes. *Cell* **21** 627–638.

Soll, D. & Roberts, R. J. (eds) (1984) *The application of computers to research nucleic acids*. IRL Press, Oxford, U.K. Parts 1 & 2.

Thomas, E. D. (1986) Marrow transplantation and gene transfer as therapy for hematopoietic diseases. *Cold Spring Harbor Symp. Quant. Biol.* **51** 1009–1012.

Watson, J. D. & Crick, F. H. C. (1953) Molecular structure of nucleic acids. *Nature* **171** 737–738.

Watson, J. D., Hopkins, N. H., Roberts, J. W., Steitz, J. A., & Weiner, A. M. (1987) *Molecular biology of the gene*. 4th edn, Vols. 1 & 2. Benjamin/Cummings, California.

Weatherall, D. J. (1985) *The new genetics and clinical practice*. 2nd edn. Oxford University Press.

Whitehouse, H. L. K. (1972) *Towards an understanding of the mechanism of heredity*, 3rd edn., Edward Arnold, London.

Wyman, A. R. & White, R. (1980) A highly polymorphic locus in human DNA. *Proc. Nat. Acad. Sci.* **77** 6754–6758.

## GENERAL READING

For an historical account of the chromosome theory of Mendelian inheritance and the development of the science of genetics:

Carlson, E. J. (1966) *The gene theory: a critical history,* Saunders, Philadelphia.

Whitehouse, H. L. K. (1972) see references.

For an elementary text on human genetics:

Hartl, D. L. (1985) *Our uncertain heritage: genetics and human diversity* 2nd edn. Harper & Row, New York.

For an account of the application of molecular biology to the diagnosis, treatment and understanding of human disease:

Weatherall, D. J. (1985) see references.

For a general account of the structure and function of DNA:

Watson, J. D. *et al.* (1987) see references.

Lewin, B. (1987) *Genes*. 3rd edn. Wiley, New York.

For an introduction to the principles of biochemistry:

Stryer, L. (1981) *Biochemistry* 2nd edn. W. H. Freeman, San Francisco.

# 2

# DNA in the cell: chromatin

**Leigh A. Burgoyne**
Department of Biological Sciences, Flinders University, Sturt Road, Bedford
Park, South Australia 5042

## 2.1  INTRODUCTION

With the exception of mitochondrial DNA, the bulk of cellular DNA resides in the
nucleus of the cell, and all but a minute proportion of the nuclear DNA, is found
within the chromosomes in a DNA/protein complex called **chromatin**.

In all life forms, truly naked DNA is probably a rarity, its very high charge density
causing it to weakly bind a large variety of proteins. Some classes of proteins are
bound much more tightly than others forming complexes with the bulk of the DNA,
and are thus not very sequence specific. The special proteins that complex to DNA in
this relatively general way are called **histones** and **protamines**. They are characteristic
of the eukaryotes, the histones being found in normal somatic cells and the
protamines in sperm cells.

These tight, DNA-specific, but not very sequence specific complexes are traditionally referred to as chromatin or, if they come from the nucleus, **nucleochromatin**.

Bacterial DNA and mitochondrial DNA are not usually so tightly bound to such a
complement of basic proteins, and they are thus often loosely referred to as **naked
DNA** to contrast them with the DNA that is tightly complexed to histones or
protamines.

Besides the intrinsic interest of nuclear structure, from the perspective of the
forensic scientist, it is important to understand the organization of the DNA and the
other components of these structures, in order to assess the quality of biological
starting material, to understand how DNA may be best recovered from various
materials, and the practical significance of the various environmental variations and
contaminations.

The application of molecular biology in forensic science is still novel, and any
worker who wishes to follow its developments must understand the underlying
molecular facts as well as understanding how to excecute the currently useful
protocols.

In addition, one of the most striking features of DNA preparation is the way that the various methods of preparation of DNA tend to require different protocols for different tissues. For example, some procedures attack the tissue directly and make no attempt to pre-purify the chromatin or nuclei from the tissue, while other tissues are best handled by first extracting semipurified chromatin from it and then extracting the DNA from the chromatin. After this, the procedures for extracting DNA from the chromatin depend on the type of chromatin concerned, particularly whether it is somatic or sperm chromatin.

Good preparation technique is essential. To be successful in general DNA studies it is most important to begin with clean DNA, as contaminants such as basic proteins, acidic carbohydrates, and RNA, may cause technical problems. Large excesses of contaminating RNA and some acidic carbohydrates tend to block the action of restriction endonucleases, and contaminating basic proteins may block the restriction endonucleases' access to the DNA. More seriously, contaminating basic proteins may also inhibit the entry of DNA into agarose gels and thus cause the DNA to give ill-resolved smears on gel electrophoresis. In addition, RNA, minute traces of phenol, or contaminating aromatic amino acid rich proteins may simply cause a loss of any observable results. This is usually because these impurities cause an overestimate of the amount of DNA present in an extract, which results in too little DNA being submitted to the nucleases and gel analysis.

Thus an understanding of the structure and properties of chromatin is central to the practical application of human molecular genetics.


## 2.2  CHROMOSOMES AND TISSUES

Normal cells contain a spherical, densely staining nucleus that consists of a membrane surrounding a mass of DNA-containing material, chromatin.

### 2.2.1  Chromatin and chromosomes

Chromatin is actually made up of separate lumps called **chromosomes.** These are long, unbroken, DNA molecules that have an equal weight of protective protein bound to the DNA. The resultant DNA/protein complexes are always referred to as chromatin, and thus chromatin is the substance of chromosomes. It is very important to note that in the human genome, the chromatin proteins of normal nuclei are totally different from the chromatin proteins of the mature sperm head.

In mammals, sperm 'chromosomes' probably never exist as separate entities in the way that somatic chromosomes or egg cell chromosones can. The chromatin of sperm never has to go through the division processes of mitosis or meiosis, as it is created after the last spermatic division and then converted back into normal chromatin after fertilization. Thus, although the sperm chromatin can probably be said to have chromosomes in that the appropriate number and size pieces of DNA are present, this chromatin is probably not physically capable of generating separate, observable, chromosomes. Thus the study of the morphology of chromosomes is largely the study of the structure of normal, somatic, histone-type chromatin.

Through most of the cell cycle the somatic, nuclear chromatin exists as a shapeless conglomeration, but in cell division this shapeless mass undergoes a minor conformational change and resolves itself into a set of dramatically distinctively shaped chromosomes. There are 46 chromosomes per normal, adult, human nucleus, that is to say, 46 separate pieces of packaged DNA to make up the information complement of a normal adult. The structure of the DNA within them was considered in Chapter 1.

It should be noted that even when somatic chromatin looks like a featureless mass, it is known that the chromosomes are still present and intact (see review by Newport & Forbes 1987). Thus the term chromosomes not only applies to the observable chromosomes that can be seen during cell division, but is just as properly used for the highly intertangled and thus cryptic forms that are characteristic of the rest of the cell cycle.

### 2.2.2   The observable chromosome

The observable chromosomes are relatively unusual structures in the sense that they can only rarely be visualized in normal tissue preparations. Although always present within both the normal and the sperm cell, the chromosomes are observable only during the cell cycle or, best of all, in cells that have been deliberately locked in the 'metaphase' of the cell cycle by the use of antimitotic drugs such as Colchicine and Colcemid.

These drugs interfere with the spindle apparatus and thus lock the cell cycle when chromosomes are at their 'condensed' state, (that is, tightly contracted, compacted, and highly stainable, and thus observable). Thus the direct study of human chromosomes usually requires culturing of living cells from the subject, and there are now various protocols available for the staining and observation of human chromosomes (see, for example, Sandstrom *et al.* 1982).

In the human being, the shapes, sizes, and other features of the observable chromosomes are now well described in chromosomal maps or atlases in a defined, conventional shorthand language. (Bergsma *et al.* 1978). Fig. 2.1 shows an example.

### 2.3   THE STRUCTURE OF NORMAL, SOMATIC, CHROMATIN

Although the full details of the structure of chromatin are not yet clear, a great deal is already known. Firstly, the sperm chromatin is radically different in structure from somatic cell chromatin; it is discussed below as a separate topic. Somatic chromosomes are approximately 50% by weight proteins, with most of these proteins belonging to a group of simple, very positively charged proteins called histones (DeLange & Smith 1971, McGhee & Felsenfeld 1980). It is the histones that are mainly responsible for packing the DNA within the nucleus of the normal (somatic) human cell. They do this by aggregating into a large number of small octamers. These positively charged octamers are made up of four types of histone molecules, each with two molecules per unit giving a total of eight. These structures wrap a small piece, 140 base pairs, of the overall DNA length around them. The resultant complexes of DNA and histones are roughly disc shaped, approximately 5 by 10 nm, and are called the core particles of nucleosomes. When this core particle accepts an additional molecule of a different histone, called H1, then it binds still more DNA, usually a further 60 base pairs of DNA, to make a total of approximately 200 bases of DNA, and each single microcomplex of DNA and histones is then called a **nucleosome**. Note that the figure of 200 base pairs is not precise and shows characteristic deviations from this number between organisms and between tissues.

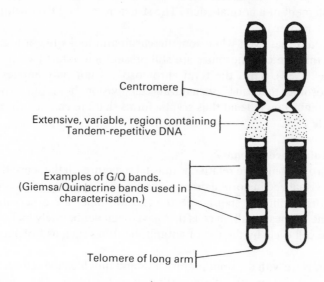

Centromere

Extensive, variable, region containing
Tandem-repetitive DNA

Examples of G/Q bands.
(Giemsa/Quinacrine bands used in
characterisation.)

Telomere of long arm

Fig. 2.1 — HUMAN CHROMOSOME 9 — A stylized diagram of human chromosome 1
stained by the Giemsa procedure. Note the bands caused by variations in stainability. These act
as identification marks for the classification of chromosomes (see Bergsma *et al.* 1978).

The DNA of chromatin is usually completely bound up into a linear series of
thousands or millions of these nucleosomal complexes per DNA molecule. Fig. 2.2A
depicts a single example of such a complex, and Fig. 2.2B shows how a series of them
may be arranged along a DNA molecule to form a nucleofilament. Fig. 2.3A shows
what these structures actually look like under the electron microscope.

Having considered the overall arrangement of protein and DNA it is now
necessary to look at this structure in more detail to lay the foundation for examining
how to go about releasing DNA.

There are four core, histone molecules, a combination of two of each (giving a
total of eight) which together form the body of the nucleosome. The H3 and the H4
form a central tetramer flanked by dimers of the H2A-H2B pair (Richmond *et al.*
1984). The core of the nucleosome is thus a hetero-octamer.

Outside of this core structure, there is the other, larger histone of the H1 group.
This class of molecule is usually approximately twice the size of the individual core
histones, and is rich in the amino acid lysine as opposed to the more arginine rich core
histones. The H1 class of histones are currently thought to bind to the DNA molecule
as it makes its passage across the centre of the nucleofilament from core particle to
core particle (see Fig. 2.2).

The histones that make up the core structure are evolutionarily stable, and their
primary structure varies very little from organism to organism or from tissue to tissue
so they have no value for personal or even species identification purposes. However,

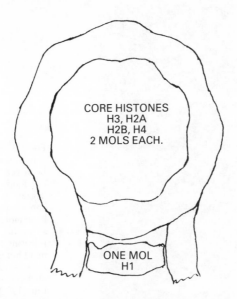

CORE HISTONES
H3, H2A
H2B, H4
2 MOLS EACH.

ONE MOL
H1

DNA COILS AROUND OUTSIDE OF STRUCTURE WITH
1.75 TURNS (140 BP) PER NUCLEOSOME.

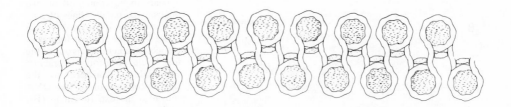

Fig. 2.2 — The structure of a nucleosome and a series of nucleosomes forming a nucleofilament. A— The approximate arrangement of the DNA in relation to the central histone hetero-
octamer and the more 'external' H1 histone. This is a face view of the disc-shaped structure.
B— The conformation of the nucleosomes or nucleosomal complexes that may be formed along
a DNA molecule to make a nucleofilament. Note the 'zigzag' arrangement of the complex sites.
Each complex site commonly involves approximately 200 base pairs of DNA.

the histone of the H1 category is much more variable and shows great variations
between organisms and even between tissues.

When chromatin is attacked by proteases such as trypsin, there is a well defined
order of susceptibility of the histones, the H1 and the H3 being first attacked,
followed by the other histones. (Saccone *et al.* 1983). Such changes in the histones
are relatively easily observed by electrophoretic analysis of acid extracts of tissues
(see, for example, Saccone *et al.* 1983). If they can be detected, it is a strong

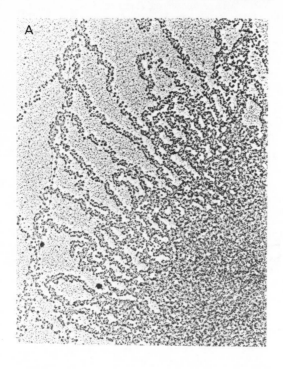

Fig. 2.3 — A comparison of chromosomal chromatin that has been gently lysed so as to loosen out loops of the relatively native 'zigzag' nucleofilament with chromosomal chromatin that has been more severely treated so as to strip the histones from it, also releasing loops of the neucleofilament but as the naked DNA.

A— 'Zigzag' loops of the native nucleofilament. From Rattner & Lin (1984) *Cytogenetics and Cell Genetics*, **38**, from the journal's title page. With permission of the editor, S. Karger, AG Basel, and the author, J. B. Rattner.

Note how the single nucleofilament, although a monofilament, appears to be composed of two opposing or parallel lines of nucleosomes. This duplex appearance arises from the 'zigzag' format of the monofilament that is one of the first results of histones interacting with DNA. Compare to the smooth contours of the free DNA shown in the experiment in (B). Scale: Each 'zigzag' nucleofilament is approximately 30 nm wide.

B— Smooth loops of the histone-depleted chromatin. The loops of near naked DNA. (Copyright held by Cell Press.) From Paulson & Laemmli (1977), *Cell* **12** 819. With permission of the editors of *Cell* and the author U. K. Laemmli.

Note the thin, smooth loops of DNA expanding away from the residual chromosomal skeleton. The loss of 'zigzag' appearance is as expected from the loss of the histones induced in this experiment, but the general pattern or format of great loops escaping a central chromosomal axis remains the same. Scale: The bar = 2 μm.

indication that nuclear-DNA damage is either under way or imminent as protease attack helps gelatinize the chromatin and render the DNA more exposed to attack from nucleases.

There are other, 'non-histone', proteins with both packing and non-packing functions. There is a wide variety of non-histone proteins, but they make up only a small proportion of the total nuclear protein, and with the exception of the DNA-destroying nucleases, the properties of this group are not of major importance to the forensic investigator. Some of these minor proteins are briefly discussed in the section dealing with the nucleoscaffold, below.

## 2.4   THE INTERACTION OF DNA AND THE HISTONE-PROTEINS OF THE CHROMOSOME

The most striking feature of chromatin is that it achieves an enormous contraction of each long DNA molecule, from DNA molecules several centimeters in length to chromosomes that are only micrometres in length. Thus the primary function of the protective histone proteins is to force the DNA into highly folded, or coiled, and/or looped conformations. The primary force associating the DNA and the histones is the charge attraction between the positively charged histones and the negatively charged DNA. The overall, final charge is usually slightly negative.

Free DNA strongly resists being sharply bent and tightly coiled because of its double helical structure which resists bending owing to steric considerations arising from its interior structure. Moreover, its external negative charges tend to repulse each other and so further favour extended, non-coiled conformations. Because of these two effects, solutions of unbroken, protein-free DNA usually form into gel-like semisolids even when the DNA is at low concentrations of well below 1%. The exact values of minimal-gelling-concentration are highly variable and are a very sensitive indicator of the average length of the extended DNA molecules.

The packaging protein can be artificially detached from the DNA by the following agents: ionic detergents such as sodium dodecyl sulphate (SDS), salt concentrations above approximately 1 Molar, and the action of specific protein destroying enzymes, proteases such as 'Protease-K'. Most de-proteinizations of DNA use some combination of these agents.

It should be noted that the full length of a human chromosome's DNA molecule *in situ* is always far larger than that which is mechanically stable in an extract or solution. The actual length of a population of human DNA fragments in solution depends on the handling and preparation procedures, and does not ever reflect the original length of the human DNA in the chromosome from which it was extracted.

## 2.5   FOLDING/COILING OF TRANSCRIPTIONALLY INACTIVE SOMATIC CHROMATIN

There are a variety of structures known to exist in somatic chromatin. For example, transcriptionally active chromatin has a distinctly different structure from the non-transcriptionally active chromatin (Pederson *et al.* 1986) and is probably structurally heterogeneous. At any one time, the bulk of the chromatin, over 95%, is in an inactive state which currently appears to be very similar in structure to the visible chromosome. The rest of this discussion will be concerned with this predominant form of chromatin.

The details of somatic chromatin folding are currently of minor importance to the forensic investigator simply wishing to extract DNA. However, they are outlined here as they may be of some importance to future investigators who wish to distinguish various forms of chromatin, one from another.

### 2.5.1 The lowest level of structure of normal human chromatin
The histone-protein that makes up the chromosome is responsible for a hierarchy of folding and/or coiling. The finest or lowest level of coil/folding is due to the histone-proteins forming the disc-like octamers of approximately 5 by 10 nm, the nucleosomes, discussed above.

Each nucleosome is arranged with opposing configuration to its neighbours (see Fig. 2.2) so that the DNA finally describes a complex zig-zagged path from double loop to double loop. (Thoma *et al.* 1979, Woodcock *et al.* 1984).

### 2.5.2 The intermediate level of structure
The intermediate level is currently subject to dispute. There are two main sets of opinions. The first, is that the zig-zag nucleofilament, as described above, is coiled in some way. A recent publication with this viewpoint is that of Walker & Sikorska (1987). The second opinion is that the next level of chromatin is obtained by folding the nucleofilament in some way. A recent publication with this particular viewpoint is that of Davis & Burgoyne (1987).

There is still no consensus on the details of this level of compaction.

### 2.5.3 The 'large-loop' level of structure
At the large-loop level the nucleofilament is arranged in gross loops along the chromosomal axis. Loops of this type are shown in Fig. 2.3. This looped structure has long been observed in a type of loosely structured chromosomes known as 'lamp-brush chromosomes', and it is becoming accepted that it is a general feature of all chromosomes but is directly observable only in highly transcriptionally active chromatin. (Rattner *et al.* 1981, Bjorkroth *et al.* 1988).

These loop systems are the first level of structure that is visible, albeit with difficulty, to the light microscope.

### 2.5.4 The gross shape of the condensed chromosome
The visible, condensed, chromosome of the human being has a definite shape with minor bulges and constrictions (Bergsma *et al.* 1978) that are quite characteristic of that chromosome and are highly inherited. Some features are very common and without obvious genetic effect, such as the pericentric heterochromatin of chromosome 9, but others cause recognizable genetic diseases such as mental retardation. For example, 'Fragile-X' (Sutherland 1983). All these special chromosomal features are in addition to the systems of G/Q stained bands discussed below.

There has been considerable debate about this highest level of structure, the 'nucleoscaffold', what causes it, and what stabilizes it (see, for example, Mirkovitch *et al.* 1984). However, the presence of a nucleoscaffold analogous to the cytoplasmic cytoskeleton, was graphically demonstrated by Paulson & Laemmlii (1977). More recently, these conclusions have been confirmed by Homberger & Koller (1988).

The skeletal proteins are a mixture, but, unlike the histones, they are not strongly basic. One interesting component is the enzyme Topoisomerase II (Earnshaw *et al.* 1985). The topoisomerases are enzymes that are responsible for putting torsional tension into DNA molecules and taking torsional tension out of DNA molecules, Thus this enzyme may be both the engine and the anchor structure which drives elastic tensions into and out of the nucleofilament and so controls the ratios of its various folding and/or coiling forms.

## 2.6  TRANSCRIPTIONALLY ACTIVE CHROMATIN

Transcriptionally active chromatin is the small subset of chromatin that is actually having its genes transcribed at any one time, and it is usually 5% or less of the genome at any one time. Thus although it is this category of the chromatin that is of critical importance for the operation of the cell at that time, it is never a major component of the nucleus. Almost none of the above discussion of chromatin structure applies to transcriptionally active chromatin. This is a field of itself. However, in summary only, the DNA in these transcriptionally active regions acts as if it were much less covered with histones than is normal nucleoprotein, and it is thought to contain many more of the 'non-histone' proteins such as RNA polymerases and sequence-specific control proteins.

## 2.7  THE STRUCTURE OF SPERM CHROMATIN

Mammalian sperm chromatin does not form recognizable chromosomes. It seems to have adopted a form of DNA packing that is highly specialized to the peculiar requirements of the sperm head, and it is assembled during the formation of the sperm and disassembled soon after penetration of the egg. It thus exists only during the short lifetime of the sperm. During this period, the histones that are found in normal chromosomes and nuclei, and which are relatively deficient in the amino acid cysteine, are almost completely replaced by cysteine-rich protamines (Kolk & Samuel 1975, Bouvier 1977). However, it should be noted that there are claims that a small but measurable proportion of sperm chromatin remains in the old, somatic, histone-type form. This histone-type chromatin seems to be a normal and definite subset of the genome (Gatewood *et al.* 1987). It is not a random internal fault or due to whole immature sperm heads, even though some infertile sperm heads are known to have unusual chromatin (Foresta *et al.* 1987, Kvist *et al.* 1987).

Compared to somatic chromatin, sperm chromatin is a physically stable material that has been aptly described as behaving like a 'porous keratinoid' (Bril-peterson & Westenbrinik 1963), keratin being the name for the proteins of hair and nails, etc. Unlike normal, histone-type-chromatin, sperm chromatin is stable to detergents of all types and is highly resistant to exogenous proteases, whilst its own endogenous proteases readily attack it under reducing conditions (Marushige & Marushige 1975). Both the resistance to detergents and the resistance to proteases is dependent on the integrity of a large number of disulphide crosslinks that are formed between the cysteine residues of the protamine protein. Hence the similarity to keratin, where disulphide crosslinks are an important feature (Evenson *et al.* 1978). In contrast to the somatic histones of the nucleosome core, the cysteine-rich protamines are not evolutionarily conserved (Calvin 1975).

Mature sperm chromatin is then markedly destabilized by reducing agents and, conversely, is extremely stable in the absence of reducing agents. This is a most important and useful feature of sperm chromatin, and one that allows it to be readily discriminated from any normal, histone-type chromatin with which it may be mixed, i.e. semen mixed with vaginal secretion. This is the basis of various methods of discrimination between the gamete chromatin of a male and the somatic chromatin from blood or vaginal tissues. During aging and storage of sperm, protamines do not protect the sperm DNA as well as might be expected because, although mechanically stable, the structure is highly porous (unpublished studies). Thus once the sperm's outer membranes have been ruptured, nucleases can interpenetrate it to a considerable degree. As a result, external nucleolytic activity on membrane-stripped sperm heads results in a large reduction in the molecular weight of the DNA inside the sperm head even without its dissolution (Naras Lapsys 1988). It is thus important, if very high quality DNA is desired, to inactivate nucleases quickly and as fully as possible, before stripping the sperm of its protective membranes. This is an important consideration when developing protocols for the extraction of sperm DNA.

It should also be noted that the structure and properties of sperm chromatin are not constant and appear to be dependent on the state of maturity of the sperm heads. As the sperm chromatin matures it loses zinc from zinc–thiol complexes. The thiols then oxidize to give the final, more stable, disulphide bonds. The zinc-thiol complexes are thought to be an earlier, looser form of bonding between the cysteines of the sulphur-rich protamines, and the disulphides a later and tighter form of bonding (Kvist *et al.* 1980, 1987).

## 2.8   THE PRINCIPLES BEHIND THE EXTRACTION OF DNA FROM SOMATIC CELLS

Often, DNA is extracted directly from a tissue without any attempt to first extract the chromatin. In these procedures the tissue is treated as if it was a mass of relatively impure chromatin. However, higher molecular weight and cleaner DNA can be obtained by first extracting the chromatin from the tissue and then the DNA from the chromatin.

Both sperm chromatin and somatic cell chromatin are, in their native state, totally insoluble complexes that can be washed and handled to almost any degree without any likelihood of damaging the DNA by fluid shearing forces (the mechanical tearing of DNA that occurs when handling in solutions).

However, in contrast to the protection from shearing, the structure of chromatin provides only a partial and incomplete protection of the DNA from enzymic or other attack and very little protection at all from the attack of low molecular weight reactive species such as acidic protons.

### 2.8.1   Chromatin disruption for DNA preparation; the problems

First, it should be noted that the moment that the chromatin structure begins to be made soluble in any way, the DNA becomes susceptible to shear forces and is also much less protected from enzymic attack. The insoluble chromatin does strongly protect the DNA from enzymic attack, but this protection is not complete and has a number of distinctive features.

Various reports of 'soluble' chromatin are actually studies of partially disrupted materials that are usually derivatives of classic 'histone-type' chromatin in which the H1 histone has been partially or totally removed and then the resultant, semi-soluble gel has been made physically tractable by breaking the continuity of the DNA with severe shear forces such as those obtained in mechnical food homogenizers of the rotating blade type.

However, in both sperm and normal 'histone-type' chromatin, as the chromatin structure is damaged its components do become progressively more soluble and thus progressively more susceptible to even more damage, both shearing and chemical. Thus chromatin breakdown tends to be a self-accelerating process.

The techniques for the deliberate disruption of chromatin and the subsequent preparation of DNA are relatively standard, although there are a large number of variations and, as already stated, difficulties can arise if the chromatin is not first semipurified from its source tissue.

The actual procedures used for extraction depend on the source tissue. Usually they rely on the fact that at physiological salt concentrations in the presence of chelating agents, a combination of low-speed homogenization together with the action of low levels of a non-ionic detergent (such as Nonidet P40 or Triton X-100) renders most cellular materials soluble, or into very small particles, so that the remaining chromatin can be centrifuged out at low speed. The insoluble chromatin is then subjected to a series of simple washes by mild mechanical resuspension, never sonication, and then pelleting from similar solutions. Sometimes high density cushions of sucrose solutions are used to further separate the relatively dense and coarse particles of chromatin from the less dense and/or much smaller particles of other cellular components.

There are a number of points to note in these sorts of preparations.

#### 2.8.1.1   The problem of premature lysis during the preparation

During handling, the chromatin can slowly lyse. The word 'lyse' generally implies the solublization of a particle, and usually implies that the products of lysis are non-sedimentable, clear solutions. Thorough lysis of chromatin does, indeed, give such a final product, a non-sedimentable, viscous solution. However, the incomplete lysis of chromatin usually gives a transitory but very long-lived phase in which intractable globules of semi-solution-gel centrifuge out and pack into coherent masses at the bottom of centrifuge tubes.

These masses of gel may become impossible to resuspend for further washing or further lysis, without the use of violent mechanical agitation, with its unavoidable problem of DNA-shearing. This whole difficulty is often prevented by taking care to postpone lysis until the chromatin is thoroughly washed. Premature lysis can also be prevented by the presence of a multicharged ion such as $Mg++$ or $Ca++$ or

Spermine++++ and/or Spermidine+++ all at millimolar or near millimolar concentrations. Spermidine and spermine are simple, low molecular weight, polypositive aliphatic amines that are ubiquitous in micro organisms and tissues, and are present in very high levels in some natural fluids such as semen. Their natural function seems to be to act as counter ions for nucleic acids, thus making these molecules less mutually repulsive.

Despite the fact that many old procedures certainly do use calcium or magnesium *in vitro* for this purpose (that is, to make nucleic acid complexes less gelatinous), it is now advised that use of either calcium or magnesium is avoided when stabilizing chromatin. These two metals can activate both endogenous and exogenous nucleases that can attack the DNA *in situ* in the chromatin (see, for example, review by Burgoyne & Hewish 1978).

If stabilization is necessary, it is preferable to use polyamines in the presence of chelating agents. Ideal conditions vary between materials, and some buffer mixtures are quite complex, for example the 'buffer-A' of Burgoyne *et al.* (1970), with the addition of 2 mM EDTA and 0.5 mM EGTA, has been used quite effectively. (EDTA = Ethylene diamine tetra acetate; EGTA = ethylene glycol-bis-(2-aminoethyl ether)-$N,N'$-tetraacetic acid.)

However, mixtures are usually in the range of 0.25 nm spermine tetra hydrochloride with 1 or 2 nm EDTA in tris-buffered physiological saline at a pH slightly above neutral, for example, pH 8.0.

### 2.8.1.2   Premature proteolysis
The chromatin can also be subjected to premature proteolysis and thus premature exposure of the DNA to other agents. Proteases are nearly ubiquitous biological contaminants and some forms of chromatin even have endogenous proteases (see, for example, Chong, *et al.* 1974, Bartley & Chalkley, 1970).

There is a range of commercially available protease inhibitors that can be used in cocktails to inhibit protease activity. Some examples are: phenyl methyl sulphonyl fluoride (PMSF), leupeptin, pepstatin, chloro tosyl amido amino heptanone (TLCK), chloro tosyl amido phenyl butanone (TPCK), and diisopropylfluorophosphate (DFP). These should be used with caution as some are extremely toxic. The most commonly used is PMSF.

### 2.8.1.3   Nucleases; nucleolytic damage
Nucleases that attack DNA are found in chromatin and tissue fluids and are produced by bacteria. Nucleases are classified into two broad classes: the exonucleases which attack the ends of DNA molecules, and the endonucleases that attack the DNA at a large variety of widely distributed sites. The exonucleases are of no real significance until there has already been extensive endonuclease activity, so they can usually be ignored, and it is the activity of the endonucleases that is critically important in understanding the types of damage that occur to DNA while it is still in chromatin. The first point to note is that, with few exceptions, the endonucleases tend to be strongly inhibited by a combination of alkaline conditions in the presence of chelating agents. Alkaline conditions in the absence of chelating agents do not inhibit the major nucleases, and the nucleases that operate under slightly acid conditions are less inhibited by chelating agents.

The endonucleases that commonly contaminate chromatin preparations are only very weakly specific with respect to the base sequences that they will attack. Thus their attack is random or merely spaced according to the spacing of whatever protective proteins may remain attached to the DNA (this contrasts with the restriction endonucleases that are very highly specific for base sequences. Their use will be discussed in subsequent chapters). However, although the common DNA-attacking endonucleases are poorly specific for base sequence (that is, relatively unaffected by base sequence), they are strongly affected by the chromatin proteins that are bound to the DNA. This 'blocking' effect of chromatin proteins has now been used in a great many basic studies of chromatin structure. From the practical point of view of the forensic scientist, the main types of damage that may be observed in DNA from somatic chromatin are as follows:

(a) Nucleolytic attack at the DNA where it is exposed at the short bridge region between nucleosomes (see Fig. 2.2B). This type of damage is readily recognizable because on examining the fragmented DNA by electrophoresis, it is found to form a series of broad molecular weight classes that are all multiples of approximately 200 base pairs (200 bp), that is, approximately 200, 400, 600, etc. This effect is character-istic of the common Ca–Mg endonuclease of mammalian chromatin (Burgoyne & Hewish 1978) and is also characteristic of some bacterial nucleases such as micrococ-cal nuclease (Noll 1974b).

(b) Nucleolytic attack on the nucleosomes themselves. This results in a mixture of fragments. At low levels of digestion, there may be a very ill-defined series of fragments that fall in a series of approximately 400, 600, 800, base pairs, etc. This is considered to be the consequence of the nuclease attacking at a very few places, and then only on the body of the most exposed nucleosomes (Burgoyne & Skinner 1981). However, if the damage has progressed further, then the breaks start to appear at very small intervals in the region of 80 base pairs, reflecting the approximate size of the turns the DNA makes (nearly twice) around each nucleosome. This phase is accompanied and followed by a terminal stage characterized by the appearance of a great many small subpeaks at 10 base pair intervals (Noll 1974a).

Overall, the three stages described always overlap; the first two stages reflecting the way the detail of the nucleosome structure interferes with the nucleolytic attack, and the last stage, of intense nucleolytic attack, more reflecting the way that the double helix of DNA lying against any protective surface will have a 10 base pairs periodic susceptibility that simply reflects the one-side protection that a helix with a 10 base pairs period gains from the surfaces it is bound to.

Nucleases that attack like this are often of the DNAase-I type, and would be expected to be magnesium dependent and stimulated by, or dependent upon, calcium also.

### 2.8.2  Summary: a 'typical' DNA extraction procedure
(a) Wash tissue homogenate in mildly alkaline chelating agents; if washing is to be extensive, a little spermine may be desirable.

(b) Physically detach the nucleoproteins from the DNA with anionic detergents and a number of hours digestion with a commercial protease.

(c) Extraction with an organic solvent such as phenol (to remove protease, detergent, and remnants of undigested protein).

(d) Precipitate the DNA from solution with alcohol and some salt such as sodium or ammoniun acetate.

First, the contaminating DNAases are inhibited with alkaline conditions and chelating agents such as EDTA. Then the histones are partly detached from the DNA with a detergent such as sodium dodecyl sulphate or sarcosinate. The detergents also inhibit DNAases, but not quickly enough to prevent damage of the DNA in the absence of EDTA.

It is usually the addition of the detergent that causes the DNA to expand away from the chromatin masses and raise the viscosity of the solution. If the viscosity is intractably high, then this lysate is often gently sheared by shaking or passing through a hypodermic needle a few times. The remainder of the procedure for DNA preparation usually consists of the digestion of the histones with one of the commercially available detergent-resistant proteases, followed by extraction with liquid phenol or chloroform, or phenol chloroform mixtures. This is to remove the protease, much of the detergent, and any remaining protein. The DNA is then commonly precipitated from the aqueous phase with alcohol. The final steps, stages (c) and (d) above, are often repeated once or twice.

At some stage during the procedure, the enzyme RNAase is added in order to degrade RNA. Pancreatic RNAase-A is commonly used because this enzyme is remarkably stable and thus easy to handle and keep pure. Neutral solutions of it are activated by a few minutes at 100°C, conditions that inactivate most contaminating enzymes. Anionic detergents do inhibit it to some degree, but it still slowly operates in their presence. It is only removed by phenol or slowly destroyed by the proteases used in preparing DNA such as protease-K.

So long as financial economy is not a serious consideration it is usually most convenient to add an excess of boiled RNAase-A very early in the DNA preparation. It will then quietly operate during the whole of the procedures until phenol or proteolytic digestion stops it. It is not inhibited by chelating agents.

## 2.9 THE PRINCIPLES BEHIND EXTRACTION OF DNA FROM SPERM CHROMATIN

The sperm chromatin also packages the DNA in a shear-resistant state, and it also provides a large degree of protection of the DNA from enzymic attack. However, as was the case for somatic chromatin, this protection is not complete.

The critical practical difference between the properties of sperm chromatin and somatic chromatin lie in the fact that the dissolution of sperm chromatin is very difficult unless there are reducing agents such as thiols or borohydrides present to break the S–S disulphide crosslinks. In the absence of reducing agents, proteolysis is slow and detergents have negligible effect on the structure. Herein lies the principle that allows the separation of somatic DNA from sperm DNA in mixtures of both. A mixture such as semen with other body fluids, may have chelating agents and anionic detergents added to it in order to selectively lyse the less structurally stable somatic chromatin. The somatic chromatin then selectively unravels, and its DNA can then be sheared and washed away from the sperm chromatin which still remains as compact masses, often still in the shape of the original sperm heads. The sperm heads may be further purified by other procedures such as gradient centrifugation, then washed, and are lysed by the addition of a reducing agent such as 2-mercaptoethanol or dithiothreitol.

Once the sperm heads have been subjected to reductive conditions the preparation of DNA from them is essentially the same as from somatic chromatin.

### 2.9.1   Patterns of nucleolytic damage of sperm chromatin

As only a negligible proportion of sperm chromatin is nucleosomal (Young & Sweeny 1979, Gatewood *et al.* 1987), patterns of fragments produced by nucleolytic attack are different. They have not been studied in as much detail as those from somatic chromatin, but it appears that the first and most noticeable product of endonuclease attack may be fragments first claimed to be approximately 20 kb (Wagner & Yun 1981) but probably nearer to 50 kb (Naras Lapsys 1988), and the final, most resistant category of fragments is approximately 72 bp (Young & Sweeny 1979). As noted by Young & Sweeny, the sperm head structure does strongly protect the DNA from attack until reducing agents are present.

### 2.10   SOME FINAL PROBLEMS WHICH MAY AFFECT THE QUALITY OF EXTRACTED DNA FOR FORENSIC INDIVIDUALIZATION

### 2.10.1   Microbial contamination

The enormous variety of microbial contaminations makes only a few broad generalizations possible.

Prokaryotic (i.e. common bacterial) chromatin is usually less tightly complexed to proteins than is human chromatin. However, the bacterial cell wall commonly remains intact during the first stages of preparation, and, even when dead, still encapsulates its DNA. This encapsulation, commonly but not invariably, prevents the DNA escaping even after the microbe has been killed by the detergents and chelating agents used to lyse chromatin. Thus it may be possible to remove much bacterial contamination by taking advantage of this, for example, by high-speed centrifugation of freshly lysed chromatin, after the addition of anionic detergents, chelating agents, and salt, but before the addition of the proteases. In the case of sperm chromatin, the best strategy may be to separate all DNA-containing, salt stable, particles on a caesium gradient. However, as there is an enormous variety of possible microbial contaminants, it seems unlikely that there can ever be any completely reliable, single set of principles for dealing with them.

Thus, contamination of human tissues with microbes is probably best handled at a much later stage in investigative procedures, the stage when the DNA is being probed. Probes that are known to be highly specific for the human genome should be selected.

### 2.10.2   Shearing of DNA and chromatin

DNA within the somatic or the sperm chromatin complex is relatively stable to shearing damage except for the most vigorous shearing, but is not stable to sonication. However, very early in the dissolution of any mass of chromatin, DNA and partially disrupted chromatin usually expand away from the mass and tend to gel the solutions around it. It is then much more susceptible to shear forces. This creates an unavoidable dilemma in the preparation of DNA from chromatin. If the chromatin suspension is dilute, then the preparation procedure was inefficient and the DNA is more easily damaged and/or lost as minute, wispy precipitates. However, if the DNA is too concentrated, then the solutions will be too viscous to extract and handle.

There is no ideal solution to this problem, and the worker must always expect that the ordinary handling of the chromatin lysate, pouring and pipetting, must break the DNA into random pieces that are commonly longer than 25 kilobases but shorter than approximately 60 kilobases. The actual size depends on the particular care of stirring and handling during preparation. Thus, if on analysis on agarose gel electrophoresis the DNA is observed to have a mean molecular weight well below 20 kilobases, then it is reasonable to presume that there had been chemical or enzymic degradation either before or during the process of lysing the chromatin.

One or two passages of DNA solutions through a fine-bored hypodermic syringe needle will reduce DNA molecular weights to approximately 20 kilobases, and a few seconds of sonication from ultrasonic devices of the type used to disrupt cells will usually reduce the molecular weight below approximately 2 kilobases, but not below approximately 200 base pairs.

### 2.10.3   Non-enzymic chemical damage of DNA during DNA and chromatin isolation procedures

Chemical damage by free radicals and other active species is common and diverse, and usually bears little relationship to the structure of chromatin. However, a number of points are worth noting.

It is desirable to carry out chromatin and DNA preparations in subdued light, particularly when they are impure, because biologically ubiquitous chromophores such as lumichrome can transfer light energy to nucleic acids and cause extensive damage to them (see, for example, Sussenbach & Berends 1963).

It is also desirable to avoid transition metals, particularly iron and zinc, and to add EDTA to chelate the remainder because although DNA is not highly susceptible to metal damage (unlike RNA), transition metals do catalyze the destruction of nucleic acid components, both directly or by facilitating attack of oxidative species (Singer & Fraenkel-Conrat 1965, Butzow & Eichorn 1975).

### 2.11   SUMMARY

Free DNA with a relaxed structure is not commonly found in cells as its great length and high tendency to extend rather than bend result in a material that could not be contained within cells unless there was very little of it per cell. This was, apparently, evolutionarily unacceptable.

Thus the DNA within cells is always found to be compacted, coiled, or folded in various ways. In the human being, these foldings and coilings are understood reasonably well at the lowest levels of coiling, and have been described. However, they are less clearly understood at some of the higher orders of folding or coiling.

The structures formed by these hierarchies of compaction are known as chromosomes.

The DNA of eukaryotes such as the human being, exists bound in a variety of complexes of which the most common is the histone-type complex of somatic cells.

The other complex of interest is the protamine-type complex of sperm cells.

With care, the DNA can be differentially extracted from these two types of complex, and this is the basis of forensically useful separations of male and female DNA in mixtures of sperm and other fluids. The procedures for these differential extractions are still not fully developed, and this is one obvious set of advances that still waits to be completed.

Isolation of DNA is principally a procedure for separating the protein of chromatin from the DNA while minimizing damage to the DNA. These forms of damage have been discussed.

When extracting DNA from chromatin, it is important to keep the molecular weight as high as is practical. This is usually more important for DNA destined to be used in RFLP (restriction fragment length polymorphisms) studies than in PCR (polymerase chain reaction) studies, as the molecular weights of the regions of interest are usually smaller for PCR analysis than for RFLP analysis.

## REFERENCES

Bartley, J. & Chalkley, R. (1970) Further studies of a thymus nucleohistone associated protease. *J. Biol. Chem.* **245** 4286–4292.

Bergsma, D., Lindsten, J. E., Klinger, H. P., Hamerton, J. L., & Geffner, E. S. (1978) An international system for human cytogenic nomenclature. *Cytogenetics and Cell Genetics.* **21** 309–403. Reprint requests to publishers: S. Karger, Basel, Arnold-Bocklin-Strasse 25, CH-4011 Basel. Switzerland.

Bjorkroth, B., Ericson, C., Lamb, M. M., & Daneholt, B. (1988) Structure of the chromatin axis during transcription. *Chromosoma* **96** 333–340.

Bouvier, D. (1977) Chemical aspects of histone acetylation and replacement in mouse spermatids at different stages of maturation. *Cytobiologie* (*European Journal of Cell Biology*) **15** 420–437.

Bril-peterson, E. & Westenbrinik, H. G. K. (1963) A structural basic protein as a counterpart of deoxyribonucleic acid in mammalian spermatozoa. *Biochim. Biophys. Acta* **76** 152–154.

Burgoyne, L. A., Anwar Wagar, M., & Atkinson, M. (1970) Calcium-dependent priming of DNA synthesis in isolated rat liver nuclei. *Biochem. Biophys. Res. Comms.* **39** 254–259.

Burgoyne, L. A. & Hewish, D. R. (1978) The regular substructure of mammalian nuclei and nuclear Ca–Mg endonuclease. *The cell nucleus* (ed. Busch, H.) **4** 47–74.

Burgoyne, L. A. & Skinner, J. D. (1981) Chromatin superstructure: the next level of structure above the nucleosome has an alternating character. A two-nucleosome based series is generated by probes armed with DNAase I acting on isolated nuclei. *Biochem. Biophys. Res. Comms.* **99** 893–899.

Butzow, J. & Eichorn, G. (1975) Different susceptibility of DNA and RNA to cleavage by metal ions. *Nature* **254**, 358–359.

Calvin, H. I. (1976) Comparative analysis of the nuclear basic proteins in rat, human, guinea pig, mouse, and rabbit spermatozoa. *Biochimica et Biophysica Acta* **434** 377–389.

Chong Ming Ta, Garrard, W. T., & Bonner, J. (1974) Purification and properties of a neutral protease from rat liver chromatin. *Biochemistry* **13** 5128–5134.

Davis, S. J. & Burgoyne, L. A. (1987) The DNAase I generated disomal series is coherent to 16N. *FEBS Letters* **226** 88–90.

DeLange, R. J. & Smith, E. L. (1971) Histones: structure and function. *Annual Reviews of Biochemistry* **40** 279–314.

Earnshaw, W. C., Halligan, B., Cooke, C. A., Heck, M. M. S., & Lui, L. F. (1985) Topoisomerase ii is a structural component of mitotic chromosome scaffolds. *J. Cell Biol.* **100** 1706–1715.

Evenson, D. P., Witkin, S. S., De Harven, E., & Bendich, A. (1978) Ultrastructure of partially decondensed human spermatozoal chromatin. *J. Ultrastructure Research* **63** 178–187.

Foresta, C., Indino, M., Mioni, R., Scannelli, G., & Scandellari, C. (1987) Evidence of sperm nuclear heterogeneity in ex-cryptorchid subjects. *Andrologia* **19** 148–152.

Gatewood, J. M., Cook, G. R., Balhorn, R., Bradbury, E. M., & Schmid, C. W. (1987) Sequence specific packaging of DNA in human sperm chromatin. *Science* **236** 962–964.

Homberger, H. & Koller, T. (1988) The integrity of the histone–DNA complex in chromosome fibres is not necessary for the maintainance of the shape of mitotic chromosomes. *Chromosoma* **96** 197–204.

Kolk, A. R. H. & Samuel, T. (1975) Isolation, chemical and immunological characterisation of two strongly basic nuclear proteins from human Spermatozoa. *Biochem. Biophys. Acta* **393** 307–319.

Kvist, U., Afzelius, B. A., & Nilsson, L. (1980) The intrinsic mechanism of chromatin decondensation and its activation in human spermatozoa. *Develop., Growth and Differ.* **22**(3) 543–554.

Kvist, U., Bjorndahl, L., & Kjellberg, S. (1987) Sperm nuclear zinc, chromatin stability and male fertility. *Scanning Microsc.* **1**, 1241–1247.

Marushige, Y. & Marushige, K. (1975) Enzymic unpacking of bull sperm chromatin. *Biochim. Biophys. Acta* **403** 180–191.

McGee, J. D. & Felsenfeld, G. (1980) Nucleosome structure. *Annual Reviews of Biochemistry* **49** 1115–1156.

Mirkovitch, J., Mirault, M. E., & Laemmlli, U. K. (1984) Organisation of the chromatin loop: Specific DNA attachment sites on the nuclear scaffold. *Cell* **39** 223–232.

Naras Lapsys (1988) Honours thesis. Flinders University. May 1988.

Newport, J. W. & Forbes, D. J. (1987) The nucleus: structure, function and dynamics. *Annual Reviews of Biochemistry* **56** 535–565.

Noll, M. (1974a) Internal structure of the chromatin unit. *Nucleic Acids Research* **1** 1573–1578.

Noll, M. (1974b) Subunit structure of chromatin. *Nature* **251** 249–251.

Paulson, J. R. & Laemmli, U. K. (1977) The structure of histone-depleted metaphase chromosomes. *Cell* **12** 817–828.

Pederson, D. S., Thoma, F., & Simpson, R. T. (1986) Core particle, fibre, and transcriptionally active chromatin structure. *Ann. Rev. Cell. Biol.* **2** 117–147.

Rattner, J. B., Goldsmith, M. R., & Hamalko, B. A. (1981) Chromosome organisation during male meiosis in *Bombyx mori. Chromosoma* **82** 341–351.

Rattner, J. B. & Lin, C. C. (1984) Ultrastructural organisation of double minute chromosomes and HSR regions in human colon carcinoma cells. *Cytogenet. Cell. Genet.* **38** 176–181.

Richmond, T. J., Finch, J. T., Rushton, B., Rhodes, D., & Klug, A. (1984) Structure of the nucleosomal core particle of 7 A resolution. *Nature* **311** 532–537.

Saccone, G. T. P., Skinner, J. D., & Burgoyne, L. A. (1983). Resistance of chromatin superstructure to tryptic digestion modulated by conjugated polyacrylamide. *FEBS* **157** 111–114.

Sandstron, M. M. H., Beauchesne, M. T., Kustashaw, K. M., & Latt, S. A. (1982) Prenatal cytogenic diagnosis. *Methods in Cell Biology*, (ed. Latt, S. A. & Darlington, G. J.) **26** 35–66.

Singer, B. & Fraenkel-Conrat, H. (1965) Effects of light in the presence of iron salts on RNA and model compounds. *Biochemistry* **4** 226–233.

Sussenbach, J. S. & Berends, W. (1963) Photosensitised inactivation of deoxyribonucleic acid *Biochim. Biophys. Acta* **76** 154–156.

Sutherland, G. R. (1983) The fragile X chromosome. Int. Rev. Cytology **81** 107–143.

Thoma, F., Koller, T., & Klug, A. (1979) Involvement of histone H1 in the organisation of the nucleosome and the salt dependent substructures of chromatin. *J. Cell Biol.* **83**, 408–427.

Wagner, T. E. & Yun, J. S. (1981) Human sperm chromatin organisation: isolation of homogenous (25K bp) DNA fragments from human sperm cells. *Archives of Andrology* **6** 47–51.

Walker, R. P. & Sikorska, M. (1987) Chromatin structure. *Jour. Biol. Chem.* **262** 12223–12227.

Woodcock, C. L. F., Frado, L. Y., & Rattner, J. B. (1984) The higher order structure of chromatin: evidence for a helical ribbon arrangement. *J. Cell Biol.* **99** 42–52.

Young, R. J. & Sweeny, K. (1979) The structural organisation of sperm chromatin. *Gamete Research* **2** 265–282.

# 3

# Experimental techniques for the isolation and analysis of DNA from forensic materials

**Ivan Balazs, Michael Baird, Keven McElfresh,** and **Robert Shaler**
Lifecodes Corporation, Sawmill River Road, Valhalla, NY 10595 USA

## 3.1  INTRODUCTION

The main objective of this chapter is to provide general information on the basic procedures used in the processing of samples for DNA profiling. The main topics covered are: sample preservation, extraction of DNA from evidentiary material, estimation of the integrity and amount of DNA, and effect of environment on recovered DNA. The final part of this chapter gives a general outline of the procedures utilized for the fractionation and analysis of extracted DNA.

## 3.2  SAMPLE PRESERVATION

The first and probably most asked question by those concerned with the collection of samples from the crime scene, is how to store evidence that contains biological material so as to minimize the destruction of the DNA present in it. This destruction or degradation occurs as a result of the action of enzymes that randomly degrade DNA starting from the end of the molecule (exonucleases) or by producing double strand breaks (endonucleases). These enzymes are present in the cell or in contaminating bacteria, and begin their action after cell death. Sterile blood in tubes with EDTA or citrate, as preservatives, can be kept for several days at room temperature and many years at 4°C. However, once opened, blood samples in citrate are readily contaminated, and the stability of DNA is reduced. Blood collected in heparinized tubes will clot in a few days, and the yield of DNA will be greatly reduced. Probably the safest and simplest procedure for preserving samples is freezing. This procedure is applicable to any biological material since it will stop both bacterial growh and the activity of enzymes that cleave DNA. The best temperature to store biological materials for an unlimited period is at −70°C or over liquid nitrogen. For a period in the range of a few weeks it can be stored at −20°C, preferably in a non-frost free freezer. Storage in ice is recommended for only a short period, ideally for a few hours and no more than a few days. After a sample has been frozen it should not be thawed and frozen repeatedly since this will promote cell breakage and facilitate DNA degradation. Similar recommendations for blood storage have been made by Madisen *et al.* (1987).

Another set of conditions that can be used to preserve evidence is to air-dry the liquid samples on filter paper (McCabe *et al.* 1987) or on clean cotton fabric. Items such as blood or semen have been preserved for several years as dried stains in sealed plastic envelopes (to protect them from exposure to humidity) and stored at 4 or −20°C.

Preservation of tissues in formaldehyde or similar chemicals is not recommended since DNA degrades during prolonged storage. A tissue sample which has been fixed should be rinsed with normal saline solution and then kept refrigerated or frozen until ready to process.

A major advantage of DNA over proteins is that, while environmental conditions readily affect the properties of proteins due to changes from a native to a denatured state the secondary structure of DNA is much more resistant to denaturation. The most significant effects of the environment upon DNA are hydrolytic and oxidative cleavages. These degradations frequently result in cleavage and occur at near-random sites along the DNA molecule. The analytical tests described in the following sections (i.e. analysis of DNA polymorphisms) require that, to generate a result, the DNA region to be examined has to be intact. Therefore it is not only important to recover a sufficient amount of DNA for a particular test, but the DNA sample should contain a sufficient amount of DNA larger than the pieces to be studied, and this usually means larger than 10 or 20 kb.

## 3.3   EFFECT OF THE ENVIRONMENT ON THE INTEGRITY OF DNA

An important aspect of the application of an identity test to forensic samples is to understand the ways in which their exposure to the environment can affect the outcome of the test. Since the chemical and physical properties of DNA are well understood it is possible to predict that prolonged exposure to sunlight, warm temperatures, and high humidity will result in the degradation of DNA. As mentioned earlier (section 3.1), even in the absence of external factors, the nucleases released upon cell death may cause the degradation of DNA. However, because this breakdown occurs at near-random sites the probability of generating particular DNA fragment size(s) by a restriction endonuclease will depend on how extensive was the DNA degradation and the size of the DNA fragment(s) to be detected. The larger DNA polymorphic fragments are more likely to become a target for random breaks. A common observation with samples of partially degraded DNA is that the largest size alleles gradually disappear while the smaller ones remain. Therefore, when examining DNA polymorphisms it is important to analyze each locus individually. This will facilitate the interpretation of the results and the statistical calculations associated with it (see Chapter 6). Studies using semen and blood stains indicate that DNA, suitable for restriction fragment length polymorphism (RFLP) analysis, have been recovered from samples several years old (Gill *et al.* 1985, Giusti *et al.* 1986, Kanter *et al.* 1986). Similarly, experiments have been performed to test the effect of humidity, heat, ultraviolet radiation, and soil contamination on the quality and quantity of DNA recovered from blood stains (Gill *et al*. 1987, McNally *et al*. 1989). The results showed that several days of incubation at 37°C, or at different degrees of humidity, did not change the pattern of RFLP detected in those samples. Prolonged exposure to ultraviolet decreased the amount of high molecular weight DNA recovered, but it did not have any effect on the pattern of RFLP. However, the addition of any type of soil to a blood stain greatly decreased the chances for DNA recovery, and much of the DNA recovered was of bacterial origin. Another factor in the recovery of DNA from bloodstains is the type of substrate on which the sample is found. Studies by McNally *et al*. (1989a) show that the DNA recovered from scrapings, plastic bags, synthetics, and denim is, generally, either high molecular weight or only partially degraded and suitable for RFLP analysis. However, DNA recovered from carpet was usually degraded probably as a result of its interaction with dirt or soil. In general, evidence recovered from soiled materials is more likely to be degraded than that from relatively clean substrates. Also, putrefied biological material, as judged by its characteristic smell, commonly yields degraded DNA that is not suitable for RFLP analysis.

The most useful information that this type of study provides is whether, from a particular evidentiary sample, sufficient quality and quantity of DNA might be recovered by the forensic scientist to obtain a DNA profile.

Another aspect related to sample quality is the effect of bacterial, yeast, or fungal contamination in the RFLP analysis. In many instances the DNA recovered from a sample consists of a mixture of human and bacterial DNA. In addition, plasmids might be present in the bacteria. Although human DNA probes are not homologous to bacterial DNA, plasmid DNA may crossreact with residual plasmid vector which may be present in a DNA probe. None of these possible contaminants can lead to false inclusions and the best way to account for the additional bands that might be present is to hybridize the DNA sample to probes consisting of plasmid DNA and bacterial ribosomal DNA. Since the sequence of bacterial ribosomal genes are highly conserved, they commonly expose the presence of DNA derived from bacteria (unpublished results).

## 3.4 PROCESSING OF EVIDENTIARY MATERIAL FOR DNA PURIFICATION

The main objective of this first step in the analysis of a forensic sample, especially where the amount of material is limiting, is to maximize the recovery of the cellular material containing the DNA. At the same time the method used to process the sample should also be gentle enough so as not to mechanically shear the DNA.

### 3.4.1 Blood

By and large the simplest source from which to prepare DNA is liquid blood. Unfortunately, with the exception of samples collected as exemplars, only on rare occasions is this type of sample available from the scene of a crime.

The first step in the processing of blood is to lyse the erythrocytes, which account for over 99% of blood cells, while leaving the nuclei of the other cells intact. This step is also important since it eliminates the haemoglobin from the red cells. The iron present in haemoglobin causes the degradation of DNA by catalyzing the cleavage of phosphodiester bonds (Zamenhof 1957). Blood samples are mixed with four volumes of a blood lysis buffer (0.32 M sucrose, 10 mM Tris HCl, pH 7.6, 5 mM magnesium chloride, 1% Triton X-1000). The nuclei are pelleted by centrifugation at $1000 \times g$ for 10 min at 4°C, and the process repeated a second time (Kanter *et al.* 1986). Similarly, blood stains can be left soaking overnight at 4°C in blood lysis buffer and the released nuclei recovered by centrifugation. However, it should be noted that over-long extraction in the presence of magnesium and cellular debris often results in degradation of the DNA.

The nuclear pellet is resuspended in nuclei lysis buffer (10 mM tris hydrochloric acid, 10 mM sodium chloride, 10 mM EDTA final pH 7.4). Proteinase K is then added to a final concentration of 100 µg/ml, followed by sodium dodecylsulphate (SDS) to a final concentration of 0.2%, and gently mixed. The lysate is incubated for 2 hrs at 65°C.

### 3.4.2  Semen
The recovery of spermatozoa from semen is aided by the fact that this type of cell is more resistant to lysis than somatic cells. Sperm from vaginal swabs are obtained by soaking the cotton swabs with physiological saline and pelleted by centrifugation for 10 min at 3600 rpm, 4°C (Giusti *et al.* 1986). Dried semen stains are processed by cutting the material into small pieces and soaking them, with mild agitation, overnight at 4°C in phosphate buffered saline (PBS) containing 2% Sarcosyl. Sperm released into solution are recovered by centrifugation. To decrease the number of, or totally eliminate, nuclei from female cells, a possible contaminant of the sperm recovered from a vaginal swab or semen stain, the sperm pellet is resuspended in PBS containing 1% sodium lauryl sulphate and 100 µg/ml of proteinase K and incubated for 2 h at 65°C with mild agitation. The sperm heads are subsequently lysed by resuspension in the same solution with the addition of 10 mM dithiothreitol, 50 mM EDTA followed by incubation for 4 h at 65°C. This procedure is similar to those described by Gill *et al.* 1985 and Giusti *et al.* 1986.

### 3.4.3  Soft tissues
To maximize recovery of DNA the tissue has to be ground. This ensures that all cells are lysed by the DNA lysis buffer (see section 3.4.2). On fresh or decomposed tissue this is performed by cutting the tissue, with a scalpel or scissors, into fragments a few mm in size followed by further disruption at 4°C in a tissue homogenizer such as a Dounce, Virtis, or similar apparatus. This homogenization is carried out in normal saline or blood lysis buffer. Cells and or nuclei are collected by centrifugation (1000 $\times g$ for 10 min). Alternatively, frozen tissue is processed by breaking it into small fragments in a mortar followed by grinding in a blender, equipped with a stainless steel cup, with liquid nitrogen. The frozen powder is placed into DNA lysis buffer, followed by addition of proteinase K and SDS (see section 3.4.1).

### 3.4.4  Bones
The best source of cellular material is the bone marrow, but cells are also embedded in the bone matrix. After mechanically opening a bone, the central soft tissue can be scraped off and subjected to a standard lysis protocol. Solid bone should be broken

into small pieces a centimetre or less in size and placed into the metal vessel of a Waring blender with liquid nitrogen and homogenized to a fine powder. The powdered sample can be processed as described for soft tissues. This method is simlar to that described by Perry *et al.* (1988) to isolate DNA from human rib bone.

### 3.4.5  Formalin and paraffin-embedded samples

Although prolonged storage of tissue in formalin results in the degradation of DNA, there are instances in which this material can be the only potential source of DNA. We have been successful in purifying undegraded DNA from tissues that have been kept for several weeks in formaldehyde and also from samples that had been subsequently embedded in paraffin. This is consistent with results obtained with histopathological specimens by Goelz *et al.* (1985).

Formalin fixed tissues can be processed by first rinsing the tissue with saline solution, followed by mincing into small fragments. These fragments can then be further homogenized in a blender with cold saline solution. The homogenized tissue is pelleted by centrifugation and resuspended in DNA lysis buffer, followed by the addition of proteinase K and SDS, as described for fresh tissue. Alternatively, the tissue can be frozen at $-70°C$ and pulverized by homogenization in a blender with liquid nitrogen followed by digestion with proteinase K as above.

Paraffin-embedded tissues can be processed by first removing the excess paraffin surrounding the tissue and slicing the tissue block into small sections with a razor blade. The rest of the paraffin can be removed by washing the tissue with xylene followed by ethanol. Finally the sample is resuspended in DNA lysis buffer, proteinase K (500 µg/ml), and 1% SDS and digested for 2 h at 37°C (Impraim *et al.* 1987, Mark *et al.* 1987).

### 3.5  PURIFICATION OF DNA

There are innumerable variations on the general procedures, described below, that will result in the isolation of DNA. In addition, there are a number of potentially simpler, if not as general, methods to obtain DNA suitable for analysis. Therefore, only a general outline of some of them will be given here. To be usable for DNA profiling the main criterion that the DNA sample has to meet is that it is completely digested with restriction enzymes. To reach this objective the proteins in the cellular lysate are digested with a general purpose protease, proteinase K (as described earlier). The proteins remaining in the lysate are then removed by addition of sodium perchlorate (1 M final concentration) and gently mixed for 15 min with an equal volume of 90% phenol. The phases are separated by centrifugation ($5000 \times g$ for 15 min) and the extraction process repeated with an equal volume of solvent (phenol:chloroform (1:1)) and then finally chloroform. This is followed by dialysis against three changes, at 4 h intervals, of TE buffer (10 mM tris hydrochloric acid, 10 mM EDTA at pH 7.4) or by ethanol precipitation of the DNA (in 0.3 M ammonium acetate, 70% ethanol) overnight at $-20°C$. Ethanol precipitated DNA is recovered by centrifugation at $12\,000 \times g$ for 15 min, and the precipitate is resuspended in TE buffer.

Deproteinization with solvents is not essential for restriction enzyme digestion although it probably facilitates it. Alternatively, lysis can be performed with cells trapped in an agarose gel (Schwartz & Cantor 1984, Williams 1987), with subsequent elimination of detergent and proteinase K by soaking the gel in TE buffer. A different method of purifying DNA is to add caesium chloride (CsCl) to the cell lysate. Samples are centrifuged at high speeds to band the DNA (Weeks *et al.* 1986). It is possible to concentrate DNA by dialyzing the cell lysate against polyethylene glycol (PEG) (Longmire *et al.* 1987). This is by no means an exhaustive coverage of DNA purification methods, and many more can be found in the literature (Gautreau *et al.* 1983, Leadon & Cerrutti 1982, McCabe *et al.* 1987, Miller *et al.* 1988). All of those described above should yield high molecular weight DNA that is suitable for digestion with restriction endonucleases. The final choice of a DNA purification procedure is a subjective matter ultimately determined by how easily a particular laboratory adapts any of them to their needs.

## 3.6   TESTING DNA SAMPLE FOR QUALITY AND QUANTITY

Whatever extraction and purification protocol is adopted, it is necessary to check the purity (quality) and the amount (quantity) of DNA before restriction and further analysis.

Several procedures for measuring the amount of DNA recovered from biological materials are available (Table 3.1). A frequently used method is to measure the

**Table 3.1** — Methods to quantitate DNA

| Method | Sensitivity |
|---|---|
| Diphenylamine (Burton 1956) | $6\times10^{-6}$ g |
| UV absorption | $1\times10^{-6}$ g (in 0.2 ml) |
| Fluorescence with Hoechst | $1\times10^{-8}$ g |
| Fluorescence in gel with ethidium bromide | $1\times10^{-8}$ g |
| Hybridization to Alu-DNA sequence | $<1\times10^{-10}$ g |

absorbance of a solution containing purified DNA at 260 nm. Although the results are accurate when used with purified samples, this method is limited in its usefulness if the sample contains large amounts of RNA or any chemical that also absorbs at that wavelength. It has the advantage of being nondestructive to the sample. Chemicals that specifically bind or react with DNA have also been popular. One such method is based on the reaction of diphenylamine to deoxyribose (Burton 1956). Because of its specificity, RNA does not interfere. Its major drawback is that it is slow and it destroys the DNA sample.

More sensitive tests utilize dyes that specifically bind or intercalate into DNA such as DABA (Vytasek 1982), Hoechst 33258 (Cesarone *et al.* 1979), DAPI (Kapuscinski & Skoczylas 1977), and Ethidium Bromide, EtBr, (Luttke *et al.* 1980). These tests are based on the property of the dyes to form a fluorescent complex upon binding to DNA. In addition this binding is generally reversible, therefore nondestructive, and the DNA sample can be saved for later processing.

The most sensitive method to detect human DNA is by hybridization to repeated DNA sequences. For example, denatured human DNA bound to a nylon filter (dot or slot blot) is annealed to a clone containing a highly repeated DNA sequence (e.g. clone pBLUR8 containing an Alu sequence; Jelineck *et al.* 1980). The relative intensity of the radioactive signal is compared to samples containing a known amount of DNA.

The above procedures only provide information about the quantity of DNA but not about the quality or integrity of the DNA sample. A simple method that will provide both types of information is the 'yield or degradation' gel. A 0.5% agarose gel is loaded with the following: one lane containing size markers made of HindIII-digested DNA from lambda bacteriophage, several standards containing known amounts of undigested lambda DNA (e.g. 5, 10, 20, 50 ng/lane), and an aliquot from each DNA sample under question. Electrophoresis is performed for 1 or 2 h at 50 V/cm in a submarine gel apparatus with an electrophoresis buffer containing 50 µg/ml of EtBr. The DNA is visualized in a UV-transilluminator (302 nm) and photographed with a Polaroid film. Samples containing mostly intact DNA (i.e. >20 kb) will appear as a tight fluorescent band at approximately the same distance from the origin as the intact, undigested standards. A completely degraded sample will migrate at a size of less than 2 kb, while a partially degraded sample will produce an intermediate pattern. The amount of intact DNA in the sample can be closely estimated by comparing the amount of fluorescence of the unknown to those of DNA concentration standards (Fig. 3.1A). It is also possible to increase the sensitivity of this test by gel hybridization, of the DNA samples, to a highly-repeated human DNA sequence (e.g. Alu sequence) using the procedure described by Purrello & Balazs (1983). The results of such experiments are shown in Fig. 3.1B,C.

### 3.7   SEX DETERMINATION

For a number of forensic cases it is useful to know the sex of the individual from whom a DNA sample originated. The existence of repeated DNA sequences preferentially located in the Y chromosome can help establish the presence of DNA that, with rare exceptions, is characteristic of male individuals.

Several such repeated sequences have been cloned and used for sexing. Two cloned DNA fragments have been described by Cooke *et al.* (1982), LWES5 and pHY2.1, that recognize respectively a 3.4 and a 2.1 kb DNA fragment in HaeIII digested DNA. The DNA fragments recognized by these probes represent repeated DNA sequences from the long arm of the Y-chromosome and have been used for sex determination in prenatal and forensic samples (Gosden *et al.* 1984, Gill 1987). Another, Cosmid Y97, is a clone containing an alphoid repeat that hybridizes to a 5.5 kb EcoRI fragment from the centromere of the YH-chromosome (Wolf *et al.* 1985).

Probe Y-190 detects a 3.5 kb fragment in HindIII digested male DNA that is repeated approximately 100-fold and is localized in the short arm of the Y-chromosome (Muller *et al.* 1987).

We have used a cloned DNA fragment, pAC004, that has properties similar to LWES5 described by Cooke *et al.* (1982). The clone pAC101 contains a 3.4 kb

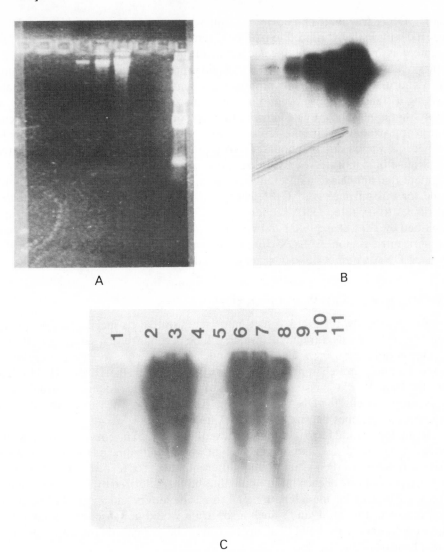

Fig. 3.1 — Sensitivity of the yield/degradation gel. High molecular weight human DNA was loaded into a 0.5% agarose gel and fractionated for 2 h by electrophoresis at 50 V/cm in the presence of EtBr. After electrophoresis the gel was placed on a UV-transilluminator and photographed. (A) lane 1 to 5: high molecular weight human DNA (0.2, 1, 5, 20, 100 ng/lane respectively) and lane 6 bacteriophage lambda DNA digested with HindIII. (B) The above gel was dried; the DNA trapped in the gel was denatured by alkaline treatment and hybridized to human Alu sequence. After washing, the gel was exposed for 6 h at −70°C, with X-ray film and intensifying screens. (C) Autoradiogram of a gel containing human DNA from evidentiary material. Lane 1:1 ng of control human DNA. Lane, 2, 3, 6, 7, and 8: high molecular weight human DNA from blood and semen stains. Lane 10, 11: partially degraded human DNA from bloodstains (exposed for 3 h at −70°C).

HaeIII DNA fragment cloned into a Bluescript plasmid vector. Human DNA digested with PstI, hybridized to pAC004, generates a 3.6 kb DNA fragment. This fragment is Y-chromosome specific (DYZ1) and represents approximately 100 copies of the sequence. Since this 3.6 kb band is present only in the Y-chromosomal DNA, normal females do not produce any bands. However, abnormal females carrying a translocation between the X-chromosome and the long arm of the Y-chromosome may show this band, but this type of inherited rearrangement occurs only in approximately 1 in 3000 females (Cooke & Noel 1979). With normal females it is necessary to be sure that human DNA is present in the sample, thus the negative result must be confirmed by hybridizing the same DNA sample to a cloned DNA fragment that anneals to a different human repeated DNA sequence. One suitable clone for this purpose is pAC101 which is a 2.0 kb BamHI DNA fragment that hybridizes to repeated DNA sequences (DXZ1). This type of sequence has been described by Yang *et al.* (1982) and Willard *et al.* (1983) and shown to be localized in the pericentric region of the X-chromosome and a number of autosomes. In PstI digested DNA a number of bands are detected predominantly at 4.1 and 2.0 kb.


## 3.8   METHODS USED IN RFLP ANALYSIS

For RFLP analysis, the DNA is 'cut' into pieces so that its specific base sequence creates a series of DNA fragments which will be peculiar to that sample of DNA.

This is done by using a class of endonucleases known as restriction endonucleases. Examples which appeared in section 3.7 included HaeIII, EcoRI, HindIII, PstI and BamHI. These enzymes locate short, defined base sequences (usually four or six long) and 'cut' the DNA at that point. The spacing of the chosen specific base sequences determines the size of the DNA fragments.

An analogy would be to consider the text of this page. The enzyme chosen would recognize one word, say 'and'. At each point where 'and' appears the text would be broken. It is easy to then visualize that different lengths of text would be created.

Each page of text of each book would thus be characterized by a spectrum of text pieces, each piece having a length equal to all the letters and spaces between two occurrences of the word 'and'. Such a spectrum would not strictly be unique to a single book, but the probability of any two books having exactly the same spectrum would be astronomically low.

In practice, the choice of probe limits the study of the genome to a very small subset (much less than one chapter of the book!). After that the nuclease is chosen from the greater than one hundred available to us, to give a conveniently analyzable spectrum of DNA pieces.

The basic techniques required for RFLP analysis, such as gel electrophoresis, transfer of DNA to a membrane, labelling of DNA, and hybridization are extensively covered in laboratory manuals such as those of Maniatis *et al.* (1982), Ausubel *et al.* (1987), and Berger & Kimmel (1987), and they are applicable to any type of DNA sample. What follows is a basic description of these laboratory procedures.


### 3.8.1   Fractionation of DNA by agarose gel electrophoresis

Electrophoretic fractionation of DNA through a gel is based on the principle that DNA, in a near neutral solution, is negatively charged. Therefore, DNA placed in an electrical field will migrate from the negative pole (cathode) to the cathode pole (anode). The rate of migration is inversely proportional to the log of the fragment size. The smaller fragments move through the gel much faster than the larger ones. The voltage applied is commonly uniform, but pulsed fields have been used for specialized purposes. Constant voltage electrophoresis of DNA through an agarose gel is a very powerful procedure for fractionating DNA fragments. The main advantages are: it is a simple and reproducible procedure. It produces excellent resolution of mixtures of different DNA fragment sizes up to a limit, near 40 kb, that is determined by gel concentration and voltage gradient. The fractionated DNA can be visually detected in the gel by staining with a dye that binds to DNA (e.g. ethidium bromide) and thus to follow the progression of the DNA fractionation.

The general procedure used for agarose gel electrophoresis of DNA consists in first casting the gel in an appropriate size tray or mould. While the gel is liquid, a comb is placed near one end. Once the gel has hardened, the comb is removed, leaving troughs or wells in which samples will be loaded. The gel is then placed into a horizontal electrophoresis apparatus and covered by buffer. Samples are loaded into the wells and the current is applied for a predetermined time (Fig. 3.2).

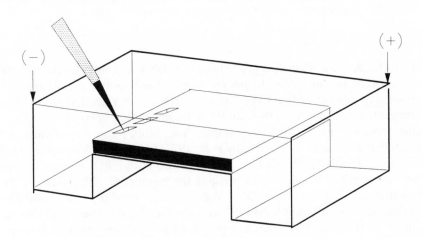

Fig. 3.2 — Horizontal agarose gel electrophoresis of DNA. Sample being loaded into a well cast in the agarose gel. The agarose gel has been placed into an electrophoresis 'tank' or 'box' to which electric current will be applied to perform the electrophoresis.

### 3.8.2   Capillary transfer of DNA (Southern procedure)
This procedure was invented by Southern (1975), and it is used to transfer the DNA in the gel to a filter membrane, to which it becomes immobilized, for subsequent hybridization to a tagged DNA or RNA probe.

After electrophoresis, the steps are: the DNA is denatured by soaking the gel in alkali. The gel is then commonly soaked in neutralizing solution depending on the membrane used for transfer. A membrane e.g. (nitrocellulose or nylon) is placed on one side of the gel and the DNA is allowed to transfer by capillary suction, using a setup similar to that shown in Fig. 3.3.

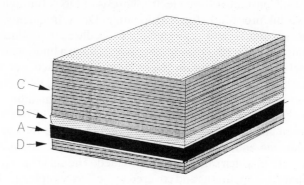

Fig. 3.3 — Transfer of DNA from the gel to membrane, by the Southern procedure. Basic components: A. agarose gel; B. transfer membrane; C. stack of filter paper; D. absorbent material (i.e. filter or sponge) saturated with transfer solution.

### 3.8.3   Hybridization of labelled probe to specific DNA sequences on the membrane

The size of particular DNA fragments immobilized in the membrane can be determined by incubating (i.e. hybridizing) the DNA with a labelled probe. A probe is a reagent consisting of a DNA or RNA fragment that is complementary to a specific sequence in the human genome. The probes can be labelled with a radioactive isotope such as $P^{32}$ (Rigby *et al.* 1977, Feinberg & Vogelstein 1983) or with a non-radioactive molecule (e.g. biotin; Langer *et al.* 1981). After hybridization the unreacted probe is removed by washing the membrane with a buffer solution. Probes that detect polymorphic DNA regions in the human genome will identify DNA fragments at different locations along the membrane. Their positions can be visualized, in the case of a radioactive probe, by autoradiography (i.e. by exposing the membrane to an X-ray film) or for a biotinylated probe, by an appropriate colour reaction.

Methods used in analyzing small fragments of DNA below the kilobase level have assumed importance with the introduction of polymerase chain reaction (PCR) technology. These are considered elsewhere in chapter 7.

### REFERENCES

Ausubel, F. M., Brent, R., Kingston, R. E., Moore, D., Seidman, J. G., Smith, J. A., & Struhl, K. (1987) *Current protocols in molecular biology*. Wiley & Sons, New York.

Berger, S. L. & Kimmel, A. R. (ed.) (1987) Guide to molecular cloning techniques. *Methods in Enzymology* **152**. Academic Press, New York.

Burton, K. (1956) A study of conditions and mechanism of the diphylamine reaction for the colorimetric estimation of deoxyribonucleic acid. *Biochem. J.* **62** 315–322.

Cesarone, C. F., Bolognesi, C., & Santi, L. (1979) Improved microfluorometric DNA determination in biological material using 33258 Hoechst. *Anal. Biochem.* **100** 188–197.

Cooke, H. J. & Noel, B. (1979) Confirmation of Y/autosome translocations using recombinant DNA. *Hum. Genet.* **50** 39–44.

Cooke, H. J., Schmidtke, J., & Gosden, J. R. (1982) Characterization of a human Y chromosome repeated sequence and related sequences in higher primates. *Chromosoma* **87** 491–502.

Feinberg, A. P. & Vogelstein, B. (1983) A technique for radiolabeling DNA restriction endonuclease fragments to high specific activity. *Anal. Biochem.* **132** 6–13.

Gautreau, C., Rahuel, C., Cartron, J. P., & Lucotte, G. (1983) Comparison of two methods of high-molecular-weight DNA isolation from human leukocytes. *Anal. Biochem.* **134** 320–324.

Gill, P., Jeffreys, A. J., & Werrett, D. J. (1985) Forensic application of DNA 'fingerprints'. *Nature* **318** 577–579.

Gill, P. (1987) A new method for sex determination of the donor of forensic samples using a recombinant DNA probe. *Electrophoresis* **8** 35–38.

Gill, P., Lygo, J. E., Fowler, S. J., & Werrett, D. J. (1987) An evaluation of DNA fingerprinting for forensic purposes. *Electrophoresis* **8** 38–44.

Giusti, A., Baird, M., Pasquale, S., Balazs, I., & Glassberg, J. (1986). Application of deoxyribonucleic acid (DNA) polymorphisms to the analysis of DNA recovered from sperm. *J. Forens. Sci.* **31** 409–417.

Goelz, S. E., Hamilton, S. R., & Vogelstein, B. (1985) Purification of DNA from formaldehyde fixed and paraffin embedded human tissue. *Biochem. Biophys. Res.* **130** 118–126.

Gosden, J. R., Gosden, C. M., Christie, S., Cooke, H. J., Morsman, J. M., & Rodeck, C. H. (1984) The use of cloned Y chromosome-specific DNA probes for fetal sex determination in first trimester prenatal diagnosis. *Hum. Genet.* **66** 347–351.

Impraim, C. C., Saiki, R. K., Erlich, H. A., & Teplitz, R. L. (1987) Analysis of DNA extracted from formalin-fixed, paraffin-embedded tissues by enzymatic amplification and hybridization with sequence-specific oligonucleotides. *Biochem. Biophys. Res. Commun.* **142** 710–716.

Jelinek, W. R., Toomey, T. P., Leinwand, L., Duncan, C. H., Biro, P. A., Choudary, P. V., Weissman, S. M., Rubin, C. M., Houck, C. M., Deininger, P. L., & Schmid, C. W. (1980) Ubiquitous, interspersed repeated sequences in mammalian genomes. *Proc. Nat. Acad. Sci. USA* **77** 1398–1402.

Kanter, E., Baird, M., Shaler, R., & Balazs, I., (1986) Analysis of restriction fragment length polymorphisms in deoxyribonucleic acid (DNA) recovered from dried bloodstains. *J., Forens. Sci.* **31** 403–408.

Kapuscinski, J. & Skoczylas, B. (1977) Simple and rapid fluorometric method for DNA microassay. *Anal Biochem* **83** 252–257.

Langer, P. R., Waldrop, A. A., & Ward, D. C. (1981) Enzymatic synthesis of biotin labeled nucleotides: novel nucleic acid affinity probes. *Proc. Nat. Acad. Sci. USA* **80** 6633–6637.

Leadon, S. A. & Cerutti, P. A. (1982) A rapid and mild procedure for the isolation of DNA from mammalian cells. *Anal. Biochem.* **120** 282–288.

Longmire, J. L., Albright, A. K., Meincke, L. J., & Hildebrand, C. E. (1987) A rapid and simple method for the isolation of high molecular weight cellular and chromosome-specific DNA in solution without the use of organic solvents. *Nucleic Acids Res.* **15** 859.

Luttke, A., Lurquin, P. F., & Bonotto, S. (1980) Rapid method for the detection of small amounts of DNA in CsCl gradients with ethidium bromide. *Anal. Biochem.* **108** 1–5.

Madisen, L., Hoar, D. I., Holroyd, C. D., Crisp, M., & Hodes, M. E. (1987) DNA banking: the effects of storage of blood and isolated DNA on the integrity of DNA. *Am. J. Med. Genet.* **27** 379–390.

Maniatis, T., Fritsch, E. F., & Sambrook, J. (1982) *Molecular cloning. a laboratory manual.* Cold Spring Harbor Laboratory, New York.

Mark, A., Trowell, H., Dyall-Smith, M. L., & Dyall-Smith, D. J. (1987) Extraction of DNA from formalin-fixed paraffin-embedded pathology specimens and its use in hybridization (histo-blot) assays. Application to the detection of human papilloma virus DNA. *Nucleic Acid Res.* **15** 8565.

McCabe, E. R. B., Huang, Shu-Zhen, Seltzer, W. K., & Law, M. L. (1987) DNA microextraction from dried blood spots on filter paper blotters: potential applications to newborn screening. *Hum. Genet.* **75** 213–216.

McNally, L., Shaler, R. C., Giusti, A., Baird, M., Balazs, I., DeForest, P., & Kobilinsky, L. (1989) Evaluation of DNA isolated from human blood stains exposed to ultraviolet light, heat, humidity and soil contamination. *J. Forens. Sci.* **34** 1059–1069.

McNally, L., Shaler, R. C., Giusti, A., Baird, M., Balazs, I., Kobilinsky, L., & DeForest, P. (1989a) The effects of environment and drying surfaces on DNA: The use of casework samples from New York City. *J. Forens. Sci.* **34**, 1070.

Miller, S. A., Dykes, D. D., & Polesky, H. F. (1988) A simple procedure for extracting DNA from human nucleated cells. *Nucleic Acid Res.* **16** 1215.

Muller, U., Donlon, T. A., Kunkel, S. M., Lalande, M., & Latt, S. M. (1987) Y-190, a DNA probe for the sensitive detection of Y-derived marker chromosomes and mosaicism. *Hum. Genet.* **75** 109–113.

Perry, W. L., Bass, W. M., Riggsby, W. S., & Siotkin, K. (1988) The autodegradation of deoxyribonucleic acid (DNA) in human rib bone and its relationship to the time interval since death. *J. Forens. Sci.* **33** 144–153.

Purrello, M. & Balazs, I. (1983) Direct hybridization of single-copy DNA sequences to DNA in agarose gels. *Anal. Biochem.* **128** 393–397.

Rigby, P. W. J., Dieckmann, M., Rhodes, C., & Berg, P. (1977) Labelling deoxyribonucleic acid to high specific activity in vitro by nick translation with DNA polymerase I. *J. Mol. Biol.* **113** 237–251.

Southern, E. (1975) Detection of specific sequences among DNA fragments separated by gel electrophoresis. *J. Mol. Biol.* **98** 503–517.

Schwartz, D. C. & Cantor, C. R. (1984) Separation of yeast chromosome-sized DNAs by pulse field gradient agarose gel electrophoresis. *Cell* **37** 67–75.

Vytasek, R. (1982) A sensitive fluorometric assay for the determination of DNA. *Anal. Biochem.* **129** 243–248.

Weeks, D. P., Beerman, N., & Griffith, O. M. (1986) A small-scale five-hour procedure for isolating multiple samples of CsCl-purified DNA: application to isolations from mammalian, insect, higher plant, algal, yeast, and bacterial sources. *Anal. Biochem.* **152** 376–385.

Willard, H. F., Smith, K. D., Sutherland, J. (1983) Isolation and characterization of a major tandem repeat family from the human X chromosome. *Nucleic acids Res.* **11** 2017–2033.

Williams, G. T. (1987) High-efficiency preparation of DNA from limiting quantities of eukaryotic cells for hybridization analysis. *Gene* **53** 121–126.

Wolf, J., Darling, S. M., Erichson, R. P., Craig, I. W., Buckle, V. J., Rigby, P. W. J., Willard, H. F. K., & Goodfellow, P. N. (1985) Isolation and characterization of an alphoid centromeric repeat family from the human Y chromosome. *J. Mol. Biol.* **182** 477–485.

Yang, T. P., Hansen, S. K., Oishi, K. K., Ryder, O. A., & Hamkalo, B. A. (1982) Characterization of a cloned repetitive DNA sequence concentrated on the human X chromosome. *Proc. Nat. Acad. Sci. USA* **79** 6593–6597.

Zamenhof, S. (1957) Preparation and assay of deoxyribonucleic acid from animal tissue. In: Colowick, S. P. & Kaplan, O. (eds), *Methods in enzymology* **3,** Academic Press, New York, 696–704.

# 4

# Hypervariant probes and DNA 'fingerprinting'

**Arie Geursen**
Auckland Regional Blood Donor Centre, Auckland Hospital, Private Bag, Auckland, New Zealand

## 4.1 INTRODUCTION

Variations in the human genome have been observed for many years. These variations or 'polymorphisms' were first observed as differences in gene products (that led to biochemical variations) such as enzymes which behaved differently on electrophoretic analysis or changes in structure which could be recognized by antibodies. These variations are called the phenotype of the individual. Indeed, forensic biologists make use of the many different blood group phenotypes such as ABO, Rhesus, Lewis, Hp, Gc, PGM, and EAP, to name but a few, to identify the genetic origin of the blood or body fluid sample that they are testing. All of these systems suffer from the fact that they have a relatively low exclusion power. In a paternity dispute, for example, Phosphoglucomutase (PGM) phenotyping by cellulose acetate electrophoresis will exclude approximately 25% of falsely accused fathers. The reason for this is that one of the two isozymes detected by this method is found in 75% of the population. However, this does vary with individuals of various ethnic groups (Woodfield *et al.* 1987). Using isoelectric focusing, it is possible to detect subtypes of these isozymes, thereby greatly improving the probability of exclusion in this system. When all the blood tests, including HLA (tissue) typing, are done the combined discriminating power is of the order of 99%. In practice, however, it is much more difficult to get reliable results for tests on blood stains or body fluids obtained at the crime scene. This is either because the tests cannot be performed on the small and frequently old samples, or there is often a mixture of body fluids present. There is, therefore, a need for a test which is able to identify the origin of a biological sample with the same degree of certainty as is obtained with a fingerprint.

In this chapter we look at how the advances in recombinant DNA techniques have made it possible to analyze the composition and structure of DNA (the genetic material contained in all living cells) which make every individual different, with the exception of monozygotic (identical) twins.


## 4.2  RESTRICTION LENGTH POLYMORPHISMS AS GENETIC MARKERS

Restriction endonucleases are enzymes (usually purified from bacteria) which will cleave double stranded DNA only at a specific sequence of bases known as a restriction site. The enzyme Pst I, for example, will only cleave the DNA every time it detects the following sequence:

Some enzymes, like Pst I, will recognize a sequence of six bases, while others recognize only four. For a particular enzyme there are many thousands of restriction sites randomly distributed throughout the human genome. Therefore, restriction endonuclease digestion of human genomic DNA results in a mixture of DNA fragments of various lengths depending on the distance between the cutting sites.

These fragments can be fractionated according to size by electrophoresis in an agarose gel. The smaller fragments are able to migrate faster through the gel matrix than the larger ones. Once separated according to size, it is not possible to identify a specific fragment because there are so many of them that they appear as a long smear in the gel matrix. Therefore, the size separated fragments are denatured into single stranded fragments and immobilized onto a nylon membrane by a process known as Southern Blotting (Southern 1975), as described in Fig. 4.1.

The immobilized DNA fragments can then be analyzed by hybridization with a suitably labelled probe. DNA probes are themselves a short, single stranded piece of DNA complementary to a known gene or region of the genome, and are often referred to as cDNA probes (cDNA=complimentary DNA). Hybridization of the membrane bound genomic DNA in the presence of the probe will result in base pairing between the probe and that fragment containing the original base sequence. Visualization is made possible by labelling the probe DNA in the laboratory with a reporter molecule such as a radioisotope (frequently $^{32}$p — dCTP). Subsequent exposure of the nylon membrane to an X-ray film will result in a pattern of bands (See Fig. 4.1). This variation in fragment length of restriction digested genomic DNA is known as **restriction fragment length polymorphism** (RFLP).

The discovery of genetic variation in restriction endonuclease cutting sites (Kan & Dozy 1978) led to the suggestion that these variations or polymorphisms, which could be detected by cDNA probes derived from cloned functional genes, could be useful not only for forensic purposes but also for medical genetic diagnosis (Fig. 4.1). Indeed, an ever growing list of genetic diseases such as sickle cell anaemia (Chang & Kan 1982), haemophilia A and B (Antonarakis *et al.* 1985, Giannelli *et al.* 1984), Huntington's disease (Gusella *et al.* 1983), Alzheimer disease (St John-Hyslop *et al.* 1987), to name but a few, are now able to be diagnosed by RFLP. Most RFLPs are believed to be derived from a single base substitution resulting in the gain or loss of a recognition site for the restriction enzyme used to fragment the genomic DNA but

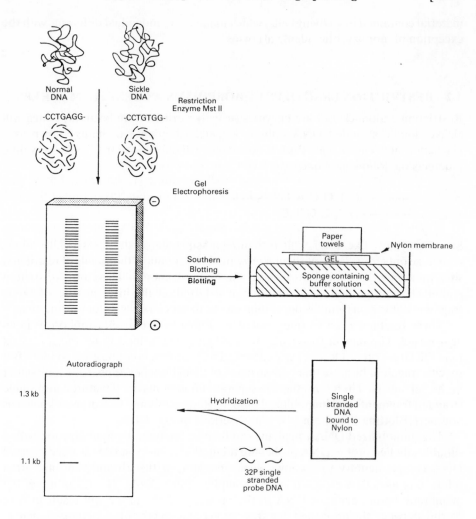

Fig. 4.1 — Schematic presentation in the use of restriction fragment length polymorphism (RFLP) analysis in the diagnosis of sickle cell anaemia. Most restriction length polymorphisms are brought about by the gain or the loss of a restriction site as a result of a point mutation. For example, sickle cell anaemia is caused by the substitution of a T for an A in codon 6 of the beta globin gene resulting in an abnormal globin molecule. The enzyme Mst II is able to cleave DNA from normal individuals at this site but not that of afflicted individuals. Hence a probe to the globin gene will detect a fragment of 1.1 kilobases in size in a normal individual, and a larger (1.3 kb) fragment in patients with sickle cell anaemia.

without resulting in a change in the gene product. Unfortunately, human DNA in the coding regions does not vary very much between members of the species, with roughly 999 out of every 1000 base pairs being the same in two unrelated individuals (Jeffreys 1979, Urlich *et al.* 1980). It follows, therefore, that the degree of polymorphism detected by **single copy probes** (probes derived from sequences which occur once per genome) is not very high, and as a result no information can be gained about critical individuals in a pedigree.

## 4.3   VARIABLE LENGTH POLYMORPHISMS

The structure of eukaryotic genes is considerably more complex than was first thought, with many non-coding sequences interspersed in the coding sequences of the genes themselves. These non-coding regions are called **introns,** while the coding regions themselves are called **exons** (for a review on their origin see Lewin 1982). Studies on the globin gene family located on chromosome 11, showed that there were large segments of 'spacer' DNA that do not code for protein (Proudfoot & Maniatis 1980, Little 1982).

It is not known whether spacer DNA is merely 'junk' DNA in the human genome and is there purely as a result of random events over many, many years of evolution, or if it is there because it in some way benefits the organism. Frequently the spacer DNA is larger than the actual coding regions of the genes themselves. If the globin cluster of genes is typical of most genes, then only about 10% of a chromosome would actually code for protein. It follows, therefore, that there is a large portion of the human genome, which could serve as a potential genetic marker, which could never be detected by relying on studying the protein products of genes.

Wyman & White (1980) first identified a highly variable locus in different individuals. It consisted of at least 8 homologous restriction fragments that appeared to be due to DNA rearrangement rather than base substitution. These became known as **variable length polymorphisms.** Subsequently, other variable length polymorphisms have been observed near the alpha-related globin gene (Higgs *et al.* 1981, Proudfoot *et al.* 1982, Goodbourn *et al.* 1983), human insulin gene (Bell *et al.* 1982), c-Harvey Ras oncogene (Capon *et al.* 1984), and the type II collagen gene (Stoker *et al.* 1985). During 1985, Professor Alec Jeffreys, from the University of Leicester, described exciting new applications for the variable length polymorphisms.

### 4.3.1   Tandem-repetitive DNA hybridization probes and DNA 'fingerprints'
In the course of studies on the gene for myoglobin, a protein which stores oxygen in muscle, Jeffreys and colleagues (Weller *et al.* 1984) observed a 33 base pair (bp) sequence tandemly repeated four times in the intron region. This was called a **minisatellite** since it resembled the much longer repeated sequences called satellite DNA which will be discussed in the following chapter.

Jeffreys and colleagues (Jeffreys *et al.* 1985a) purified the minisatellite region and ligated it head to tail a number of times. The resulting polymer was then cloned into the plasmid vector pUC and used as a probe to screen a human genomic library. Numerous clones containing human DNA sequences homologous to the constructed probe were discovered in this genomic library. Of these, eight were randomly chosen and sequenced. They all differed in their base sequence, number of repeat units, and, consequently, length. However, careful analysis of their base sequence revealed a common 'core' sequence of 10 to 16 bp embedded in each repeat unit. Although the mechanism by which minisatellites with different repeat numbers are generated is not understood, one possible method is by unequal crossing over during DNA replication. Interestingly, there is a highly conserved region at the 3′ end of the core sequence which strongly resembles the generalized recombination sequence observed in *Escherichia coli* (Smith *et al.* 1981). This suggests that the core sequences may be the signal for recombination hot spots in eukaryotes (Jeffreys *et al.* 1985a).

Purely by chance, one of the clones detected in the human genomic library consisted entirely of 26 repeats of the core sequence. When a probe was made from this clone itself and used in Southern blotting and hybridization of human DNA digested with the restriction enzyme, Hinf I, it was found that this myoglobin minisatellite detected many other human satellites, all of different base length. Each individual's hybridization pattern, particularly in the larger fragments, was different from all others (Fig. 4.2). This pattern, likened to a bar code, was called a genetic

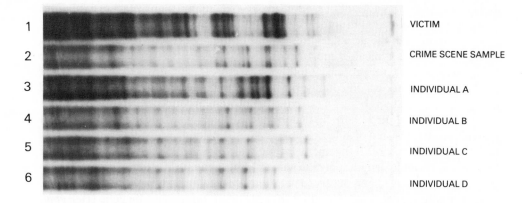

Fig. 4.2 — DNA profiling, using hypervariant probes. DNA profiles were obtained from blood samples taken from a rape victim (lane 1) and four suspects (lanes 3–6). These were compared with the DNA profile from a human body fluid sample obtained at the crime scene (lane 2). The results show that the banding pattern for each individual is different. Further, the banding pattern of the crime scene sample is clearly distinguishable from that of the victim, and matches that obtained with blood from suspect B. This work was carried out by Drs Cordiner & Chambers, using human minisatellite probe 33.15 provided by Prof. Alec Jeffreys.

fingerprint (Jeffreys *et al.* 1985b, Gill *et al.* 1985). Hinf I was chosen as the restriction enzyme to digest the genomic DNA because it does not have a recognition sequence within the minisatellite region. The enzyme does, however, have many cutting sites in the flanking regions and would, therefore, be expected to release the whole repetitive region. Indeed, when the genomic DNA was digested with other restriction enzymes, the banding pattern was either significantly altered or had completely lost its unique characteristic, presumably because the repeat sequences had been cut (Jeffreys *et al.* 1985b).

Realizing the significance of their find, Jeffreys and his colleagues undertook considerable work to characterize these probes. Classical Mendelian genetics shows that an individual inherits one chromosome from the mother and the other from the father. It follows then that a band in a DNA profile represents either one of two alleles from a single locus, or two alleles of the same size from the same locus, or two or more coincidentally migrating alleles derived from two or more loci. A family study revealed that each variable fragment could be traced from a parent to some of its offspring and in turn back to that parent's own parents (Jeffreys *et al.* 1985a, 1986). Careful pair-wise comparison of all the large, resolvable, bands in the DNA profile of a large family group revealed that only a few fragments could always be paired as they segregated from either mother or father to their children. In general, if one observed any given pair of bands in a parent, the children in the large family inherited both, none, or one of the two bands in approximately equal proportion. Further, of all the pairs of bands scored no more than 3 or 4 pairs could be shown to be either alleles at the same locus or linked (side by side on the same chromosome). Allelic pairs of bands are those where one or the other band of the pair but never both, are inherited by all of the offspring, while linked pairs of bands are always inherited together. From this it was concluded that, indeed, each band in a DNA profile represents one of the two alleles at a single locus. The other allele is presumably much smaller in size and would be found among the unresolved bands at the bottom of the gel (Jeffreys *et al.* 1986). As expected, the banding pattern for monozygotic twins was identical (Jeffreys *et al.* 1985b, Hill & Jeffreys 1985). With improved electrophoretic techniques it was found that two of the most polymorphic probes (33.6 and 33.15) identified about 60 scorable autosomal loci between them (Jeffreys *et al.* 1986). Obviously, for minisatellites to be inherited they must be present in the germ cells that give rise to other cells. Indeed, the banding pattern in blood and sperm of the same individual are indistinguishable (Jeffreys *et al.* 1985b). Further, it was found that DNA profiles could be obtained from dried blood, seminal stains, and even from the roots of hairs (Gill *et al.* 1985, 1987).

### 4.3.2  Statistical analysis

Jeffreys *et al.* (1985c) used DNA profiling to provide proof of both paternity and maternity in a difficult immigration case. This work was remarkable in a number of respects: the putative father was unavailable for testing, it was alleged that the child's maternal aunt was the true mother, and finally, the overwhelming statistical certainty with which DNA profiling resolved this matter. While to many the science of statistics is a mystery, the principles underlying the probability that a randomly selected individual possesses all the same bands in a given DNA profile are relatively simple.

If we assume that co-migrating bands in DNA profiles of unrelated individuals are always the same allele at a given locus, then the frequency ($f$) with which each allele, or band, occurs in the population can easily be determined by comparing how often a band of particular size appears in randomly selected DNA profiles. Analysis with probe 33.15 of 20 randomly chosen caucasians revealed that minisatellite frequencies were extremely low (0.04) especially for the large ones (Jeffreys *et al.* 1985b). Once the frequency is known, the probability ($p$) that an allele in individual A is also present in another is given by: $p=2f-f^2$. Since the frequency is low, $f^2$ will be negligible, therefore, the probability can simply be estimated as $p=2f$. Finally, the probability that *all* the fragments ($n$) present in one individual are present in a second randomly chosen individual is given by $p^n$.

The mean probability that a fragment in the DNA profile of one person is present in a second randomly selected individual for European caucasians is approximately 0.2 (Jeffreys *et al.* 1985b). The statistical chance that a randomly selected individual could share, for example, 15 bands with another individual is $0.2^{15}=3\times10^{-11}$ or 1 in 30 000 million. Obviously, closely related individuals such as siblings share bands more frequently than randomly chosen individuals. For example, siblings from non consanguineous marriages would be expected to share bands approximately $\frac{1}{2}$ of the time (for a more precise estimate see Jeffreys *et al.* 1985c). Thus the probability that two sibs share all 15 scored bands in a DNA profile is: $0.5^{-15}=3\times10^{-5}$ or about 1 in 30 000!

In these statistical analyses it is assumed that each band in the profile is a single allele derived from a different locus. While, in theory, only one of an allelic or linked pair should be scored in the statistical calculation, in practice, however, it is not possible to identify these without an extensive family study which is not possible on a crime sample or in a paternity dispute. While, Jeffries (1986) did observe some allelic and linked bands, their frequency is not high relative to the number of bands being scored. By contrast, it should be remembered that in practice not all bands of the same molecular weight in DNA profiles of different individuals are alleles derived from the same locus. Some, if not all, could be expected to be derived from a different locus but by chance are electrophoretically indistinguishable. Therefore, any frequencies determined by comparing the occurrence of a particular band in randomly selected DNA profiles would, at best, be a gross overestimate of their true frequency. This was confirmed in latter work which used locus specific probes derived from minisatellites where randomly selected individuals shared bands at a locus only seldom (Wong *et al.* 1986, 1987).

### 4.3.3  Further characterization of minisatellite fragments

To conclusively establish the properties of the bands that make up a DNA profile, a number of the larger fragments from DNA profiles have been isolated and subcloned (Wong *et al.* 1986, 1987). When hybridization probes were prepared from these subcloned minisatellites they were shown to hybridize to a single locus in the human genome. As predicted from earlier segregation analysis of the bands in a DNA profile, each locus does indeed consist of two bands which are extremely variable in length with heterozygosities ranging from 90–99%. The purified minisatellites were located on chromosomes 1, 5, 7, and 12 with no evidence of clustering. This, and the fact that the inheritance of minisatellites is not sex linked, confirms that other minisatellites in a DNA profile are dispersed all over the autosomes. Sequence analysis of the cloned minisatellites confirms that they consist of a repetitive sequence with a small flanking region of genomic DNA. Interestingly, in no minisatellite was the repeat unit sequence completely homogeneous. A question frequently asked is: 'If cDNA probes hybridize to exactly complementary sequences in the genomic DNA, how is it that a probe consisting of tandemly repeated core sequences detects many, many minisatellites which are not homogenous in their sequence?' The answer to this is that by manipulating hybridization conditions, such as temperature or ionic strength, the molecular biologist is able to relax the accuracy with which the probe hybridizes to like sequences in the genomic DNA. In general, poorly matched hybrids between probe and target DNA are formed at lower temperature and/or high salt concentration, while only very closely matched hybrids are formed at high temperature (68°C) and low salt concentrations. In the case of hypervariant probes, DNA profiles are generated at relatively low hybridization and washing stringencies so that the probe detects repetitive sequences even though there are minor differences in their sequence composition (Fig. 4.3). In this way,

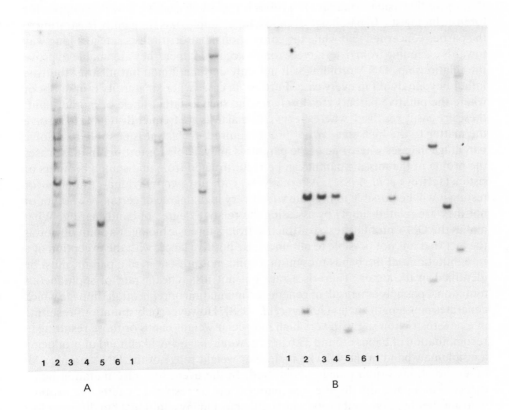

1 2 3 4 5 6 1                               1 2 3 4 5 6 1

A                                                    B

Fig. 4.3 — DNA profiles generated at high and low stringency washes. DNA from a family was digested with the restriction endonuclease Pst I. After electrophoresis and Southern blotting, the nylon membranes were hybridized with a probe to the hypervariable region 3′ to the x globin gene. Panel A shows the DNA profile obtained after a low stringency wash (5× SSC, 0.1% SDS at 55°C for 20 min). Panel B shows the same nylon filter washed at high stringency (0.1× SSC, 0.1% SDS at 65°C for 60 min). Lanes were loaded as follows; Father, 2; Mother, 5; Children, 3, 4, 6; lambda DNA digested with Hind III, 1. Panel A was exposed to the X-ray film for 4 hours while Panel B was exposed for 24 hours.

human hypervariant probes have been used with equal success to DNA profile other species such as birds (Burke & Bruford 1987), mice (Jeffreys *et al.* 1987), and even whales (Hoelzel & Amos 1988). Greatly increasing the washing stringency leaves only the pair of bands corresponding to the locus from which the probe was originally derived (Fig. 4.3). The forensic applications of these probes will be discussed in Chapter 6.

## 4.4  DISCUSSION

DNA profiling using hypervariant probes is providing exciting new possibilities for forensic biologists. In parentage disputes, for example, it is frequently frustrating to the parties concerned that while the conventional battery of tests can go a long way towards excluding from paternity a wrongly accused father, they are unable to prove the relationship. DNA profiling will not only exclude a man but identify the true father beyond doubt in every case. Further, in cases where maternity is in doubt or where the putative parents are closely related such as father/uncle or mother/aunt, these are easily resolved, whereas conventional tests are frequently unable to resolve the matter to the high standard of proof required. In fact, it is possible to resolve parentage in cases where one of the parents is unavailable for testing. In these cases the profile of the missing parent can be reconstructed from undisputed brothers or sisters (Jeffreys *et al.* 1985c). Alternatively, with just two individuals available for testing it will be possible to indicate with a very high degree of certainty whether or not they are related simply by assessing the relative degree of band sharing. What makes the DNA profiling test so attractive from a forensic biologist's point of view is the fact that it is not possible to obtain a false positive since, with the exception of a rare mutation, all the bands present in a child, not present in one parent, must be identified in the other. There is a rare but not insignificant rate of spontaneous mutations, possibly as a result of genetic recombination or replication slippage which generates new length alleles (Jeffeys *et al.* 1988). However, only mutations resulting in a new restriction site with very high molecular weight bands or those resulting in recombination of bands around 3 kb in size, would have any likelihood of producing a visible new band in the 4–20 kb molecular weight range of the DNA profile. All other mutations would remain undetected. In the event of a rare mutation being detected in a paternity dispute, the matter could be resolved by either re-probing with another hypervariant probe which will detect many additional but different loci or by further investigation using a battery of single locus probes which detect a maximum of two discrete bands in each individual, one inherited from the mother, the other from the father (only one band will appear in homozygotes). If all these match up, there can be no doubt that parentage is established. Hill (1986) applied a more rigorous statistical analysis to the DNA profile data which resulted in probabilities of the same order as those obtained by using the assumptions and methods described above.

It is, however, in rape cases that DNA profiling will have its greatest impact. Semen stains obtained at the crime scene are frequently contaminated with vaginal fluid. If the victim and the offender have the same conventional markers, it is not possible to positively identify the origin of crime scene material. Fortunately, sperm heads do not lyse when washed in the absence of a sulphydryl agent such as dithiothreitol while female cells do (see Chapter 2). Therefore, by washing the crime sample in the absence of sulphydryl agents, female material including DNA is able to be preferentially removed from the mixture before it is treated with a sulphydryl agent to release the DNA from the sperm heads. In this way the resulting DNA profile is entirely that of sperm. This is clearly demonstrated in Fig. 4.2 (lane 2) where the DNA profile obtained from the crime sample is entirely different from that of the victim but matches the DNA profile of individual B. Further, once extracted, DNA remains stable and undegraded (Madison *et al.* 1987), allowing comparisons of DNA profiles generated from crime scene material and the alleged offenders to be made many years later.

Despite its obvious advantages over conventional testing there remain challenges ahead for genetic identification by DNA profiling. While the large number of bands produced by these hypervariant probes under low stringency result in the often quoted overwhelming odds of 30 thousand million to one against mistaken identification, it is virtually impossible to interpret a profile generated from a sample to which more than one person has contributed. In these cases the single locus probes would be more useful in that each individual would contribute a maximum of two bands to the profile, with the likelihood that these bands are shared is small although not insignificant. Similarly, contamination of the crime scene sample with material from another species could result in additional bands in a hypervariant, multi-locus, profile leading to false exclusions. Hence it may well be necessary to validate the analysis by using single-locus probes at high hybridization and washing stringency and/or with a human specific probe. A further limitation in the use of hypervariant probes for generating a multi-locus DNA profile is that a relatively large amount (10 µg) of undegraded DNA is required. Frequently, crime scene material is not discovered until some considerable delay, resulting in degradation of the DNA, or alternatively, the recovered sample is so small as to yield insufficient DNA for analysis. Recent advances in DNA amplification using the DNA polymerase chain reaction have allowed DNA typing of a single hair (Higuchi *et al.* 1988) or sperm (Li *et al.* 1988). While this has exciting prospects for solving the problems of degradation and insufficient material encountered in forensic samples, it is unlikely that the DNA so amplified will be suitable for analysis with hypervariant, multi-locus, probes and their high probabilities of inclusion or exclusion.

Finally, while the techniques required for DNA profiling are routine in molecular biology laboratories, their introduction on a routine basis has not been without difficulty. The techniques are very labour intensive, and a considerable expertise in reading and interpreting the banding pattern is required. Clearly each laboratory will be required to obtain this expertise and validate it by extensive family and population testing. All this has been made considerably more difficult by the fact that the probes have been patented for exclusive use by commercial concerns (Newark 1986). This makes independent verificiation of results, which is a fundamental requirement of any forensic test, impossible (Newark 1987). In the interim a number of hypervariant loci have been detected and characterized (Higgs *et al.* 1986: Buroker *et al.* 1987, Nakamura *et al.* 1987, Vassart *et al.* 1987, Wainscoat *et al.* 1987). This should lead to probes and methods becoming freely available, perhaps in kit form, and should ultimately facilitate their introduction to routine use.

Looking to the future, it may well be that with improved electrophoretic techniques and greatly improved computer technology to actually read autoradiographs, store, and identify DNA banding profiles in databases, DNA profiles produced by hypervariant probes will be used in the same manner as is currently the case with conventional fingerprints.

## ACKNOWLEDGEMENTS

I would like to thank Dr S. J. Cordiner, Chemistry Division, DSIR, and Dr G. K. Chambers, Victoria University, Wellington, New Zealand, for providing Fig. 4.2 and Prof. D. J. Weatherall, Oxford University, UK, for providing the probe to the hypervariable region 3′ to the x globin gene.

## REFERENCES

Antonarakis, S. E., Copeland, K. L., Carpenter, R. J., Carta, C. A., Hoyer, L. W., Caskey, C. T., Toole, J. J., & Kuzazian, H. H. (1985) Prenatal diagnosis of haemophilia A by factor VIII gene analysis. *Lancet* I 1407–1409.

Bell, G. I., Selby, M. J., & Rutter, W. J. (1982) The highly polymorphic region near the human insulin gene is composed of simple tandemly repeating sequences. *Nature* **295** 31–35.

Burke, T. & Bruford, M. W. (1987) DNA fingerprinting in birds. *Nature* **327** 149–152.

Buroker, N. E., Bufton, L., Surti, U., Leppert, M., Kumlin, E., Sheehy, R., Magenis, R. E., & Litt, M. (1987) A hypervariable region at the D19S11 locus. *Hum. Genet.* **76** 90–95.

Capon, D. J., Chen, E. Y., Levinson, A. D., Seeburg, P. H., & Goeddel, D. V. (1983) Complete nucleotide sequences of the T24 human bladder carcinoma oncogene and its normal homologue. *Nature* **302** 33–37.

Chang, J. C. & Kan, Y. W. (1982) A sensitive new prenatal test for sickle-cell anemia. *N. Eng. J. Med.* **307** 30–32.

Giannelli, F., Anson, D. S., Choo, K. H., Rees, D. J. G., Winship, P. R., Ferrari, N., Rizza, C. R., & Brownlee, G. G. (1984) Characterization and use of an intragenic polymorphic marker for the detection of carriers of haemophilia B (factor IX deficiency). *Lancet* I 239–241.

Gill, P., Jeffreys, A. J., & Werrett, D. J. (1985) Forensic application of DNA 'fingerprints'. *Nature* **318** 577–579.

Gill, P., Lygo, J. E., Fowler, S. J., & Werrett, D. J. (1987) An evaluation of DNA fingerprinting for forensic purposes. *Electropheresis* **8** 38–44.

Goodbourn, S. E. Y., Higgs, D. R., Clegg, J. B., & Weatherall, D. J. (1983) Molecular basis of length polymorphism in the human α-globin gene complex. *Proc. Natl. Acad. Sci. USA* **80** 5022–5026.

Gusella, J. F., Wexler, N. S., Conneally, P. M., Naylor, S. L., Anderson, M. A., Tanzi, R. E., Watkins, P. C., Ottina, K., Wallace, M. R., Sakaguchi, A. Y., Young, A. B., Shoulson, I., Bonilla, E., & Martin, J. B. (1983) A polymorphic marker genetically linked to Huntingtons disease. *Nature* **306** 234–238.

Higgs, D. R., Goodbourn, S. E. Y., Wainscoat, J. S., & Weatherall, D. J. (1981) Highly variable regions of DNA flank the human α-globin genes. *Nuc. Acids Res.* **9** 4213–4224.

Higgs, D. R., Wainscoat, J. S., Flint, J., Hill, A. V. S., Thein, S. L., Nicholls, R. D.,

Teal, H., Ayyub, H., Peto, T. E. A., Falusi, A. G., Jarman, A. P., Clegg, J. B., & Wetherall, D. J. (1986) Analysis of the human α-globin gene cluster reveals a highly informative genetic locus. *Proc. Natl. Acad. Sci. USA* **83** 5165–5169.

Higuchi, R., von Beroldingen, C. H., Sensabaugh, G. F., & Erlich, H. A. (1988) DNA typing from single hairs. *Nature* **332** 543–546.

Hill, A. V. S. & Jeffreys, A. J. (1985) Use of minisatellite DNA probes for determination of twin zygosity at birth. *Lancet* Dec. 1394–1395.

Hill, W. G. (1986) DNA fingerprint analysis in immigration test cases. *Nature* **322** 290–291.

Hoelzel, A. R. & Amos, W. (1988) DNA fingerprinting and 'scientific' whaling. *Nature* **333** 305.

Jeffreys, A. J. (1979) DNA sequence variants in the $^E\gamma$, $^A\gamma$, δ, and β-globin genes of man. *Cell* **18** 1–10.

Jeffreys, A. J., Wilson, V., & Thein, S. L. (1985a) Hypervariable 'minisatellite' regions in human DNA. *Nature* **314** 67–73.

Jeffreys, A. J., Wilson, V., & Thein, S. L. (1985b) Individual-specific 'fingerprints' of human DNA. *Nature* **316** 76–79.

Jeffreys, A. J., Brookfield, J. F. Y., & Semeonoff, R. (1985c) Positive identification of an immigration test-case using human DNA fingerprints. *Nature* **317** 818–819.

Jeffreys, A. J., Wilson, V., Thein, S. L., Weatherall, D. J., & Ponder, B. A. J. (1986) DNA 'fingerprints' and segregation analysis of multiple markers in human pedigree. *Am. J. Hum. Genet.* **39** 11–24.

Jeffreys, A. J., Wilson, V., Kelly, R., Taylor, B. A., & Bulfield, G. (1987) Mouse DNA 'fingerprints': analysis of chromosome localization and germ-line stability of hypervariable loci in recombinant inbred strains. *Nuc. Acid Res.* **15** 2823–2837.

Jeffreys, A. J., Royle, N. J., Wilson, V., & Wong, Z. (1988) Spontaneous mutation rates to new length alleles at tandem repetative hypervariable loci in human DNA. *Nature* **322** 278–281.

Kan, Y. W. & Dozy, A. M. (1978) Polymorphism of DNA sequence adjacent to human α-globin structural gene: relationship to sickle mutation. *Proc. Nat. Acad. Sci. USA* **75** 5631–5635.

Lewin, R. (1982) On the origin of introns. *Science* **217** 921–922.

Li, H., Gyllensten, U. B., Cui, X., Saiki, R. K., Erlich, H. A., & Arnheim, N. (1988) Amplification and analysis of DNA sequences in single human sperm and diploid cells. *Nature* **335** 414–417.

Little, R. F. R. (1982) Globin pseudogenes. *Cell* **28** 683–684.

Madisen, L., Hoar, D. I., Holroyd, C. D., Crispe, M., & Hodes, M. E. (1987) DNA banking: The effects of storage of blood and isolated DNA on the integrity of DNA. *Am. J. Med. Genetics* **27** 379–390.

Nakamura, Y., Leppert, M., O'Connell, P., Wolfe, R., Holm, T., Culver, M., Martin, C., Fujimoto, E., Hoff, M., Kumlin, E., & White, R. (1987) Variable number of tandem repeat (VNTR) markers for human gene mapping. *Science* **235** 1616–1622.

Newark, P. (1986) DNA fingerprints go commercial. *Nature* **321** 104.

Newark, P. (1987) Dispute over who should do DNA fingerprinting in murder hunt. *Nature* **325** 97.

Proudfoot, N. J. & Maniatis, T. (1980) The structure of a human globin pseudogene and its relationships to α-globin gene duplication. *Cell* **21** 537–544.

Proudfoot, N. J., Gil, A., & Maniatis, T. (1982) The structure of the human zeta-globin gene and a closely linked, nearly identical pseudogene. *Cell* **31** 533–563.

Smith, G. R., Kunes, S. M., Schultz, D. W., Taylor, A., & Triman, K. L. (1981) Structure of chi hotspots of generalized recombination. *Cell* **24** 429–436.

Southern, C. M (1975) Detection of specific sequences among DNA fragments separated by gel electrophoresis. *Jour. Mol. Biol.* **98** 503–517.

St George-Hyslop, P. H., Tanzi, R. E., Polinsky, R. J., Haines, J. L., Nee, L., Watkins, P. C., Myers, R. H., Feldman, R. G., Pollen, D., Drachman, D., Growdon, J., Bruni, A., Foncin, J.-F., Salmon, D., Frommelt, P., Amaducci, L., Sorbi, S., Piacentini, S., Stewart, G. D., Hobbs, W. J., Conneally, P. M., & Gusella, J. F. (1987) The genetic defect causing familial Alzheimer's disease maps on chromosome 21. *Science* **235** 885–890.

Stoker, N. G., Cheah, K. S. E., Griffin, J. R., Pope, F. M., & Solomon, E. (1985) A highly polymorphic region 3′ to the human Type II collagen gene. *Nuc. Acids Res.* **13** 4613–4620.

Ullrich, A., Dull, T. J., & Gray, A. (1980) Genetic variation in the human insulin gene. *Science* **209** 612–615.

Vassart , G., Monsieur, R., Brocas, H., Christophe, D., Georges, M., & Lequarre, A. S. (1987) A sequence in M13 phage detects hypervariable minisatellites in human and animal DNA. *Science* **235** 683–584.

Wainscoat, J. S., Pilkington, S., Peto, T. E. A., Bell, J. I., & Higgs, D. R. (1987) Allele-specific DNA identity patterns. *Hum. Genet.* **75** 384–387.

Weller, P., Jeffreys, A. J., Wilson, V., & Blanchetot, A. (1984) Organization of the human myoglobin gene. *EMBO J.* **3** 439–446.

Wong, Z., Wilson, V., Jeffreys, A. J., & Thein, S. L. (1986) Cloning a selected fragment from a human DNA 'fingerprint': isolation of an extremely polymorphic minisatellite. *Nuc. Acids Res.* **14** 4605–4617.

Wong, Z., Wilson, V., Patel, I., Povey, S., & Jeffreys, A. J. (1987) Characterization of a panel of highly variable minisatellites cloned from human DNA. *Ann. Hum. Genet.* **51** 269–288.

Woodfield, D. G., Simpson, L. A., Seber, G. A. F., & McInerney, P. J. (1987) Blood group and other genetic markers in New Zealand Europeans and Maoris. *Ann. Hum. Biol.* **14** 29–37.

Wyman, A. L. & White, P. H. (1980) A highly polymorphic locus in human DNA. *Proc. Natl. Acad. Sci. USA* **77** 6754–6750.

# 5

# Polymorphism in the major human repetitive DNA sequences: theory, practice, and comparison with other methods of measuring human genome variation

**Craig Fowler**
Forensic Science Centre, 21 Divett Place, Adelaide, South Australia 5000

## 5.1  OUTLINE

In this chapter human genome structure is briefly reviewed with particular emphasis being given to the nature, properties, and distribution of the major human repetitive DNA species. Some of these repetitive sequences present complex restriction fragment length polymorphisms (RFLPs) which are potentially useful in forensic analyses. These are described.

Recent technical advances in DNA manipulation and analysis are then briefly described or referenced, concentrating upon those elements which go to make up a typical 'Southern' analysis.

Finally, the discrimination of individual genomes by 'Southern' analysis of DNA is compared with methods based upon the prior amplification of short DNA segments, using the polymerase chain reaction (PCR). This comparison draws attention to recent information regarding their relative merits and disadvantages, and should serve to signpost some of the pitfalls which have the potential to undermine the reliable application of DNA technology in legal matters.

## 5.2  STRUCTURE OF THE HUMAN GENOME: MAJOR REPETITIVE DNA SEQUENCES

### 5.2.1  Introduction

Single-stranded deoxyribonucleic acid (DNA) is a long linear polynucleotide constructed from four different nucleotide monomers. The ordering of these monomers defines DNA sequence. Double-stranded DNA consists of two such polymers held together by hydrogen bonding via specific nucleotide pairs, such that the sequence of one strand defines the sequence of its 'homologous' strand. The resultant double-stranded DNA is twisted in a helix and structurally stabilized by packaging around nuclear proteins called histones. The combined complex is then called chromatin. Chromatin may be condensed to varying levels of compactness, and microscopically it is seen in its most compact state as chromosomes. The DNA in the human genome is distributed unequally among 23 pairs of chromosomes, these totalling some $6 \times 10^9$ nucleotides per diploid genome (Alberts *et al.* 1983). (Refer to chapters 1 and 2 for detailed explanations regarding DNA and chromatin structure.)

Two important practical points arise from the above.

First, removal of the protein scaffold upon which the DNA is supported is generally necessary before DNA analysis is possible. This inevitably leaves the DNA more susceptible to mechanical or enzymatic damage, thus further disrupting its integrity. Further, if the DNA is to be recovered from dried and aged biological stains, its integrity even before protein digestion may be much less than favourable. Any method will thus have a threshold for both DNA quantity and integrity below which results will be unattainable.

Second, the fidelity of DNA base pairing: G–C, A–T: is essential, not only to life itself (Radman & Wagner 1988), but also to all *in vitro* DNA manipulations, for example, DNA probe preparation, 'Southern' hybridizations, DNA sequencing, or polymerase chain reaction (PCR) amplifications. An appreciation of the experimental conditions which influence and maintain the fidelity of this pairing is paramount. (See Chapters 1 and 2).

These two points serve as a platform from which DNA technology is launched. The first is its major limitation (loss of DNA sequence destroys its only distinguishing feature) and the second is its major strength (the ordering of nucleotides can be mapped and measured by the precision of its hydrogen bonding). This holds true, regardless of the genomic region being studied and regardless of the purpose and techniques chosen for such studies.

The structure of the human genome is now described in greater detail, with particular reference to its major repetitive DNA species and those which show inter-genome variation.

### 5.2.2  Major repetitive DNA sequences of the human genome

The genomes of higher eukaryotes, such as humans, consist of DNA sequences of known function (e.g. genes — whose sequences 'code' for the amino acid sequence of a protein and regulate their degree of expression in any tissue at any time) and DNA sequences for which no clear function has been established or for which no function may exist. Such 'non-coding' DNA may either be in single copy acting as 'spacer', sequences between 'coding' regions, or be in multiple copies. This is termed repetitive DNA and accounts for as much as 30% of the human genome with many such sequences having little or no transcriptional or translational capacity (Singer 1982, Hardman 1986, Jelinek & Schmid 1982, John & Miklos 1979, Beridze 1986, Verma 1988, Deininger & Daniels 1986). They have, however, been able to amplify in number and spread themselves through the genome. Such behaviour may be of little benefit to the genome itself, and is hence termed 'selfish' (Orgel & Crick 1980, Ridley 1985).

### 5.2.2.1 *Discovery, nomenclature, and classification*

The discovery of repetitive DNA sequences in higher eukaryotes was generally made by one of three methods (Singer 1982):

(a) after denaturing (melting to single strands) the DNA, some of it reannealed (reformed double strands) very rapidly. These are sequences existing in multiple copies;
(b) centrifugation of genomic DNA in caesium chloride (CsCl), fractionated DNA into different buoyancy or 'satellite' bands to the main band. These 'satellites' were found to contain repetitive DNA sequences;
(c) digestion of genomic DNA with particular restriction enzymes showed some fragments to be of uniform size and in multiple copy number when separated by electrophoresis, indicating them to be repeated.

The classification of repetitive DNA sequences is based upon their structure and their copy number. (See Table 5.1). Two major classes are now recognized; the

Table 5.1 — Classes of repetitive DNA in the human genome

| Repetitive DNA sequences (20 to 30% of the genome) | | | |
| --- | --- | --- | --- |
| Tandemly repeating DNA (~10% of the genome) | | Interspersed repeating DNA (~10 to 15% of the genome) | |
| 'Classical' satellites e.g. Sat I-IV. alphoid | 'Mini- satellites' e.g. Jeffreys *et al.* 1987 | LINES (>500 bp) e.g. L1 or Kpn family | SINES (<500 bp) e.g. Alu family |

tandemly repeating DNA species and the interspersed repeating DNA species. The former are characterized by blocks of DNA of some common sequence which is repeated in a head-to-tail tandem fashion. The latter are characterized by being single units, of some common sequence but being dispersed more generally throughout the genome, and only occasionally arranged as clusters or tandem arrays.

### 5.2.2.2 *Tandem repetitive sequences*

The human genome contains four major tandem repeat classes: Satellite I, II, III, and IV (Singer 1982). These total about 5% of the genome and correspond to the 'satellite' bands separated by CsCl centrifugation of genomic DNA. Their sequences have been found to be tandemly repeating, and consequently the term 'satellite' has been adopted for all tandem repeating sequences, whether separable by centrifugation or not. Each of the Satellites I to IV represents a heterogenous mixture of DNA species, similar in DNA base composition, and thus buoyancy, but not necessarily similar in DNA sequence. For example, a further major tandemly repeating DNA species is the alphoid class, constituting some 2% or more of the genome (Willard &

Waye 1987a, Alexandrov *et al.* 1988). Although mostly co-buoyant with Satellite II and III, alphoid DNA is quite distinct from these in sequence.

The consensus base sequences, that is to say the smallest tandemly repeating units of Satellites I to IV and alphoid satellite, are known (Prosser *et al.* 1986, Frommer *et al.* 1982, Hollis & Hindley 1988, Waye & Willard 1987). This may be as small as 5 bp in the case of Satellite III, but is more often larger, such as the 170 bp alphoid repeat. The size of these repeat units is generally constant within each class. However, sequence divergence within each class may generate related families of sequences (Waye & Willard 1987), with different members sometimes being associated with specific chromosomes (see 5.2.2.4).

### 5.2.2.3  *Non-tandem repetitive sequences*
The non-tandem or interspersed repetitive DNA sequences occupy some 10 to 15% of the human genome (Singer 1982, Hardman 1986, Jelinek & Schmid 1982). They consist of a short single unit and have been classified into two class sizes (Singer & Skowronski 1985): short interspersed elements (SINES, less than 500 bp) and long interspersed elements (LINES, greater than 500 bp).

The Alu repeat is the most repetitive SINE, amounting to about 5% of the human genome or some $3 \times 10^5$ copies per haploid genome (Quentin 1988, Slagel *et al.* 1987, Willard, C. *et al.* 1987, Bains 1986). The unit is about 300 bp and has a moderately well conserved sequence (Kariya *et al.* 1987).

The L1 (Kpn) element is the most abundant LINE, amounting to about 1–2% of the human genome or some $1–4 \times 10^4$ copies per haploid genome. It is variable in size, ranging from 7 kb down to 0.5 kb, with the smaller examples being shortened from their 5′ end (Fanning & Singer 1987).

SINES and LINES are believed to be examples of mobile genetic elements (transposons). Both may be transcribed (into RNA) and then the new copy reintegrated as DNA, via reverse transcription, into other suitable genomic sites. This is believed to occur in a manner similar to retroviral integration into eukaryotic genomes (Fanning & Singer 1987, Hardman 1986, Deininger & Daniels 1986).

### 5.2.2.4  *Distribution and role in the genome*
Information is emerging regarding the distribution of repetitive sequences in the human genome, their relationship one unto another, as well as the inter-chromosomal variation between tandemly repeating DNA of related sequence.

The normal human karyotype consists of 46 chromosomes identified by their size and 'banding' (alternate light and dark staining along the length of the chromosome). This 'banding' may be induced in chromosomes in a number of different ways (Benn & Perle 1986). These are, for example: pre-treatment with a protease and staining with Giemsa (G banding), or staining with a fluorescent dye such as quinacrine (Q banding — the results from which are similar to G banding), or staining with acridine orange (called 'reverse' R banding as it highlights those chromosome segments 'unstained' in G and Q banding), or pre-treatment with mild alkali solutions and staining with Giemsa (C banding — which stains centromeres and the long arm of the Y chromosome).

Chromosome 'banding' is believed to result from differences in the structure and function of the chromatin located along the length of each chromosome (Benn &

Perle 1986). The major human repetitive DNA sequences could, in part, account for these differences because evidence suggests there is a correlation between chromosome banding and the location of the major repetitive sequences. In particular, Alu sequences appear to be non-randomly distributed in the genome (Filatov *et al.* 1987) and are perhaps most clustered into R bands (Korenberg & Rykowski 1988). The L1 sequences, however, apparently predominate in G/Q bands, but neither Alu nor L1 repeats occur to any great extent in C banded centric and pericentric ('heterochromatic') chromosome regions (Korenberg & Rykowski 1988).

These centric C banded regions are predominantly constructed of the major human tandem repeats, Satellites I to IV and alphoid, and represent the largest 'blocks' of tandemly repeating DNA sequences in the genome (John & Miklos 1979, Singer 1982, Korenberg & Rykowski 1988). However other tandemly repeating DNA sequences, whose array size is generally smaller than centric tandem repeats, have been found interspersed throughout the genome with evidence of 'clustering' in telomeric regions (Cooke *et al.* 1985, Royle *et al.* 1988). These tandem repeats have been termed 'minisatellites', their array size (number of tandem repeats) often being highly variable and thus discriminating of individual genomes (see detailed description in other chapters). There are, though, other categories of satellite sequence which also possess much genetic variation (see 5.3).

Models for the initiation and accumulation (size expansion) of satellite DNA sequences suggest their initiation is most likely to occur by slipped-strand mispairing in very short (e.g. <10 bp) DNA segments which by chance alone have some repeat features (Levinson & Gutman 1987). Their further size expansion would depend upon sequence amplification mechanisms, such as *de novo* DNA synthesis; and mechanisms for copy number control, such as Darwinistic selection in conjunction with non-reciprocal recombination (Charlesworth *et al.* 1986, Stephan 1986, 1987, Walsh 1987).

Centric and pericentric regions are known to be zones of suppressed recombination (Hotta & Stern 1978, Fang & Jagiello 1988), and this could in part account for the large size of C banded satellite sequences. The relatively low frequency of non-reciprocal (unequal) recombination which does occur in such regions would tend to redistribute the tandemly repeating blocks of DNA (Stephan 1986, 1987, Walsh 1987). Such an event may also therefore explain the highly variable size of heterochromatin e.g. 9qh and Yq (Wahedi & Pawlowitzki 1987, Hsu *et al.* 1987) and occasional saltatory (sudden jump) alteration of heterochromatic size in related individuals (e.g. Craig-Holms *et al.* 1975).

Evidence indicates that much of the human centromeric and pericentromeric DNA has evolved in a chromosome specific manner or at least as if isolated on their chromosomes so that the random divergence takes on a chromosome specific character. Alphoid DNA thus exists in sequence related families, individual members of which may be chromosome specific or near specific (Willard & Waye 1987a, Alexandrov *et al.* 1988). Similar evidence exists for Satellite III and Satellite II sequences (Burk *et al.* 1985, Moyzis *et al.* 1987, Higgins *et al.* 1985, Schwarzacher-Robinson *et al.* 1988). It is from these 'macrosatellites' that examples of both relatively simple and complex RFLPs have emerged as a means of discriminating between individuals (see 5.3.1 and 5.3.2).

The functions, if any, of the major repetitive sequences in the human genome are not solidly established. It has been speculated that Alu sequences, for example, are origins of DNA replication in humans (Johnson & Jelinek 1986). The functions of the major tandem repeats (reviewed by John & Miklos 1979) have been speculated as including cellular speciation and evolution, chromosome recognition, and nucleus organization. If sequence conservation is taken to be a major indicator of some cellular function, then a most convincing example is the extreme sequence conservation found in the simple tandem repeats which characterize telomeric caps of mammalian, bird, and reptile chromosomes (Moyzis *et al.* 1988). The sequences at chromosome centromeres, and in particular the constancy of their tandem repeat phasing, best seen in alphoid sequences, would also suggest some cellular function (Miller DA. *et al.* 1988, Vig 1987).

## 5.3   POLYMORPHISM IN CLASSICAL MACROSATELLITE SEQUENCES

Length-polymorphisms arising from tandemly repeated DNA are a consequence of a restriction enzyme digesting the DNA into fragments that contain variable numbers of the tandemly repeating species. These may then be separated electrophoretically and identified by their core or consensus sequence. Two different mechanisms have been established:

(a)  by restriction at two specific restriction sites which are external to a variable number of short repeat sequences ('minisatellites'). This has been summarized elsewhere (Fowler *et al.* 1988a) and is described in detail in other chapters;

(b)  restriction may occur within the long tandemly repeating sequence at some mutatable site and at which an unusual point mutation/deletion/insertion has occurred, thereby generating a new or deleted restriction site. If such mutations occur at random locations within the long tandem repeat, then inter-individual differences arise. The complexity of the resultant 'Southern' patterns then depends upon the genomic/chromosomal specificity of the probe sequence. This is demonstrated by alphoid and Satellite III DNA sequences.

### 5.3.1   Alphoid sequences

Alphoid RFLPs are best revealed by using chromosome specific (or near specific) probe sequences at high stringency of hybridization. Published examples are listed in Table 5.2. The resultant patterns are generally a simple progression of restriction fragments in a ladder-like fashion, starting from a 'monomer' fragment(s) through to larger 'multimer' fragments. The monomer size, and its multiples, reflect the configuration and evolution of alphoid sequences at the centromere of just a single or very limited number of chromosomes. The absence or presence of specific multimers or 'rungs' to these ladder-like patterns display RFLPs which characterize individual DNA samples, and indicates that they probably arise by the method (b) above. The fragments have been shown to segregate in a Mendelian fashion (Willard *et al.* 1986, Jabs *et al.* 1986, Wa-ye *et al.* 1987a).

The advantage of these RFLPs as a potential forensic tool is their relative simplicity of interpretation, with generally fewer than ten fragments being present within a size range of about 15 to 0.5 kb. Some of these fragments are common to all individuals (thus being good internal controls for fragment sizing), and others are

**Table 5.2** — Examples of RFLPs occurring in alphoid satellite DNA

| Sequence type | Chromosome source | Reference |
| --- | --- | --- |
| alphoid | X | Willard *et al.* 1986 |
|  |  | Durfy & Willard 1987 |
| alphoid | 17 | Willard *et al.* 1986 |
| alphoid | 11 | Waye *et al.* 1987a |
| alphoid | 1 | Waye *et al.* 1987b |
| alphoid | 6 (mainly) | Jabs *et al.* 1986 |
|  |  | Jabs & Carpenter 1988 |
| alphoid (Sau3a) | 11 (mainly) | Kiyama *et al.* 1986 |
|  |  | Kiyama *et al.* 1988 |

variable fragments, being either absent or present, and from which chromosome specific haplotypes can be scored (Willard *et al.* 1986).

Each fragment size is likely to be present in multiple copy number, repeated either tens or hundreds of times. This is because each new variant length arising by sequence mutation will itself, in time, be amplified and fixed in the tandemly repeating blocks of alphoid sequence (Waye *et al.* 1987a). Although this may lead to some quantitative or copy number polymorphism, it also means the quantity of DNA required to obtain a result is less than with single copy sequences.

It is essential to ensure complete and equal digestion of each DNA sample, as the 'laddered' pattern could, in part, result from incomplete DNA digestion. Checking this by reprobing with an invariate single copy DNA sequence, preferably located on the same chromosome as the alphoid polymorphism, is advisable (Willard *et al.* 1987a).

### 5.3.2  Satellite III and related sequences
Human Satellite III DNA displays a highly complex RFLP (Fowler *et al.* 1987). Its cause appears to be primarily the result of a specific C to G point mutation in the pentameric sequence 5'TTCCA 3' which typifies 'pure' Satellite III sequences. This creates a TaqI (TCGA) restriction site in the pentamer, the location of which is randomly placed in the long tandemly repeating blocks of Satellite III (Fowler *et al.* 1988b). It is also therefore an example of method (b) above.

The TaqI-specific Satellite III polymorphism is best observed by resolution of the fragments in the range about 4 to 25 kb. Normally, about 10 to 20 fragments of this size range exist in any one individual, and these show Mendelian inheritance (Fowler *et al.* 1988b). The resulting polymorphic patterns can be identified by either isotopic or non-isotopic probe methods with optimal results being obtained by field inversion gel electrophoresis (Fowler *et al.* 1988c) (Figs 5.1a,b).

This presentation of restriction fragments is similar in size range and number to that identified by 'polycore' multi-locus 'minisatellite' probes (Jeffreys 1987). The results differ, however, from 'minisatellite' patterns in that firstly, the Satellite III fragments are in multiple and differing copy number so that band intensities may be

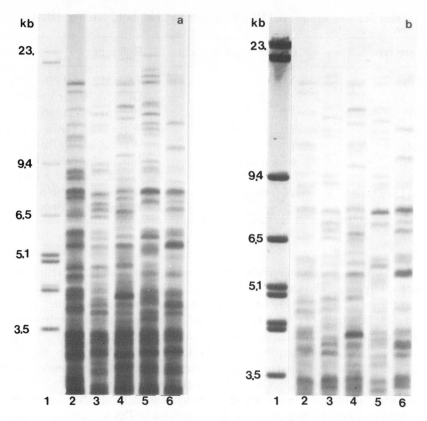

Fig. 5.1 — (a) TaqI and TaqI/ other double digests of DNA form unrelated individuals. Field inversion gel electrophoresis, Southern analysis and probing with a Satellite III sequence related probe labelled with (35S) dATP. (Reproduced with permission from Fowler *et al.* 1988c). Lane 1, lambda molecular size standard; lane 2, individual #1 (TaqI); lane 3, #2 (TaqI); lane 4, #3 (TaqI), lane 5, #4 (TaqI); lane 6, #5 (TaqI). (Reproduced with permission from Fowler *et al.* 1988c). (b) TaqI digests (only) of DNA from the same individuals as seen in 1a. Field inversion gel electrophoresis, Southern analysis and probing with the same satellite III sequence as used in 1a, but using a biotin/avidin/enzyme detection method. (Reproduced with permission from Fowler *et al.* 1988c).

variable, and secondly, some fragment sizes are relatively common in any population, while others are relatively rare (Fowler *et al.* 1988b).

The major mechanism for the Satellite III sequence related polymorphism requires the generation of TaqI sites; TTCCA to TTCGA. This would serve to decrease fragment size. The resulting $C_pG$ doublet (as in TCGA) is itself, however, highly mutable (Cooper & Youssoufian 1988). This TaqI deletion would be a secondary effect, tending to increase fragment size again. However, such a contributory cause to the Satellite III polymorphism (fragments in the size range 4 to 25 kb) is likely to be only minimal. The reason is that these TaqI-deficient fragments are extremely resistant to digestion with many other restriction enzymes e.g. HaeIII, AluI, and RsaI, suggesting their sequences to be highly homogeneous with only minimal sequence drift from the 'pure' pentameric repeat. The polymorphic patterns can thus be established by using an oligo probe constructed of pure pentameric repeats (Fowler *et al.* 1988b).

Compared to the alphoid RFLPs, the Satellite III polymorphic pattern is generally of far greater complexity. This is probably because the short, core Satellite III tandem sequence is more widespread in the genome than the 'chromosome specific' alphoid tandem sequences which may be used as probes. As much as one third of the chromosome complement in humans contributes to the Satellite III polymorphism. The polymorphic fragments are derived from autosomes only, these being predominantly the centromeric heterochromatin of chromosomes 20, 21, 22, but also chromosomes 9 and 15 (unpublished observations).

The same probe which detects the autosomal TaqI-specific Satellite III polymorphism in humans may also be used to detect another region or 'domain' of Satellite III in the genome. This is a 3.4 kb sized tandem repeat derived from Yq (long arm of the Y chromosome) upon digestion with HaeIII, and may thus be used to sex the genome (Fowler *et al.* 1988c). Although the long arm of the Y chromosome is a major region of Satellite III in the genome, the frequency of its TaqI sites is so great that it does not contribute to the large TaqI fragments characteristic of the Satellite III polymorphism.

### 5.3.3    Comparisons and contrasts with 'minisatellites'

RFLPs in 'classical' tandem sequences, such as alphoid and Satellite III, are different in a number of ways from multi- and single-locus 'minisatellite' RFLPs. These may be summarized as follows.

First, the relevant sequences are located differently in the genome. Second, there is a difference in the presumptive mechanism by which RFLPs occur in such sequences. Third, fragments from the 'classical' macrosatellites are often amplified, there then being multiple copies per haploid genome. These arise from either a centric chromosome specific cluster e.g. alphoid, or clusters dispersed at multiple loci e.g. Satellite III. By contrast, RFLPs from a single 'minisatellite' locus are thought to occur in only a single copy per haploid genome, or, in the case of a multilocus 'minisatellite', in single copies, but at multiple genomic sites. Four, the results indicate that 'minisatellite' RFLPs are more variable and thus more discriminating of individuals than RFLPs from 'classical' satellites (Fowler *et al.* 1988a).

Two other points of contrast and comparison are worthy of note. The 'classical' human alphoid and Satellite III sequences are specific to the higher primates; man, gorilla, chimpanzee, and orang utan (Miller, D. A. *et al.* 1988, Mitchell *et al.* 1981), as are therefore their associated polymorphisms. By contrast, a number of the 'minisatellite' sequences are evolutionarily apparently much more ancient (e.g. Vassart *et al.* 1987, Georges *et al.* 1988, Hill 1987, Ali *et al.* 1986).

Though there are reliable immunological techniques for speciating forensic samples, a positive response from an alphoid or Satellite III probe is higher primate specific. These 'classical' tandem repeats also allow discrimination of closely related species. For example, Satellite III and Satellite II are sequence related, the latter being a degenerate form of the same pentameric repeat. Satellite II appears to be predominantly located in the pericentric heterochromatin of chromosome 1 and 16 (Moyzis *et al.* 1987, Burk *et al.* 1985, Schwarzacher-Robinson *et al.* 1988). Digestion

of human DNA with EcoR1 and probing with a Satellite II sequence produces a
ladder-like restriction fragment series (Fig. 5.2a) which is unique to humans amongst

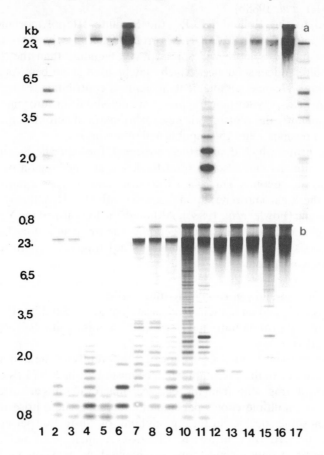

Fig. 5.2 — (a) 'Southern' analysis of human and primate (male) DNA (conventional electrophoresis). Probing with a Satellite II sequence related probe labelled with (35S) dATP. Lane 1,
lambda molecular size standard; lane 2, chimpanzee #1 (HaeIII); lane 3, chimpanzee #2
(HaeIII); lane 4, gorilla (HaeIII); lane 5, orang-utan (HaeIII); lane 6, human (HaeIII), lane 7,
chimpanzee #1 (EcoRI); lane 8 chimpanzee #2 (EcoRI), lane 9, gorilla (EcoRI), lane 10,
orang-utan (EcoRI); lane 11, human (EcoRI); lane 12 chimpanzee #1 (KpnI); lane 13,
chimpanzee #2 (KpnI); lane 14, gorilla (KpNI); lane 15, orang-utan (KpnI); lane 16, human
(KpnI); lane 17, as lane 1. Note: Human specific 'ladder' in lane 11. (Reproduced with
permission from Fowler *et al.* 1989). (b) The Satellite II sequence related probe was stripped
from the membrane (Fig. 2a) and it was then reprobed with an alphoid related sequence. Note
differences in spread and intensities of the alphoid sequence related 'ladder' fragments and the
ability to distinguish between each species, especially in the KpnI digests. (Reproduced with
permission from Fowler *et al.* 1989).

the higher primates. This sequence is near absent in other higher primates (Fig.
5.2a), consistent with previous results (Mitchell 1981). Reprobing the same digestions with an alphoid probe shows that differentation of human, chimpanzee, gorilla,
and orang-utan DNA is possible from their varying fragment patterns (Fig. 5.2b).

## 5.4   TECHNICAL DEVELOPMENTS RELEVANT TO SATELLITE RFLPs

The following is a brief resumé of some of the more recent and perhaps useful technical developments in DNA manipulation and analysis. These concern mostly the elements which go to make up a typical 'Southern' analysis for the detection of a RFLP.

### 5.4.1   DNA isolation and digestion

The most popular method of DNA isolation has been enzymatic degradation of protein, using proteinase K in aqueous buffer containing SDS, and removal of protein by organic solvent extraction. Alternative and safer procedures for protein removal after proteinase K treatment use selective precipitation of protein by salts (Miller S. A. *et al.* 1988) or denaturation with formamide and extended dialysis (Kupeic *et al.* 1987). Chemical disintegration of proteins, rather than enzymatic, has been used (Bowtell 1987, Bahnak *et al.* 1988) as well as a combination of enzymatic and chemical disintegration (Jeanpierre (1987). See also the following: (Signer *et al.* 1988a, Lindblom & Holmlund 1988, Zimmerman *et al.* 1988).

As an alternative, naked DNA may be prepared by starting with cellular tissue embedded in low melting point agarose (Mage *et al.* 1988, Williams 1987). Enzymes and reagents are then diffused into and out of the agarose. This is time consuming but is suited to microsamples, being less wasteful than conventional extractions and likely to better maintain DNA integrity.

The integrity of DNA after transport and storage of both liquid blood (Madisen *et al.* 1987, Gustafson *et al.* 1987) and dried stains (McCabe *et al.* 1987) has been evaluated. Isolation of high molecular weight DNA (apparently) from hair shafts is also possible (Kalbe *et al.* 1988). See also Lench *et al.* (1988).

Ethanol precipitation is a routine method for the precipitation of DNA from aqueous solutions. Recoveries of DNA from dilute solution are enhanced by prolonged centrifugation, this being a more important factor in DNA recovery than prolonged incubations at extremely low temperatures (Zeugin & Hartley 1985). Sodium acetate is normally used in ethanol precipitations of DNA, but by using ammonium acetate it is possible to precipitate residual proteins from solutions containing DNA before the addition of ethanol which then precipitates the DNA (Crouse & Amorese 1987). Carrier RNA may be used to improve recoveries of DNA from dilute solutions (Gallagher *et al.* 1987).

Digestion of DNA by using the appropriate restriction enzyme must clearly be carried out by using the buffer and temperature conditions stipulated by the manufacturer. Failure to do so may give only partial digestion or induce so-called enzyme 'star' reactions (see 5.5). Different restriction enzymes have differing stabilities during the course of a DNA digestion (Crouse & Amorese 1986). A 'universal' restriction buffer for all enzymes has been proposed (McClelland *et al.* 1988). Spermidine trichloride (~1 mM) may be added to digestions, its binding with DNA (Vertino *et al.* 1987) apparently improving DNA/enzyme interaction and thus digestion.

### 5.4.2   DNA electrophoresis

Separation of the DNA fragments created by enzyme digestion is conventionally carried out by electrophoresis in agarose gels in direct, uniform fields. The important experimental parameters are agarose concentration, buffer type and concentration, and temperature (Smith *et al.* 1983, West 1987). Buffer circulation between cathode and anode chambers during extended electrophoresis runs is advisable. Migration of small DNA fragments out of the end of the gel and recycling in the buffer flow can be prevented by a 'trap' placed in the extreme anodic edge of the gel (e.g. DEAE Sephadex embedded in 1% agarose makes a suitable trap for submerged gels).

Field inversion gel electrophoresis (FIGE) is one means of improving separation of DNA fragments (Carle *et al.* 1986) over that achieved when using conventional electrophoresis. Alternatively, gels of discontinuous agarose concentration may be poured to improve fragment separation (Signer *et al.* 1988b), or gels of mixed agarose and acrylamide (Jones *et al.* 1988). Chemically modified agarose is now available for separation of very small DNA fragments e.g. size range 1000 to about 20 bp (Zupanci *et al.* 1988), this being a size range normally requiring acrylamide gels.

The inclusion of ethidium bromide in electrophoresis buffers is optional, but is an additional health hazard and may induce, in combination with UV radiation, unnecessary additional damage to DNA (Cariello *et al.* 1988).

### 5.4.3   DNA blotting
Capillary blotting, rather than electrophoretic transfer, is more popularly used to transport DNA from agarose to blotting membranes, generally either nitrocellulose or nylon membranes. The speed of blotting and the extent of DNA recovery may be improved by vacuum blotting (Olszewska & Jones 1988).

Different blotting protocols have been adopted, suited to different membrane types, an informative comparative study being that of Khardjan (1987).

### 5.4.4   DNA probes and membrane hybridization: non-isotopic alternatives
Although the source of many probes will remain DNA sequences propagated by conventional cloning techniques, there appears to be an increasing trend to the use of synthetic oligonucleotide DNA sequences. Probes of short, tandemly repeating sequences are particularly appropriate in this regard for detecting multi-locus RFLPs (e.g. Edman *et al.* 1988, Schafer *et al.* 1988), as are probes to short unique sequences targeted for amplification by the 'polymerase chain reaction' (Bugawan *et al.* 1988) (also see 5.5 below). The advantages are in obtaining a large stock of stable 'pure' probe, free of vector and without the need to re-check insert sequences normally required after re-cloning. Once the optimal conditions for an oligonucleotide probe have been carefully established (e.g. Hodgson & Fisk 1987, Albretsen *et al.* 1988, Alves *et al.* 1988, Alves & Carr 1988) hybridization rate is rapid and can even be conducted within a partially dried agarose gel, eliminating the need for 'Southern' transfers (Ali *et al.* 1986).

Oligo sized probes may be conveniently labelled by direct conjugation with either an enzyme (Edman *et al.* 1988), or a hapten which is immunologically specific for an enzyme linked antibody (Schafer *et al.* 1988). Other non-radioactive methods rely upon either the enzymatic incorporation of biotinylated nucleotides (Dykes *et al.* 1986, Lo *et al.* 1988) or photochemical incorporation of biotin into DNA (McInnes *et al.* 1987). Band detection is then enzymatic, the enzyme and the biotinylated probe

DNA normally being bridged by the specificity of a biotin/avidin complex (Wilchek & Bayer 1988)l.

Enzymatic incorporation of isotopically labelled or non-isotopic nucleotides into a probe length of DNA is generally by 'nick' translation (replacement of nucleotides in double-stranded DNA with isotopic/nonisotopic analogues, using DNA polymerase I (Koch *et al.* 1986). Alternatively, 'hexamer random priming' may be used: priming DNA with hexanucleotides of random sequence and then copying the DNA with a polymerase enzyme, thereby incorporating istopic/nonisotopic nucleotide analogues (Feinberg & Vogelstein 1984).

The rate of hybridization between a probe and target DNA may be improved by high probe concentrations in specially designed buffers (e.g. Amersham rapid hybridization system), thus preventing high background signals, and/or by confinement of probe solution volume. This is best achieved by 'sandwich' hybridizations (Wilkins & Snell 1987, Nicholls *et al.* 1987).

## 5.5  SUMMARY: COMPARATIVE ANALYSIS OF RFLP AND PCR METHODS

The main objective of operational forensic biology is to reliably distinguish between biological tissues (normally human and most often blood, semen, saliva, and hair), provide information as to their likely source, and assess how common or rare such a source is in a relevant population. Traditionally, this has been done by analysis of proteins, more latterly by analysis of DNA. From both a user's (scientist's) and consumers (community, law enforcement agencies, and lawyers) point of view, five criteria will determine whether DNA technology eventually supplants, supplements, or fails to replace current forensic technologies.

These are, first and foremost, reliability, then simplicity and speed, then sensitivity, cost effectiveness, and information return. DNA technology offers two approaches which may be suitably harnessed to the objectives stated above: namely discrimination of individuals by examination of their genomic DNA for RFLPs by 'Southern' analysis; and discrimination of individuals by the analysis of micro-sequence variation at defined genomic loci, these loci and their immediate flanking sequences being initially amplified in copy number by the 'polymerase chain reaction' (PCR) (Marx 1988).

The detailed technology associated with the polymerase chain reaction is described in detail in Chapter 7, and readers unfamiliar with it are advised to read the relevant sections first.

'Southern' analyses generally assess point mutation or major insertion/deletion events in the genome. The PCR can be used to measure point mutation and very small insertion/deletion events in short genomic segments. The merits of both these methods, and their potential (and perhaps only theoretical) pitfalls, are worthy of detailed consideration.

### 5.5.1  DNA integrity and quantity

Attention should first be returned to the important issues of DNA integrity and quantity, detailed in the introduction to this chapter. All 'Southern' analyses for RFLPs require source DNA integrity (size range of isolated DNA immediately before adding a restriction enzyme) to be substantially greater than the size range of fragments created by the enzyme activity, and, more importantly, the size range of fragments sought out by the probe. Ideally, the source DNA would initially be greater than about 50 kb. PCR technology, by constrast, requires initial DNA integrity to be only greater than the 'inter-amplimer' bp length, as little as 0.5 kb. (Saiki *et al.* 1988). This is one of its major advantages as it allows the use of much more degraded material than conventional RFLPs.

'Southern' analyses for RFLPs arising from, for example, a 'minisatellite' sequence found at one or multiple loci, generally requires between 5 μg and 0.5 μg of DNA (e.g. a 'fingerprint' analysis requires at least 0.5 μg, but other single locus 'minisatellites' may be detectable from as little as 60 ng (Wong, Z. *et al.* 1987). Analysis for multicopy fragments should require still less DNA. However, prior amplification of source DNA by the PCR means that the DNA from a single cell (about $2.5 \times 10^{-12}$ g in sperm) is amenable to HLA analysis (Li *et al.* 1988). This is its second major advantage.

This degree of sensitivity may also be one of its greatest practical disadvantages to the unwary (Lo 1988). Meaningful interpretations will require scrupulous use of controls (Li *et al.* 1988). Expected 'mixtures' of DNA e.g. sperm, vaginal material, and bacterial flora on swabbings may require separations at the cellular level, rather than relying upon separations achieved by differential digestion of somatic and germ-line DNA as used in RFLP studies (Gill *et al.* 1985). Unsuspected 'mixtures' e.g. mixed blood or mixed saliva/blood (dependent upon the ratios of the mix) may provide discordant results by 'Southern' and PCR methods, the latter method is more likely to provide disproportionately strong results from the minor components of the 'mix' as (below a 50:1 mix RFLP studies would be unlikely to detect the minor component (Wong Z. *et al.* 1987).

### 5.5.2   Technique reliability
#### 5.5.2.1   *RFLP analyses*
The reliability of a RFLP analysis has two critical elements (besides the reliable comparison of DNA fragment mobility as seen after probing of the membrane). These are the fidelity with which an enzyme cuts the DNA at its precisely defined sequence, and the fidelity of probe hybridization to its target sequence.

Restriction enzymes have defined base sequence recognition sites (normally between 4 and 6 bp). However, altered base sequence specificity from 'correct' enzyme recognition sequences is known, and has been termed 'star' activity. It has been reported in circumstances such as very high enzyme concentration, lowered ionic strength, or altered di-valent ions, unfavourable pH, and presence of organic solvents such as DMSO and glycerol (e.g. Hind III, Nasri & Thomas 1986, Hsu & Berg 1978, HhaI, Malyguine *et al.* 1980, TaqI, Barany 1988). As an example, 'star' activity in EcoRI sees the enzyme retain recognition specificity for the central four nucleotides, but not the outermost nucleotides in its 'normal' hexameric recognition sequence (Polisky *et al.* 1975, Gardner *et al.* 1982).

Some restriction enzymes are sensitive to methylation of DNA. For example, MspI and HpaII restrict at the same sequence, CCGG, but if the sequence is methylated on one or both strands then MspI retains its activity, but HpaII fails to digest the DNA (Benn-Hattar & Jiricny 1988). In mammalian genomes methylation occurs on cytosine residues only (Woodcock *et al.* 1987) and is frequently tissue specific. For example, germ-line DNA is greatly undermethylated in its Satellite sequences compared with the same sequences in somatic tissue (Gama-Sousa *et al.* 1983). Consequently, digestion of DNA from sperm and that from blood from the same individual could provide discordant results if restriction is determined not only by base sequence but also by the methylation state of the DNA. Comparison of results from different tissues must therefore take account of any methylation sensitivity of the enzyme in use.

The fidelity with which a probe length of DNA hybridizes with its precisely 'homologous' sequence is practically termed 'stringency of hybridization' and is largely dependent upon the temperature used and the prevailing ionic conditions, both during hybridization of the probe to the 'target' DNA and in subsequent washings. In RFLP studies, it is these conditions which determine whether a particular sized fragment is selected and highlighted from the total fragment population as a visualized 'band'.

### 5.5.2.2   *Comparison between unique sequence PCRs and RFLPs*

If hybridization conditions are important to RFLPs, then they are much more important, even critical, to PCR techniques if 'dot-blot' probing is the only means of discriminating between samples (Higuchi *et al.* 1988, Saiki *et al.* 1986). There must be stringent control of the conditions so that a single or few base pair mismatch in a probe, normally only about 20 to 30 bp in total length, determines whether the probe will bind or not. The results may hang or fall by one or a few hydrogen bonds only. Consequently DNA sequencing, which is ideally suited to accurate assay of 2 to 3 hundred bp lengths of DNA, should always be considered a highly desirable back-up to any 'dot-blot' assay which might stand in some doubt. Failing this, the PCR product should at least be checked for its length by gel electrophoresis (Scharf *et al.* 1986).

Direct genomic sequencing is readily possible on PCR amplified mitochondrial DNA which exists in multiple copy number per cell in the genome (Wrischnik *et al.* 1987, Vigilant *et al.* 1988, Higuchi *et al.* 1988). It is also possible on amplified single copy nuclear DNA sequences (Wong C. *et al.* 1988, Stoflet *et al.* 1988, Innis *et al.* 1988). The sequence results obtained are that of the 'consensus' in the amplified population of fragments, and may be less subject to error than if only one or few clones of the same population were isolated and examined (Scharf *et al.* 1986, Paabo & Wilson 1988).

Besides the question of stringency relevant to the use of oligo-probes, the fidelity of a PCR analysis also rests upon the DNA amplification process itself. This requires an act of priming the two template DNA strands with the 'amplimers' (fidelity again determined by base sequence match) and the act of copying the template DNA by a polymerase. The polymerase of choice in the PCR is TaqI polymerase (Saiki *et al.* 1988). The reasons are as follows.

First, its optimal activity is at temperatures close to the melting point of double-stranded DNA (65°C; being conditions which would maximize the likelihood of priming on, and extension from, the precisely homologous target sequence).

Second, its resistance to denaturation (90% residual activity after pre-incubation at 70°C for 2 h, 40% at 95°C after 2 h pre-incubation (New England Biolab 1988–89 catalogue). Such high temperatures (95°C) are needed to melt the newly formed double-strand DNA, which is re-primed etc. in the next cycle of DNA synthesis. Third, its relatively high rate of processivity (rate and extent of nucleotide addition) compared with, for example, the Klenow fragment of DNA polymerase I (Saiki *et al.* 1988).

Conditions which would favour non-specific priming include extended duration of the extension reaction, excess quantities of polymerase in the initial extensions, as well as low temperature of priming (Saiki *et al.* 1988). The earlier such an error occurs in the exponential production of DNA strands, the greater the accumulation of unintended 'nonsense' DNA in the intended amplified population of fragments. Pre-fractionation of the genome by restriction enzymes and recovery of the relevant DNA size fraction by preparative gel electrophoresis prior to PCR is a further safeguard against non-specific priming (Beck & Ho 1988).

With regards to the fidelity of nucleotide incorporation, Klenow polymerase is reported to be more faithful than TaqI. However, the base substitution error rate for TaqI is still small with between 1 error in 5000 (Saiki *et al.* 1988) and 1 error in 9000 (Tindall Kunkel 1988) nucleotides incorporated (with an apparent bias from AT to GC transitions). Frameshift mutations (small insertions and deletions) by polymerase slippage occur in about 1 in 41 000 nucleotides incorporated (Tindall & Kunkel 1988). The worst scenario is for errors to occur early in the amplification process when seeking to amplify DNA containing only very few copies of the target template. This in theory would severely contaminate the fragment population with unintended or false sequences. Such contamination would probably be identified, but this could depend upon the assay method; for example assay by sizing alone, or by sequence evaluation using oligo probes, or by determination by DNA sequence. In the long term, the latter could become a standard requirement.

The PCR reaction is thus a means to amplify unique genomic fragments, up to about 6 kb in size, by the order of $10^7$ times. By contrast, the satellite sequences are sound subjects for length polymorphisms (RFLPs but are less well suited for PCR analysis, though apparently possible (Jeffreys *et al.* 1988, Horn *et al.* 1989). The PCR technique itself is not an errorless process, but the extent of error is small and moderately well predictable. In this regard, its error capacity appears better established than RFLP methods. Provided that experimental conditions are employed to contain amplification errors to a minimum, then the population of fragments created will overwhelmingly be replicas of the sequence of interest. Therefore the method is one of choice especially for degraded and small DNA samples. But unlike the RFLP methods, the final amplified product will need to be closely examined for length or sequence polymorphisms.

Finally, the information return from either RFLPs or PCR techniques for analysis of DNA is such an advance on protein methods for the discrimination of individuals, that their cost benefit analysis is positive in both cases. Analysis by PCR techniques is more amenable to automation, and, at present, more rapid than those obtained by RFLP studies. Reassuringly, both techniques have vast clinical and research application (e.g. Larzul *et al.* 1988, Loche & Mach 1988, Feldman 1988), the knowledge and experience from which will sustain and legitimize their application in forensic science.

## REFERENCES

Alberts, B., Bray, D., Lewis, J., Raff, M., Roberts, K., & Watson, J. D. (1983) *Molecular biology of the cell.* Garland Publishing Company, New York, 386.

Albretsen, C., Haukanes, B., Aasland, R., & Kleppe, K. (1988) Optimal conditions for hybridization with oligonucleotides: A study with MYC-Onco gene probes. *Anal. Biochem.* **170** 193–202.

Alexandrov, I. A., Mitkevich, S. P., & Yurov, Y. B. (1988) The phylogeny of human chromosome specific alpha satellites. *Chromosoma* **96** 443–453.

Ali, S., Muller, C. R., & Epplen, J. T. (1986) DNA finger printing by oligonucleotide probes specific for simple repeats. *Hum. Genet.* **74** 239–243.

Alves, A. M., Holland, D., Edge, M. D., & Carr, F. J. (1988) Hybridization detection of single nucleotide changes with enzyme labelled oligonucleotides. *Nucl. Acids Res.* **16** 8722.

Alves, A. M. & Carr, F. J. (1988) Dot blot detection of point mutations with adjacently hydridising synthetic oligo nucleotides. *Nucl. Acids Res.* **16** 8723.

Bahnak, B. R., Wu, Q. Y., Coulombel, L., Drouet, L., Kerbiriou-Nabias, D., & Meyer, D. (1988) A simple and efficient method for isolating high molecular weight DNA from mammalian sperm. *Nucl. Acids Res.* **16** 1208.

Bains, W. (1986) The multiple origins of human Alu sequences. *J. Mol. Biol.* **23** 189–199.

Barany, F. (1988) The TaqI 'star' reaction: strand preferences reveal hydrogen-bond donor and acceptor sites in canonical sequence recognition. *Gene* **65** 149–165.

Beck, B. N. & Ho, S. N. (1988) Increased specificity of PCR-amplified products by size-fractionation of restriction enzyme digested template genomic DNA. *Nucl. Acids Res.* **16** 9051.

Benn, P. A. & Perle, M. A. (1986) Chromosome staining and banding techniques. In: Rooney D. E., Czepulkowski, B. H. (eds) *Human cytogenetics: a practical approach.* IRL press, Oxford 57–84.

Benn-Hattar, J. & Jirincy, J. (1988) Effect of cytosine methylation on the cleavage of oligonucleotide duplexes with restriction endonucleases HpaII and MspI. *Nucl. Acids Res.* **16** 4160.

Beridze, T. (1986) *Satellite DNA* Springer-Verlag Berlin.

Bowtell, D. D. L. (1987) Rapid isolation of eukaryotic DNA. *Anal. Biochem.* **162** 463–465.

Bugawan, T. L., Saiki, R. K., Levenson, C. H., Watson, R. M., & Erlich, H. A. (1988) The use of non-radioactive probes to analyse enzymatically amplified DNA for prenatal diagnosis and forensic HLA typing. *BioTechnology* **6** 943–947.

Burk, R. D., Szabo, P., O'Brien, S., Nash, W., Yu, L., & Smith, K. D., (1985) Organization and chromosomal specificity of autosomal homologs of human Y chromosome repeated DNA. *Chromosoma* **92** 225–233.

Cariello, N. F., Keohavong, P., Sanderson, B. J. S., & Thilly, W. G. (1988) DNA damage produced by ethidium bromide staining and exposure to ultraviolet light. *Nucl. Acids Res.* **16** 4157.

Carle, G. F., Frank, M., & Olson, M. V. (1986) Electrophoretic separations of large DNA molecules by periodic inversion of the electric field. *Science* **232** 65–68.

Charlesworth, B., Langley, C. H., & Stephan, W. (1986) The evolution of restricted recombination and the accumulation of repeated DNA sequences. *Genetics* **112** 947–962.

Cooke, H. J., Brown, R. A., & Rappold, G. A. (1985) Hypervariable telomeric sequences from the human sex chromosomes are pseudoautosomal. *Nature* **317** 687–692.

Cooper, D. N. & Youssoufian, H. (1988) The CpG dinucleotide and human genetic disease. *Hum. Genet.* **78** 151–155.

Craig-Holms, A. P., Moore, F. B., & Shaw, M. W. (1975) Polymorphisms of human C-band heterchromatin. II. Family studies with suggestive evidence of somatic crossing over. *Am. J. Hum. Genet.* **27** 178–189.

Crouse, J. & Amorese, D. (1986) Stability of restriction endonucleases during extended digestions. *Focus (BRL)* **8** 1–2.

Crouse, J. & Amorese, D. (1987) Ethanol precipitation: ammonium acetate as an alternative to sodium acetate. *Focus (BRL)* **9** 3–5.

Deininger, P. L. & Daniels, G. R. (1986) The recent evolution of mammalian repetitive DNA elements. *Trends Genet.* **2** 76–80.

Durfy, S. J. & Willard, H. F. (1987) Molecular analysis of a polymorphic domain of alpha satellite from the human X chromosome. *Am. J. Hum. Genet.* **41** 391–401.

Dykes, D., Fondell, J., Watkins, P., & Polesky, H. (1986) The use of biotinylated DNA probes for detecting single copy human restriction fragment length polymorphisms separated by electrophoresis. *Electrophoresis* **7** 278–282.

Edman, J. C., Evans-Holm, M. E., Marich, J. E., & Ruth, J. L. (1988) Rapid DNA fingerprinting using alkaline phosphatase-conjugated oligonucleotides. *Nucl. Acids Res.* **16** 6235.

Fang, J. S. & Jagiello, G. M. (1988) An analysis of the human chromomere map and chiasmata characteristics of human diplotene spermatocytes. *Cytogenet. Cell Genet.* **47** 52–57.

Fanning, T. G. & Singer, M. F. (1987) LINE-1: a mammalian transposable element. *Biochim. Biophys. Acta* **910** 203–212.

Feinberg, A. P. & Vogelstein, B. (1984) A technique for radiolabelling DNA restriction endonuclease fragments to high specific activity. *Anal. Biochem.* **137** 266–267.

Feldman, G. L. (1988) Prenatal diagnosis of cystic fibrosis by DNA amplification for the detection of KM-19 polymorphism. *The Lancet* **8602** 102.

Filatov, L. V., Mamayeva, S. E., & Tomilin, N. V. (1988) Conservative and variable clusters of Alu-family DNA repeats in human chromosomes. *Mol. Biol. Reports.* **13** 79–84.

Filatov, L. V., Mamayeva, S. E., & Tomilin, N. V. (1987) Non-random distribution of Alu-family repeats in human chromosomes. *Mol. Biol. Rep.* **12** 117–121.

Fowler, J. C. S., Drinkwater, R., Burgoyne, L. A., & Skinner, J. (1987) Hypervariable lengths of human DNA associated with a human satellite III sequence found in the 3.4 kb Y-specific fragment. *Nucl. Acids Res.* **15** 3929.

Fowler, J. C. S., Burgoyne, L. A., Scott, A. C., & Harding, H. W. J. (1988a) Repetitive deoxyribonucleic acid (DNA) and human genome variation — A concise review relevant to forensic biology. *J. For. Sci.* **33** 1111–1126.

Fowler, J. C. S., Drinkwater, R., Skinner, J., & Burgoyne, L. A. (1988b) Human Satellite III DNA: an example of a 'macro' satellite polymorphism. *Hum. Genet.* **79** 265–272.

Fowler, J. C. S., Skinner, J., Burgoyne, L. A., & McInnes, J. L. (1988c) Improved separation of multi-locus hypervariable DNA restriction fragments by field inversion gel electrophoresis and fragment detection using a biotinylated probe. *Appl. and Theor. Electrophoresis* **1** 23–28.

Fowler, J. C. S., Skinner, J., Burgoyne, L. A., & Drinkwater, R. (1989) Satellite DNA and higher primate phylogeny. *Mol. Biol. Evol.* (accepted for publication).

Frommer, M., Prosser, J., Tkachuk, D., Reisner, A. H., & Vincent, P. C. (1982) Simple repeated sequences in human satellite DNA. *Nucl. Acids Res.* **10** 547–563.

Gallager, M. L., Burke, W. F., & Orzech, K. (1987) Carrier RNA enhancement of recovery of DNA from dilute solutions. *Biochem. Biophys Res. Com.* **144** 271–276.

Gama-Sosa, M. A., Wang, R. Y. H., Kuo, K. C., Gehrke, C. W., & Ehrlich, M. (1983) The 5-methylcytosine content of highly repeated sequences in human DNA. *Nucl. Acids Res.* **11** 3087–3095.

Gardner, R. C., Howarth, A. J., Messing, A. J., & Shepard, R. J., (1982) Cloning and sequencing of restriction fragments generated by EcoRI*. *DNA* **1** 109–115.

Georges, M., Lequarre, A. S., Castelli, M., Hanset, R., & Vassart, G. (1988) DNA fingerprinting in domestic animals using four different minisatellite probes. *Cytogenet. Cell Genet.* **47** 127–131.

Gill, P., Jeffreys, A. J., & Werrett, D. J. (1985) Forensic application of DNA 'fingerprints'. *Nature* **318** 577–579.

Gustafson, S., Proper, J. A., Bowie, E. J. W., & Sommer, S. S. (1987) Parameters affecting the yield of DNA from human blood. *Anal. Biochem.* **165** 294–299.

Hardman, N. (1986) Structure and function of repetitive DNA in eukaryotes *Biochem. J.* **234** 1–11.

Higgins, M. J., Wang, H., Shtromas, I., Haliotis, T., Roder, J. C., Holden, J. J. A., & White, B. N. (1985) Organization of a repetitive human 1.8 kb KpnI sequence localized on the heterochromatin of chromosome 15. *Chromosoma* **93** 77–86.

Higuchi, R., von Beroldingen, C. H., Sensabaugh, G. F., & Erlich, H. A. (1988) DNA typing from single hairs. *Nature* **332** 543–546.

Hill, W. G. (1987) DNA fingerprints applied to animal and bird populations. *Nature* **327** 98–99.

Hodgson, C. P. & Fisk, R. Z. (1987) Hybridization probe size control: optimized 'oligolabelling'. *Nucl. Acids Res.* **15** 6295.

Hollis, M. & Hindley, J. (1988) Satellite II of human lymphocytes: tandem repeats of a simple sequence element. *Nucl. Acids Res.* **16** 363.

Horn, G. T., Richards, B., & Klinger, K. W. (1989) Amplification of a highly polymorphic VNTR segment by the polymerase chain reaction. *Nucl. Acids Res.* **17** 2140.

Hotta, Y. & Stern, H., (1978) Absence of satellite DNA synthesis during meiotic prophase in mouse and human spermatocytes. *Chromosoma* **69** 323–330.

Hsu, M. & Berg, P. (1978) Altering the specificity of restriction endonuclease: effect of replacing Mg with Mn. *Biochem.* **17** 131–138.

Hsu, L. Y. F., Benn, P. A., Tannenbaum, H. L., Perlis, T. E., & Carlson, A. D. (1987) Chromosomal polymorphisms of 1,9,16, and Y in 4 major ethnic groups: A large prenatal study. *Am. J. Med. Genet.* **26** 95–101.

Innis, M. A., Myambo, K. B., Gelford, D. H., & Brow M. A. D. (1988) DNA sequencing with Thermus aquaticus DNA polymerase and direct sequencing of polymerase chain reaction-amplified DNA. *Proc. Natl. Acad. Sci. USA* **85** 9436–9440.

Jabs, E. W., Meyers, D. A., & Bias, W. B. (1986) Linkage studies of polymorphic, repeated DNA sequences in centromeric regions of human chromosomes. *Am. J. Hum. Genet.* **38** 297–308.

Jabs, E. W. & Carpenter, N. (1988) Molecular cytogenetic evidence for amplification of chromosome-specific alphoid sequences at enlarged C-bands on chromosome 6. *Am. J. Hum. Genet.* **43** 69–74.

Jeanpierre, M. (1987) A rapid method for the purification of DNA from blood. *Nucl. Acids Res.* **15** 9611.

Jeffreys, A. J. (1987) Highly variable minisatellites and DNA fingerprints. *Biochem. Soc. Trans.* **15** 309–316.

Jeffreys, A. J., Wilson, V., Neumann, R., & Keyte, J. (1988) Amplification of human minisatellites by the polymerase chain reaction: towards DNA fingerprinting of single cells. *Nucl. Acids Res.* **16** 10953–10972.

Jelinek, W. R. & Schmid, C. W. (1982) Repetitive sequences in eukaryotic DNA and their expression. *Ann. Rev. Biochem.* **51** 813–844.

John, B. & Miklos, G. L. G. (1979) Functional aspects of satellite DNA and heterochromatin. *Int. Rev. Cytol.* **58** 1–114.

Johnson, E. M. & Jelinek, W. R. (1986) Replication of a plasmid bearing a human Alu family repeat in monkey COS-7 cells. *Proc. Natl. Acad. Sci. USA* **83** 4660–4664.

Jones, C. L., Simpson, N. J., Waryas, V. L., & Pappas, M. G. (1988) Discontinuous polyacrylamide gradient agarose gels resolve a wide range of restriction fragments and optimize the efficiency of nucleic acid transfer. *Anal. Biochem.* **173** 285–288.

Kalbe, J., Kuropka, R., Meyer-Stork, L. S., Sauter, S. L., Loss, P., Henco, K., Reisner, D., Hocker, H., & Berndt, H. (1988) Isolation and characterization of high-molecular mass DNA from hair shafts. *Biol. Chem. Hoppe-Seyler* **369** 413–416.

Kariya, Y., Kato, K., Hayashizaki, Y., Himeno, S., Tarui, S., & Matsubara, K. (1987) Revision of consensus sequence of human Alu repeats. *Gene* **53** 1–10.

Khardjan, E. W. (1987) Optimized hybridization of DNA blotted and fixed to nitrocellulose and nylon membranes. *Biotechnology* **5** 165–167.

Kiyama, R., Matsui, H., & Oishi, M. (1986) A repetitive DNA family (Sau3a) in human chromosomes: Extrachromosomai DNA and DNA polymorphism. *Proc. Natl. Acad. Sci. USA* **83** 4665–4669.

Kiyama, R., Oishi, M., & Kanda, N. (1988) Chromosomal location of Sau3a repetitive revealed by in situ hybridization. *Chromosoma* **96** 372–375.

Koch, J., Kolvraa, S., & Bolund, L. (1986) An improved method for labelling of DNA probes by nick translation. *Nucl. Acids Res.* **14** 7132.

Korenberg, J. R. & Rykowski, M. C. (1988) Human genome organization: Alu, Lines, and molecular structure of metaphase chromosome bands. *Cell* **53** 391–400.

Kupiec, J. J., Giron, M. L., Vilette, D., Jeltsch, J. M., & Emanoil-Ravier, R. (1987) Isolation of high molecular weight DNA from eukaryotic cells by formamide treatment and dialysis. *Anal. Biochem.* **164** 53–59.

Larzul, D., Guidue, F., Sninsky, J. J., Mack, D. H., Brechot, C., & Guesdon, J. L. (1988) Detection of hepatitis B virus sequences in serum by using in vitro enzymatic amplification. *J. Virol. Meth.* **20** 227–238.

Lench, N., Stainer, P., & Williams, R. (1988) Simple non-invasive method to obtain DNA for gene analysis. *The Lancet* **8599** 1356.

Levinson, G. & Gutman, G., A. (1987) Slipped-strand mispairing: a major mechanism for DNA sequence evolution. *Mol. Biol. Evol.* **4** 203–221.

Li, H., Gyllensten, U. B., Cui, X., Saiki, R. K., Erlich, H. A., & Arnheim, N. (1988) Amplification and analysis of DNA sequences in single human sperm and diploid cells. *Science* **335** 414–417.

Lindblom, B. & Holmlund, G. (1988) Rapid DNA purification for restriction fragment length polymorphism analysis. *Gene Anal. Tech.* **5** 97–101.

Lo, Y. M. D., Mehal, W. Z., & Flemming, K. A. (1988) rapid production of vector-free biotinylated probes using the polymerase chain reaction. *Nucl. Acids Res.* **16** 8717.

Lo, Y. M. D. (1988) False positive results and the polymerase chain reaction. *The Lancet* **8612** 679.

Loche, M. & Mach, B. (1988) Identification of HIV-infected seronegative individuals by a direct diagnostic test based on hybridization to amplified viral DNA. *The Lancet* **8608** 418–420.

Madisen, L., Hoar, D. I., Holroyd, C. D., Crisp, M., & Hodes, M. E. (1987) DNA banking: The effects of storage of blood and isolated DNA on the integrity of DNA. *Am. J. Med. Genet.* **27** 379–390.

Mage, R. G., Harindranath, N., Hole, N. J. K., Newman, B., Perez, R., Alexander, C. B., & Young-Cooper, G. O. (1988) Genetic analysis of restriction fragment length polymorphisms using high molecular weight DNA from sperm or lymphocytes embedded in agarose. *Gene Anal. Tech.* **5** 94–96.

Malyguine, E., Vannier, P., & Yot, P. (1980) Alteration of the specificity of restriction endonucleases in the presence of organic solvents. *Gene* **8** 163–177.

Marx, J. L. (1988) Multiplying genes by leaps and bounds. *Science* **240** 1408–1410.

McCabe, E. R. B., Huang, S., Seltzer, W. K., & Law, M. L. (1987) DNA microextraction from dried blood spots on filter paper blotters: potential applications to newborn screening *Hum. Genet.* **75** 213–216.

McClelland, M., Hanish, J., Nelson, M., & Patel, Y. (1988) KGB: a single buffer for all restriction endonucleases. *Nucl. Acids Res.* **16** 364.

McInnes, J. L., Dalton, S., Vize, P. D., & Robins, A. J. (1987) Non-radioactive photobiotin-labelled probes detect single copy genes and low abundance mRNA. *BioTechnology* **5** 269–272.

Miller, D. A., Sharma, V., & Mitchell, A. R. (1988) A human derived probe p82H, hybridizes to the centromeres of gorilla, chimpanzee, and orangutan. *Chromosoma* **96** 270–274.

Miller, S. A., Dykes, D. D., & Polesky, H. F. (1988) A simple salting out procedure for extracting DNA from human nucleated cells. *Nucl. Acids Res.* **16** 1215.

Mitchell, A. R., Gosden, J. R., & Ryder, O. A. (1981) Satellite DNA relationships in man and primates. *Nucl. Acids Res.* **9** 3235–3249.

Moyzis, R. K., Buckingham, J. M., Cram, L. S., Dani, M., Deaven, L. L., Jones, M. D., Meyne, J., Ratliff, L., & Wu, J. R. (1988) A highly conserved repetitive DNA sequence, $(TTAGGG)_n$ present at the telomers of human chromosomes. *Proc. Natl. Acad. Sci. USA* **85** 6622–6626.

Moyzis, R. K., Albright, K. L., Bartholdi, M. F., Cram, L. S., Deaven, L. L., Hilderbrand, C. E., Joste, N. E., Longmire, J. L., & Schwarzacher-Robinson, T. (1987) Human chromosome-specific repetitive DNA sequences: Novel markers for genetic analysis. *Chromosoma* **95** 375–386.

Nasri, M. & Thomas, D. (1986) Relaxation of recognition sequence of specific endonuclease HindIII. *Nucl. Acids Res.* **14** 811–821.

Nicholls, P. J., Langdale, J. A., & Malcolm, A. D. B. (1987) Sandwich hybridizations using immobilized DNA. *Biochem. Soc. Trans.* **15** 140.

Olszewska, E. & Jones, K. (1988) Vacuum blotting enhances nucleic acid transfer. *Trends Genet.* **4** 92.

Orgel, L. E. & Crick, F. H. C. (1980) Selfish DNA: The ultimate parasite. *Nature* **284** 604–607.

Paabo, S. & Wilson, A. C. (1988) Polymerase chain reaction reveals cloning artefacts. *Nature* **344** 387–388.

Polisky, B., Greene, P., Garfin, D. E., McCarthy, B. J., Goodman, H. M., & Boyer, H. W. (1975) Specificity of substrate recognition by the EcoRI restriction endonuclease. *Proc. Natl. Acad. Sci. USA* **72** 3310–3314.

Prosser, J., Frommer, M., Paul, C., & Vincent, P. C. (1986) Sequence relationships of three human satellite DNA's. *J. Mol. Biol.* **187** 145–155.

Quentin, Y. (1988) The Alu family developed through successive waves of fixation closely linked with primate lineage history. *J. Mol. Evol.* **27** 194–202.

Radman, M. & Wagner, R. (1988) The high fidelity of DNA duplication. *Sci. Amer.* **259/2** 40–47.

Ridley, M. (1985) Selfish DNA comes of age. *New Scientist* **1456** 34–37.

Royle, N. J., Clarkson, R. E., Wong, Z., & Jeffreys, A. J. (1988) Clustering of hypervariable minisatellites in the proterminal regions of human autosomes. *Genomics* **3** 352–360.

Saiki, R. K., Bugawan, T. L., Horn, G. T., Mullis, K. B., & Erlich, H. A. (1986) Analysis of enzymatically amplified beta globin and HLA-DQ alpha DNA with allele specific oligonucleotide probes. *Nature* **324** 163–166.

Saiki, R. K., Gelfand, D. H., Stoffel, S., Scharf, S. J., Higuchi, R., Horn, G. T., Mullis, K. B., & Erlich, H. A. (1988) Primer-directed enzymatic amplification of DNA with a thermostable DNA polymerase. *Science* **239** 487–491.

Schafer, R., Zischler, H., & Epplen, J. T. (1988) DNA fingerprinting using oligonucleotide probes specific for simple repeats. *Nucl. Acids Res.* **16** 9344.

Scharf, S. J., Horn, G. T., & Erlich, H. A. (1986) Direct cloning and sequence analysis of enzymatically amplified genomic sequences. *Science* **233** 1076–1078.

Schwarzacher-Robinson, T., Cram, L. S., Meyne, J., & Moyzis, R. K. (1988) Characterization of human heterochromatin by in-situ hybridization with satellite DNA clones. *Cytogenet. Cell Genet.* **47** 192–196.

Signer, E., Kuenzle, C. C., Thomann, P. E., & Hubscher, U. (1988a) DNA fingerprinting: improved method for extraction of small blood samples. *Nucl. Acids Res.* **16** 7738.

Signer, E., Kuenzle, C. C., Thomann, P. E., & Hubscher, U. (1988b) Modified gel electrophoresis for higher resolution of DNA fingerprints. *Nucl. Acids Res.* **16** 7739.

Singer, M. F. (1982) Highly repeated sequences in mammalian genomes. *Int. Rev. Cytol.* **76** 67–112.

Singer, M. F. & Skowronski, J. (1985) Making sense out of LINES: long interspersed repeat sequences in mammalian genomes. *Trends Biochem. Sci.* **10** 119–122.

Slagel, V., Flemington, E., Traina-Dorge, V., Bradshaw, H., & Deininger, P. (1987) Clustering and subfamily relationships of the Alu family in the human genome. *Mol. Biol. Evol.* **4** 19–29.

Smith, S. S., Gilroy, T. E., & Ferrari, F. A. (1983) The influence of agarose-DNA affinity on the electrophoretic separation of DNA fragments in agarose gels. *Anal. Biochem.* **128** 138–151.

Stephan, W. (1986) Recombination and the evolution of satellite DNA. *Genet. Res. Camb.* **47** 167–174.

Stephan, W. (1987) Quantitative variation and chromosomal location of satellite DNAs. *Genet. Res. Camb.* **50** 41–52.

Stoflet, E. S., Koeberl, D. D., Sarkar, G., & Sommer, S. S. (1988) Genomic amplification with transcript sequencing. *Science* **239** 491–494.

Tindall, K. R. & Kunkel, T. A. (1988) Fidelity of DNA synthesis by the Thermus aquaticus DNA polymerase. *Biochem.* **27** 6008–6013.

Vassart, G., Georges, M., Monsieur, R., Brocas, H., Lequarre, A. S., & Christophe, D. (1987) A sequence in M13 phage detects hypervariable minisatellites in human and animal DNA. *Science* **235** 683–684.

Verma, R. S. (1988) heterochromatin of the human genome. *ISI Atlas Sci. Biochem.* **1** 134–138.

Vertino, P. M., Bergeron, R. J., Cavanaugh, P. F., & Porter, C. W. (1987) Structural determinants of spermidine-DNA interactions. *Biopolymers* **26** 691–704.

Vig, B. K. (1987) Sequence of centromere separation: a possible role for repetitive DNA. *Mutagenesis* **2** 155–159.

Vigilant, L., Stoneking, M., & Wilson, A. C. (1988) Conformational mutation in human mtDNA detected by direct sequencing of enzymatically amplified DNA. *Nucl. Acids Res.* **16** 5945–5955.

Wahedi, K. & Pawlowitzki, I. H. (1987) C-band polymorphisms of chromosome 9: quantitation by Ce bands. *Hum. Genet.* **77** 1–5.

Walsh, J. B. (1987) Persistence of tandem arrays: Implications for satellite and simple-sequence DNA's. *Genetics* **115** 553–567.

Waye, J. S. & LWillard, H. F. (1987) Nucleotide sequence heterogeneity of alpha satellite repetitive DNA: a survey of alphoid sequences from different chromosomes. *Nucl. Acids Res.* **15** 7549–7580.

Waye, J. S., Greig, G. M., & Willard, H. F. (1987a) Detection of novel centromeric polymorphisms associated with alpha satellite DNA from human chromosome 11. *Hum. Genet.* **77** 151–156.

Waye, J. S., Durfy, S. J., Pinkel, D., Kenwrick, S., Patterson, M., Davies, K. E., & Willard, H. F. (1987b) Chromosome-specific alpha satellite DNA from human chromosome 1: hierarchical structure and genomic organization of a polymorphic domain spanning several hundred kilobase pairs of centromeric DNA. *Genomics* **1** 43–51.

West, R. (1987) The electrophoretic mobility of DNA in agarose gels as a function of temperature. *Biopolymers* **26** 607–608.

Wilchek, M. & Bayer, E. A. (1988) Review: the avidin-biotin complex on bioanalytical systems. *Anal. Biochem.* **171** 1–32.

Willard, H. F., Waye, J. S., Skolnick, M. H., Schwartz, C. E., Powers, V. E., & England, S. B. (1986) Detection of restriction fragment polymorphisms at the centromeres of human chromosomes by using chromosome-specific alpha satellite DNA probes: Implications for the development of centromere-based genetic linkage maps. *Proc. Natl. Acad. Sci. USA* **83** 5611–5615.

Willard, C., Nguyen, H. T., & Schmid, C. W. (1987) Existence of at least three distinct Alu subfamilies. *J. Mol. Biol.* **26** 180–186.

Willard, H. F. & Waye, J. S. (1987a) Hierarchical order in chromosome-specific alpha satellite DNA. *Trends Genet.* **3** 192–197.

Willard, H. F. & Waye, J. S. (1987b) Chromosome-specific subsets of human alpha satellite DNA: Analysis of sequence divergence within and between chromosomal subsets and evidence for an ancestral pentameric repeat. *J. Mol. Biol.* **25** 207–214.

Williams, G. T. (1987) High-efficiency preparation of DNA from limiting quantities of eukaryotic cells for hybridization analysis. *Gene* **53** 121–126.

Wilkins, R. J. & Snell, R. G. (1987) Centrifugal transfer and sandwich hybridization permit 12-hour Southern blot analyses. *Nucl. Acids Res.* **15** 7200.

Wong, C., Dowling, C. E., Saiki, R. K., Higuchi, R. G., Erlich, H. A., & Kazazian, H. H. (1987) Characterization of beta thalassaemia mutations using direct genomic sequencing of amplified single copy DNA. *Nature* **330** 384–386.

Wong, Z., Wilson, V., Patel, I., Povey, S., & Jeffreys, A. J. (1987) Characterization of a panel of highly variable minisatellites cloned from human DNA. *Ann. Hum. Genet.* **51** 269–288.

Woodcock, D. M., Crowther, P. J., & Diver, W. P. (1987) The majority of methylated deoxycytidines in human DNA are not in the CpG dinucleotide. *Biochem. Biophys. Res. Comm.* **145** 888–894.

Wrischnik, L. A., Higuchi, R. G., Stoneking, M., Erlich, H. A., Arnheim, N., & Wilson, A. C. (1987) Length mutations in human mitochondrial DNA: direct sequencing of enzymatically amplified DNA. *Nucl. Acids Res.* **15** 529–542.

Zeugin, J. A. & Hartley, J. L. (1985) Ethanol precipitation of DNA. *Focus (BRL)* **7** 1–2.

Zimmerman, E. G., Akins, D. R., Planz, J. V., & Schurr, M. J. (1988) A rapid procedure for isolating mitochondrial DNA. *Gene Anal. Tech.* **5** 102–104.
Zupancic, T. J., Hilt, D. A., Zarley, C. D., & Kimball, P.C. (1988) Analysis and purification of synthetic DNA fragments with NuSieve agarose minigels. *Bio-Techniques* **6** 294.

# 6

# Properties of hypervariable single locus polymorphisms and their application to identity testing

**Ivan Balazs**
Lifecodes Corporation, Sawmill River Road, Valhalla, NY 10595 USA

## 6.1  INTRODUCTION

One of the most common procedures to date, to identify DNA polymorphisms, is to first digest the genomic DNA with a restriction enzyme, fractionate the DNA fragments by agarose gel electrophoresis, and then detect the size of the DNA fragments homologous to a probe, by nucleic acid hybridization. If the sizes of the DNA fragments detected vary from one individual to another they are considered polymorphic, and the variations detected are called restriction fragment length polymorphism (RFLP) (Botstein *et al.* 1980).

## 6.2  ORIGINS OF VARIABILITY

A variety of mutations are responsible for the generation of DNA polymorphisms. The first RFLP reported in human DNA was a point mutation (i.e. a single base change) near the β-globin gene that is in linkage disequilibrium with the sickle cell anaemia mutation (Kan & Dozy 1978).

### 6.2.1  Point mutations

Point mutations occur frequently in the human genome. However, they do not generate RFLPs efficiently, as only those affecting restriction enzyme recognition sites can be detected as RFLPs, and only if the DNA has been digested with the same enzyme that has the mutated site(s) in the region recognized by the probe. In general, this type of polymorphism will have only 2 or 3 size alleles (Fig. 6.1A). An important consideration influencing the choice of restriction endonucleases is the question of which type of restriction enzyme recognition site is more likely to suffer mutations? Studies in *E. coli* have shown that methylated cytosines are hot spots for

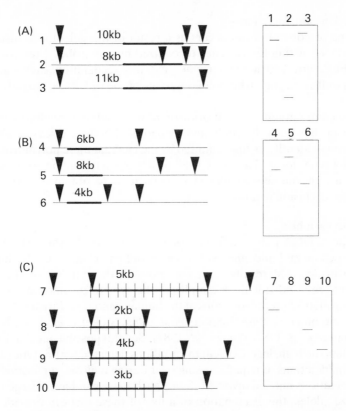

Fig. 6.1 — Examples of mutations responsible for RFLPs. The drawings at the left side represent a DNA molecule, with the arrows pointing at the site of cleavage by a restriction endonuclease. The thick line indicates the region homologous to the DNA probe. The size of the DNA fragments hybridizing to the probe are indicated in kilobases (kb). The drawings at the right side are schematic representations of the relative position of DNA fragments following fractionation in agarose gel. (A) Point mutation. [1] control DNA. [2] mutation within the region hybridizing to the probe. [3] loss of a restriction site. (B) Insertion/deletion. [4] control DNA. [5] insertion of a 2 kb DNA adjacent to the region hybridizing to the probe. [6] loss of a 2 kb DNA fragment adjacent to the region hybridizing to the probe. (C) Variations in the number of VNTRs. [7 to 10] DNA fragments containing 12, 6, 10, and 8 respectively, of a tandem repeated DNA sequence.

transition mutation. As a result it was expected that enzyme recognition sites that contain methylated cytosines would generate higher numbers of RFLPs than predicted from random mutations. However, similar analysis using human DNA has produced contradictory results as to whether the most frequent type of mutation is the cytosine (C) to guanine (G) transition (Barker *et al.* 1984, Wijsman 1984, Cooper *et al.* 1985). Therefore, it is not clear whether restriction enzyme recognition sequences (e.g. TaqI, MspI) containing one or more cytosines will produce RFLPs more frequently than expected from random mutations in human DNA. As a general rule, the more frequent a restriction enzyme recognition sequence, the larger the number of point mutations detected with that restriction enzyme.

### 6.2.2  Deletions and insertions

Another type of polymorphism occurs as a result of the deletion or insertion of a segment of DNA within the confines recognized by the probe. Therefore, for this type of RFLP, any restriction enzyme that has recognition sites flanking this mutation as well as the region homologous to the probe will reveal the polymorphism (Fig. 6.1B).

The most common genetic application of the information provided by these DNA polymorphisms has been the study and diagnosis of genetic diseases. Their application to forensic identity testing is limited by the fact that these polymorphisms have very few alleles per locus. Therefore their power of exclusion/inclusion is relatively small, and a large number would have to be used to obtain a sufficiently high probability of exclusion/inclusion.

### 6.2.3  Hypervariables

Another type of DNA polymorphism is one that consists of a short DNA sequence tandemly repeated multiple times within a gene or locus (Fig. 6.1C). In this case, the polymorphism detected results from variations in the number of these tandem repeats in different individuals. Examples of this type of polymorphism have been identified in widely scattered locations of the human genome (Ullrich *et al*. 1980, Bell *et al*. 1982, Capon *et al*. 1983, Reeders *et al*. 1985, Stoker *et al*. 1985, Knott *et al*. 1986, Nakamura *et al*. 1987, Wong *et al*. 1987). Several possible mechanisms can be used to explain the high degree of length variations detected for this type of sequence (i.e. insertion/deletions, unequal crossing over during meiosis, replication slippage) and all expectations may be involved. Since each locus can have a large number of different size alleles, the examination of a few of these loci can provide sufficient genetic information to uniquely characterize an individual.

## 6.3  SINGLE LOCUS VERSUS MULTI-LOCUS PROBES

Depending on the number of polymorphic loci detected by a probe, RFLPs can also be classified into two major classes, single and multi-locus. The general characteristics of these two classes are as follow:

### 6.3.1  Single locus DNA polymorphism

The characteristic of this type of polymorphism is that the variants detected occur at a single gene or locus. In general, this type of RFLP is detected with a probe derived from that same region of the genome. In the past ten years an enormous number of single locus polymorphisms have been identified. A summary of them can be found in the proceedings of the Human Gene Mapping Conferences 6 through 9 (1981, 1983, 1985, 1987). Of those RFLPs characterized to date, sequences containing variable number tandem repeats (VNTRs) are the ones that have proved the most informative for genetic studies. Therefore, for the detection of differences between individuals, the analysis of single locus DNA polymorphisms provides a genetically simple and extremely powerful tool.

### 6.3.2  Multi-locus polymorphism

A DNA probe that hybridizes to multiple loci at different locations in the genome is said to recognize a gene family or a multi-locus gene. If several of the loci in this gene family are polymorphic, the combination of different DNA fragments that may be present in the population can potentially be very large. An interesting property of many of the cloned DNA fragments that contain VNTR sequences is that, when used under low stringency hybridization conditions, they can recognize other closely related VNTR sequences located in different parts of the genome. The first report on this type of multi-locus genetic system was by Jeffreys *et al.* (1985). Other DNA probes that at high stringency recognize a single locus while at low stringency they recognize multiple loci, have been reported (Werret *et al.* 1988, Vassart *et al.* 1987). Another type of probe, that recognizes a multigene family of polymorphic sequences under high stringency conditions, has also been found (Ip *et al.* 1988). In the case of this probe, the number of DNA fragments detected in an individual does not change with the stringency of hybridization or washing. This property makes it potentially a very useful genetic system for identity testing.

## 6.4  GENETICS OF THE LOCI

Independent of the type of RFLP selected as a genetic marker, some of the properties of the polymorphic locus have to be known before it can be used for identity testing. These properties are: demonstration of Mendelian inheritance, chromosomal localization, whether or not the alleles are in genetic equilibrium, mutation rate, and allele frequency distribution in different populations.

### 6.4.1  Mendelian inheritance

The first test that is generally performed with a newly discovered DNA polymorphic locus is to determine whether or not it consists of independently segregating codominant alleles. This is shown by studying its inheritance in families. Another reason for this type of analysis is to determine whether the particular restriction enzyme/probe combination detects null alleles at that locus. The existence of this type of allele is indicated by the lack of inheritance of an allele, for which a parent appears to be a homozygote. The result would be an apparent case of non-paternity or non-maternity. Another indication for the existence of null alleles is the detection of an excess of homozygous individuals, at that locus, relative to the number predicted by the frequency of the demonstrable alleles. Although null alleles would not invalidate the use of a given locus as a genetic marker, it would complicate the interpretation of the results obtained in cases of disputed paternity. The most common mechanisms to generate null alleles can be technical (i.e. the size of the allele is smaller than those retained by the gel) or biological (i.e. the DNA sequence homologous to the probe has been deleted). The first situation could be corrected by selecting fractionation conditions that retain, within the gel, the entire size range of alleles. Also, depending on the particular DNA sequence and type of polymorphism, the size of the alleles can be manipulated by varying the restriction enzyme used to digest the genomic DNA. Overall, null alleles do not appear to be a common event in polymorphisms due to VNTR. Analysis of 6 such regions (Baird *et al.* 1986, Balazs *et al.* 1989) has not revealed any such cases. Thus, if null alleles exist for those loci, they are very rare.

Deviation from Mendelian inheritance could occur if the RFLP detected is not due to a mutation but rather to some *in vivo* modification of DNA (i.e. DNA methylation) that affects the sensitivity of the sequence to cleavage by a particular restriction endonuclease. This type of modification could be chromosome (e.g. inactive X-chromosome) or tissue specific (e.g. differences in DNA methylation pattern). Also, if the RFLP recognizes a mitochondrial DNA sequence it will show maternal inheritance and will have a more limited application in identity testing.

### 6.4.2   Chromosomal localization and linkage

This type of information is particularly important if several RFLPs are being used to study the DNA of an individual. To simplify the interpretation of the results, and of the probability calculations, the polymorphic loci should not be tightly linked. The reason is that the calculation used to determine the chance of two random individuals having the same genotype assumes that the loci are inherited independently of each other. Thus the frequency in the population of a genotype composed of several single loci will be equal to the product of the individual genotype frequencies. However, depending on their genetic distance, even linked loci may or may not show gametic phase equilibrium. The linkage could affect the expected frequency of a particular genotype by making it more frequent or more rare than predicted from the frequency of the individual loci. Since the genetic properties of single locus polymorphisms can be easily determined, deviations from this ideal would not invalidate their use but would require some adjustment in the frequency calculations. Such deviations from expected frequencies are referred to as linkage disequilibrium.

In large human populations disequilibrium is very rare, the only examples being between loci, i.e. between seemingly unlinked genes such as those involved in disease susceptibility. The most common examples include the major histocompatibility genes and diseases such as insulin-dependent diabetes or rheumatoid arthritis.

Similarly, for a single locus, one of the predictions of the law of inheritance is that, in populations of randomly mating individuals, the frequency of homozygotes and heterozygotes can be predicted from the frequency of the alleles. Here too, if a significant deviation from equilibrium is detected, the calculations can be corrected by using the genotype frequency instead of the allele frequency.

### 6.4.3   Mutation rate

To explain the large number of alleles associated with hypervariable regions, such as those containing VNTRs, it is assumed that the generation of diversity is the result of high mutation rate. Although new mutations do not have an effect in the matching of samples in identity tests, they could lead to false exclusions in paternity determinations.

Estimates of mutation rate have been measured for 10 VNTR-containing loci (Jeffreys *et al. et al.* 1988, Balazs *et al.* 1989). The frequency of appearance of new length alleles varies for different loci, with the most common occurring at a frequency of approximately 5% (Jeffreys *et al.* 1988). However, the results from the 688 to 1000 meiosis, examined in those studies, show that the majority of loci have a fairly low (mutation/recombination) frequency (i.e. 0 to 0.3%). Because of the uncertainty as to the real frequency of change, of those loci in which none or only a few new variants has been detected so far, it is a good practice to confirm the paternity exclusions with a second locus. By this approach, if, for example, the frequency of change at one locus is 0.4% and at the other 0.05%, the probability of falsely excluding an alleged father is only 1 in 1 000 000 (1:[0.004*0.0005*0.5]).

### 6.4.4   Population genetic studies
To predict the likelihood that a particular combination of alleles might be present in the population it is important to know the frequency of the alleles. In addition, because the individuals from a particular country or region may belong to different ethnic groups (e.g. American blacks, caucasians, orientals) it is of interest to determine whether significant differences in allele frequencies exist between them. Although it is well accepted that the use of hypervariable DNA polymorphisms provide a very powerful tool for identity testing only a few such genetic systems have been studied to compare allele frequency distributions in different ethnic groups (Baird *et al.* 1986, Harumoto *et al.* 1987, Balazs *et al.* 1989). In general it has been found that while the size distribution of the alleles in different ethnic groups is very similar, the frequency of particular sizes can vary significantly. The importance of this type of study can be illustrated with a few examples.

### Single locus allele frequency distribution of D17S79
A summary of the properties of this locus, using PstI-digested DNA, were described by Balazs *et al.* (1989). The size range of the alleles for this locus and their frequency distribution in four ethnic groups is illustrated in Fig. 6.2. The results show that the major differences between ethnic groups is in the size and frequencies of their most common alleles. For example, while in all ethnic groups the most common alleles are found in the size range between 3.3 and 3.7 kb and account for about 60 to 70% of them, in Chinese orientals (Fig. 6.2D) 40% of the alleles are between 3.3 and 3.4 kb in size. This value is about 2 times higher than in the other ethnic groups. Also it indicates that for parternity determination in Chinese orientals this locus has a lower power of exclusion than for the other ethnic groups. In the alleged fathers, not excluded by the test, the calculated paternity index for the most common allele will be only about 1.7 (i.e. 0.5/0.3).

### Allele frequency distribution of D2S44
At this locus, DNA digested with PstI has DNA fragments ranging in size from 6.7 to about 16 kb (see Fig. 6.3). In addition, the alleles detected can be further subdivided into a group of small size fragments (i.e. 6.7 to 9.3 kb) and into a group of large fragments (i.e. >9.4 kb) (Balazs *et al.* 1989). The main difference between ethnic groups, with regard to the small size fragments, is that in American blacks they are about 3 times more frequent than in the other ethnic groups. The other major characteristic of this locus is that, in Chinese orientals, approximately 70% of the total alleles can be found between 10.5 and 12 kb, while in the other ethnic groups it is only 30 to 50%. The results presented above serve to illustrate the need of population genetic studies before a polymorphic locus can be used for identity tests.

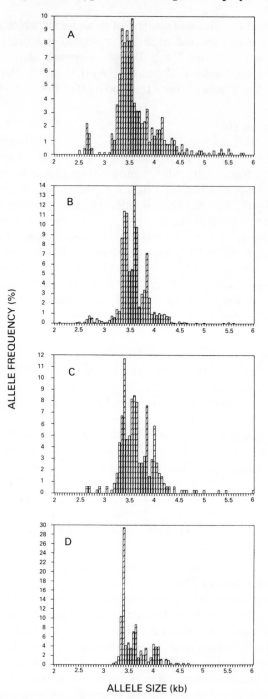

Fig. 6.2 — Frequency distribution of D17S79 alleles in PstI digested DNA from four ethnic groups. DNA from random individuals was digested with PstI and hybridized to pAC 256 (Balazs *et al.* 1989). The number of chromosomes analyzed for these figures were (A) 676 for American blacks, (B) 1468 for Caucasians, (C) 346 for Hispanics, (D) 340 for Chinese orientals.

As the results indicate, the probability of an individual having a combination of the most common alleles will be several fold higher in orientals than in the other populations analyzed so far.

## 6.5   USES OF SINGLE LOCUS VNTR

A question that is frequently asked is how many alleles are in a hypervariable locus. Since the highly polymorphic nature of these RFLPs is the result of variations in the number of VNTRs, it may be expected that the number of alleles, for a particular locus, could be equal to the difference in size between the largest and smallest allele, divided by the size of the repeat. The sizes of some of the VNTR units described vary from 3 to 40 bases (Nakamura *et al.* 1987). Therefore even a 1 kb range in allele sizes may contain a large number of different alleles. In theory, to visualize the maximum number of alleles from a polymorphic locus it would be necessary to fractionate the DNA in gels that can resolve fragment sizes smaller than the repeat unit that defines each allele. There might be some polymorphisms for which this is possible. However, for loci that are composed of alleles that vary widely in size (i.e. several kb) this is not currently practical since there is a limit to the size of the gel that the techniques allow. The gel normally used for DNA fractionation does not measure more than 25 to 30 cm. In this size gel the potential number of alleles is more than our ability to resolve them. Therefore the number of useful alleles at a locus is determined by the size measurement error (Baird *et al.* 1986) i.e. by the resolution of the procedure. To estimate the frequency of an allele and correct for this type of measurement error, Morris *et al.* (1989) have described a method that incorporates the resolution of the gel and the standard error of the size measurement to provide a conservative value for the frequency of an allele.

### 6.5.1   Paternity determinations

The most significant measure of the utility of a polymorphism, to resolve paternity cases, is its power of exclusion. This value expresses the fraction of falsely accused individuals that would be excluded as alleged fathers by a given genetic system. The probability of exclusion of polymorphic DNA loci can be calculated, by using the equation described by Ito *et al.* (1985), empirically by designing an experiment in which DNA samples from random individuals are matched to mother/child DNA samples, or by computer designed Monte-Carlo simulations of paternity cases.

The first report on the analysis of single locus hypervariable loci for paternity and identity testing was reported by Baird *et al.* (1984) and Baird *et al.* (1986) on the D14S1 and HRAS loci. The results show that the combination of those two loci, in cases of disputed paternity, have a power of exclusion similar to that obtained by typing for HLA-A and B (i.e. approximately 96% in caucasians). Other examples on the use of several single locus polymorphic loci have been reported by Dykes *et al.* (1986), Wainscoat *et al.* (1987), Wong *et al.* (1987), and Balazs *et al.* (1989).

For the analysis of paternity cases, the examination of several hypervariable loci, either sequentially or as a mixture, results in a test that on the average will exclude >99.99% of randomly selected non-fathers (Wong *et al.* 1987, Balazs *et al.* 1989). However, in the extreme situation when the accused individual is a close relative of the biological father, as in the case of brothers, the power of the genetic markers is no longer determined by their allele frequencies. Instead, for each locus there is a 50% probability for a particular allele to be present in both brothers. Thus, 4 loci will exclude approximately 94% $(1-0.5^4)$, and 8 loci 99.6% of falsely accused brothers.

### 6.5.2   Identity determinations

Just as for paternity or family studies, the extreme variability of these loci makes them invaluable tools to determine whether two or more biological samples originated from the same individual (i.e. identity testing). The chance of two random individuals having the same combined genotype, after analysis of several polymorphic loci, can be calculated by multiplying the frequency of the genotypes of the individual loci:

genotype of homozygote=(frequency of A allele)$^2$;

genotype of heterozygote=2×freq. allele A×freq. allele B).

For example, based on the allele frequency distribution of the five loci analyzed by Balazs *et al.* (1989), the chance of two random individuals having the same genotype is, on the average, about $2\times10^{-12}$. Even in the event that an individual is heterozygotus at each locus, for the most common alleles, the chance is only about $2\times10^{-9}$, while more rare alleles will generate even smaller values. The powers of identity of hypervariable loci have also been calculated for mixtures of probes that recognize five independent loci simultaneously (Wong *et al.* 1987). Those calculations show that the chance for all of the alleles from an individual to be present in a second random individual is approximately $6\times10^{-7}$.

From the results presented above it may be concluded that the examination of an individual's DNA hypervariable loci, whether one at a time or in mixtures, generates patterns which are likely to be unique for that individual or extremely rare in the population. However, at present the sequential examination of individual DNA polymorphic loci, by hybridization with one DNA probe at a time, or two loci with non-overlapping patterns, offers several advantages over mixtures of probes. It is easier to identify the presence of a mixture of biological samples from two or more individuals, and it simplifies the interpretation of results obtained with partially degraded DNA (see Chapter 2). In addition, in a mixture, the probability of detecting an allele at a particular position of the gel equals the sum of the frequencies of the individual alleles from each of the loci. The result is a loss of informational content and consequently a lower power of identity than if the probes were used individually. The major disadvantage of examining one locus at a time is that it extends the amount of time it takes to complete a test. An intermediate solution would be to use first a couple of individual probes followed by a mixture of several probes.

As discussed above, the chance of two random individuals having the same genotype, with several loci, is extremely small. However, family relatedness will increase this probability. The extreme situation occurs when the individuals to be distinguished are siblings. A common medical application of this type of identity test is to follow the results of a bone marrow transplantation or other type of tissue engraftment (Ginsburg *et al.* 1985, Knowlton *et al.* 1986). In this case, just as in

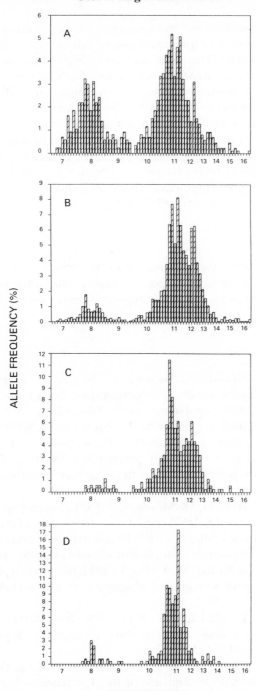

Fig. 6.3 — Frequency distribution of D2S44 alleles in PstI digested DNA from four ethnic groups. DNA from random individuals was digested with PstI and hybridized to SLi103 (Balazs *et al.* 1989). The number of chromosomes analyzed for these figures were (A) 872 for American blacks. (B) 1700 for Caucasians, (C) 346 for Hispanics, (D) 340 for Chinese orientals.

paternity testing, the fact that the loci examined are hypervariable is no longer important. Two siblings, derived from heterozygote parents, have a 25% probability of having the same genotype. Therefore, for 5 polymorphic loci, the chance of two siblings having the same combined genotype for the 5 loci is $0.25^5 = 10^{-3}$. As individuals are further separated by additional generations of random mating, the chance of maintaining the same haplotype in one of their gametes becomes very small. For example, the chance of 5 loci maintaining the same haplotype through four generations is $10^{-6}$ (i.e. $[0.5^4]^5$). If in these two individuals (e.g. cousins) the other gamete is contributed by unrelated parents, the chance of having the same genotype, for the 5 loci described by Balazs *et al.* (1989), is $1.4 \times 10^{-11}$. Depending on the degree of consanguinity between individuals, an appropriate calculation can be made, or alternatively the suspected individual(s) tested.


## 6.6 CONCLUSION

In conclusion, VNTR offers the combination of the simplicity of each pattern or profile together with a large menu of possible profiles within the population. For these reasons VNTR analysis is commonly applied to the resolution of paternity and identity testing.

## REFERENCES

Baird, M., Guisti, A., Miyazaki, L., Nicholas, L., Wexler, K., & Balazs, I. (1984) Allele frequency distribution of highly polymorphic DNA sequences in Caucasian and American black populations. *Am. J. Hum-Genet.* **36** 161S.

Baird, M., Balazs, I., Giusti, A., Miyazaki, L., Nicholas, L., Wexler, K., Kanter, E., Glassberg, J., Allen, F., Rubinstein, P., & Sussman, L. (1986) Allele frequency distribution of two highly polymorphic DNA sequences in three ethnic groups and its application to the determination of paternity. *Am. J. Hum. Genet.* **39** 489–501.

Balazs, I., Baird, M., Clyne, M., & Meade, E. (1989) Human population genetic studies of five hypervariable DNA loci. *Am. J. Hum. Genet* (in press).

Barker, D., Schafer, M., & White, R. (1984) Restriction sites containing CpG show a higher frequency of polymorphism in human DNA. *Cell* **36** 131–138.

Bell, G. I., Selby, M. J., & Rutter, W. J. (1982) The highly polymorphic region near the human insulin gene is composed of simple tandemly repeated sequences. *Nature* **295** 31–35.

Botstein, D., White, R. L., Skolnick, M., & Davis, R. W. (1980) Construction of a genetic linkage map in man using restriction fragment length polymorphisms. *Am. J. Hum. Genet.* **32** 314–331.

Capon, D. J., Chen, E. Y., Levinson, A. D., Seeburg, P. H., & Goeddel, D. V. (1983) Complete nucleotide sequence of the T24 human bladder carcinoma oncogene and its normal homologue. *Nature* **302** 33–37.

Cooper, D. N., Smith, B. A., Cooke, H. J., Niemann, S., & Schmidtke, J. (1985) An estimate of unique DNA sequence heterozygosity in the human genome. *Hum. Genet.* **69** 201–205.

Dykes, D., Fondell, J., Watkins, P., & Polesky, H. (1986) The use of biotinylated

DNA probes for detecting single copy human restriction fragment length polymorphism by electrophoresis. *Electrophoresis* **7** 278–282.

Ginsburg, D., Antin, J. H., Smith, B. R., Orkin, S. H., & Rappeport, J. M. (1985) Origin of cell populations after bone marrow transplantation. *J. Clin. Invest.* **75** 596–603.

Harumoto, T., Suzuki, K., Matsui, K., Ito, S., Matsuo, Y., Miyasaki, T., & Matsumoto, H. (1988) Allele frequency of polymorphic sequences in Japanese and its application to the paternity testing. In: Mayr, W. R. (ed), *Advances in forensic haemogenetics,* **2**. Springer, New York, 373–376.

Human Gene Mapping Conference 6 (1981) *Cytogenet Cell Genet* **32**, No. 1–4; *ibid* 7 (1983) *Cytogenet Cell Genet* **37**, No. 1–4; *ibid* 8 (1985) *Cytogenet Cell Genet* **40**, No. 1–4; *ibid* 9 (1987) *Cytogenet Cell Genet* **46** No. 1–4.

Ip, N. Y., Nicholas, L., Baum, H., & Balazs, I. (1988) Characterization of a novel multilocus DNA polymorphism. *Am. J. Hum. Genet* **43** A188.

Ito, H., Yasuda, N., & Matsumoto, H. (1985) The probability of parentage exclusion based on restriction fragment length polymorphisms. *Jpn. J. Human. Genet.* **30** 261–269.

Jeffrey, A. J., Royle, N. J., Wilson, V., & Wong, Z. (1988) Spontaneous mutation rates to new length alleles at tandem-repetitive hypervariable loci in human DNA. *Nature* **332** 278–281.

Kan, Y. W. & Dozy, A. M. (1978) Polymorphism of DNA sequence adjacent to human b-globin structural gene:Relationship to sickle mutation. *Proc. Nat. Acad. Sci. USA* **75** 5631–5635.

Knott, T. J., Wallis, S. C., Pease, R. J., Powell, L. M., & Scott, J. (1986) A hypervariable region 3' to the human hapolipoprotein B gene. Nucleic Acid Res. **14** 9215–9216.

Knowlton, R. G., Brown, V. A., Braman, J. C., Barker, D. Schumm, J. W., Murray, C., Takvorianc, T., Ritz, J., & Donnis-Keller, H. (1986) Use of highly polymorphic DNA probes for genotype analysis following bone marrow transplantation. *Blood* **68** 378–385.

Morris, J. W., Sanda, A. I., & Glassberg, J. (1989) Biostatistical evaluation of evidence from continuous allele frequency distribution DNA probes in reference to disputed paternity and disputed identity. *J. Forens. Sci.* (in press).

Nakamura, Y., Leppert, Mark, O'Connell, P., Wolff, R., Holm, T., Culver, M., Martin, C., Fujimoto, E., Hoff, M., Kumlin, E., & White, R. (1987) Variable number of tandem repeat (VNTR) markers for human gene mapping. *Science* **235** 1616–1621.

Reeders, S. T., Breuning, M. H., Davies, K. E., Nicholls, R. D., Jarman, A. P., Higgs, D. R., Pearson, P. L., & Weatherall, D. J. (1985) A highly polymorphic DNA marker linked to adult polycystic kidney disease on chromosome 16. *Nature* **317** 542–544.

Stoker, N. G., Cheah, K. S. E., Griffin, J. R., & Solomon, E. (1985) A highly polymorphic region 3' to the human type II collagen gene. *Nucleic Acid Res.* **13** 4613–4622.

Ullrich, A., Kull, T. J., Gray, A., Brosius, I., & Sures, I. (1980) Genetic variations in the human insulin gene. *Science* **209** 612–615.

Vassart, G., Georges, M., Monsieur, R., Brocas, H., Lequarre, A. S., & Christophe, D. (1987) A sequence in M13 phage detects hypervariable minisatellites in human and animal DNA. *Science* **235** 683–684.

Wainscoat, J. S., Pilkington, S., Peto, T. E. A., Bell, J. I., & Higgs, D. R. (1987) Allele Specific DNA identity patterns. *Hum. Genet.* **75** 384–387.

Werrett, D. J., Gill, P. D., Lygo, J. E., & Fowler, S. J. (1988) DNA polymorphisms — Practical use. In: Mayr, W. R. (ed.) *Advances in Forensic Haemogenetics* **2**. Springer-Werlag, Berlin, 320–338.

Wijsman, E. M. (1984) Optimizing selection of restriction enzymes in search for DNA variants. *Nucleic Acid Res.* **12** 9209–9226.

Wong, Z., Wilson, V., Patel, I., Povey, S., & Jeffreys, A. J. (1987) Characterization of a panel of highly variable minisatellites cloned from human DNA. *Ann. Hum. Genet.* **51** 269–288.

# 7

# HLA DNA identityping

**Malcolm J. Simons**
Simons Genetype Diagnostics Phy Ltd, 60–66 Hanover Street, Fitzroy, Vic 3065

## 7.1 INTRODUCTION

DNA profiling is a major advance in individual identification. Traditional individuality testing has employed indirect methods for gene typing in which the chemical products of genes are detected. From the resulting phenotype, the likely genotype is deduced. With the advent of DNA technologies, it is now possible to directly determine an individual's true genotype by typing the genes themselves. This dispenses with the need to deduce likely genotypes from the phenotype, and maximizes the potential for individualization.

DNA profiling is possible because there are individual differences in the particular genes that occur at many locations along the DNA threads of each of the 23 pairs of chromosomes that constitute the total genome. Each gene location (or locus) where such DNA molecular differences occur is known as a polymorphism, and each of the gene types is known as a polymorph, or allele.

There are two main types of DNA sequence polymorphic variation, namely SITE polymorphisms and LENGTH polymorphisms. SITE polymorphisms arise owing to mutations at the actual bases recognized by the restriction endonucleases. They can be contrasted with length polymorphisms which arise owing to different distances between the sites. LENGTH polymorphisms can be further subdivided into those occurring at a single locus, and those occurring at multiple locations throughout the 23 pairs of chromosomes.

For the non-scientist who will utilize DNA profiling information, it is important to make the effort to understand the two types because they underlie types of DNA profiling that have distinct scientific, technical, and interpretational aspects. DNA profiling is mistakenly referred to in the singular. In fact, there are three categories of DNA profiling corresponding to SITE, single locus LENGTH and multiple locus LENGTH polymorphisms. An understanding of differences between SITE and

LENGTH polymorphic systems has become imperative in view of the recent adverse publicity concerning DNA profiling by LENGTH polymorphic analysis arising from dispute over the scientific veracity of DNA data contributed to the investigation of a New York murder case (Lander 1989, Anon 1989).

## 7.2 SITE POLYMORPHISMS

SITE polymorphisms were the first to be discovered. Gene allelic variability is largely due to differences in DNA molecules at specific sequence sites. At these polymorphic loci, the presence of particular DNA chemical base components confers susceptibility to the sequence-cutting action of chemical scissors (enzymes) known as restriction endonucleases. In alternative forms of the gene (alleles) which lack the particular chemical sequences, the absence of so-called restriction sites prevents the sequence being cut by the endonuclease enzyme at that site. Thus, the presence or absence of restriction sites results in chromosomal fragments of varying lengths. The DNA fragments resulting from enzyme treatment are length-separated under electric current in a supporting gel matrix (a process known as electrophoresis). A fragment bar-code pattern results when the gel containing the size-separated fragments is 'probed', using DNA having a sequence sufficiently similar to the test DNA for the two to combine (DNA hybridization). These site polymorphisms are better known as restriction fragment length polymorphisms (RFLP), and the bar-code patterns as RFLP patterns.

## 7.3 LENGTH POLYMORPHISMS

Polymorphisms also occur owing to multiple repeats of short-length DNA segments. In each of the repeated segments the sequence is similar, but the segment length varies owing to the variable number of tandem repeats. These loci are known as Variable Number Tandem Repeat (VNTR) loci. The tandem sequences are considered to be length-based alleles since, in general, they are inherited according to classical Mendelian laws. At a population level, individuals differ greatly in the tandem length repeat varieties present at single VNTR loci. For example, one highly polymorphic locus DNA probe known as YNH24 recognizes over 70 alleles. Such VNTR loci provide for a high order of individuality discrimination.

For single VNTR loci, any one individual has two alleles, one on each chromosome. The two alleles are either of the same length, or of different lengths. Variability in sequence length is revealed as different length fragments on RFLP analysis. Thus, for single VNTR loci, each individual has either one band (i.e. a double dose of a single gene). or two bands.

Repeat sequences can also occur at multiple loci on several chromosomes. DNA probes that hybridize with repeat sequences detect allelic variation at each of the multiple loci. Dr Alex Jeffreys of Leicester University was the first to recognize that a DNA probe based on the core sequence shared by VNTR loci produced complex bar fragment patterns on RFLP analysis that were individual specific DNA 'Fingerprints' (Jeffreys *et al.* 1985).

The purpose of this introduction is to emphasize that there are two main types of polymorphism underlying DNA individuality, not just one as the singularity of

'DNA profiling' implies. LENGTH polymorphisms are described in detail in other chapters in this book. This chapter is concerned with SITE polymorphisms as exemplified by genes of the HLA complex.

## 7.4 HLA GENES

It is a widely-based misconception among forensic and disputed parentage practitioners that, with the advent of DNA profiling, HLA gene typing has been superseded as a useful gene system for individuality analysis. The misconception arises from the common use of HLA testing which employs only two HLA loci (HLA-A and HLA-B). While these two loci alone constitute a powerful individuality discriminating duo, HLA two-locus typing does not regularly provide for inclusionary probabilities of >99%. The term 'inclusionary probability' refers to the statistical chance that a putative father is the actual father. Sometimes an alternative method of expressing this is used, the paternity index, which is the inclusionary probability of the putative father over the inclusionary probability of a randomly selected male. These two terms and their calculation are dealt with in detail by Bryant (1980). It is not generally comprehended that the HLA-A and -B loci encode only two of the seven types of HLA 'antigens' that arise from HLA genes (see Fig. 7.1). It is even less well known that the HLA-A and -B loci are only two of 20 HLA loci that can contribute to individuality determination. In fact, the earliest description of what is now referred to as DNA profiling for individuality testing involved site polymorphisms of the HLA multilocus complex when in the early 1980s, Dr Henry Erlich and colleagues of Cetus Corporation, Emeryville, California, first described the detection of an HLA class II locus RFLP for the HLA-DR alpha locus (Stetler *et al.* 1985). Thus, the DNA profiling era was ushered in by HLA RFLP.

Since the late 1960s, HLA gene ('tissue') typing has been used in disputed paternity resolution. In addition to the two best known loci (HLA-A and HLA-B), the class I complex of polymorphic HLA genes also includes a third locus, HLA-C. Each locus is highly polymorphic, with approximately 20, 40, and 11 alternative forms of the genes presently recognized at the HLA-A, -B, and -C loci, respectively. HLA typing added a new dimension to individuality testing in that the polymorphic information content of the HLA-A and -B loci alone confers a 95% probability of excluding a falsely alleged father. This exclusionary power is similar to that of all the other commonly employed blood groups combined. To regularly attain paternity probabilities of >99%, current practice is to combine HLA-A and -B loci with typing of 'classical' red cell and other blood gene systems.

In addition to the three HLA class I loci (HLA-A, -B, -C), there are three main class II regions known as HLA-DR, -DQ, and -DP. In each region there are one or two loci encoding an alpha chain, and two or more loci encoding beta chains. HLA molecules are made up of both alpha and beta chains. The class II loci, like those of class I, are highly polymorphic. There are at least 25, 14, and 24 different alleles at the DR beta, DQ beta, and DP beta loci, respectively. Thus, at the class I and class II loci combined, there are over 140 recognized main alleles. Since at least some of these can be further sub-grouped, the eventual number of discriminatory alleles can be expected to number in the hundreds. Among known human gene systems, this genetic complexity of the HLA system is unique.

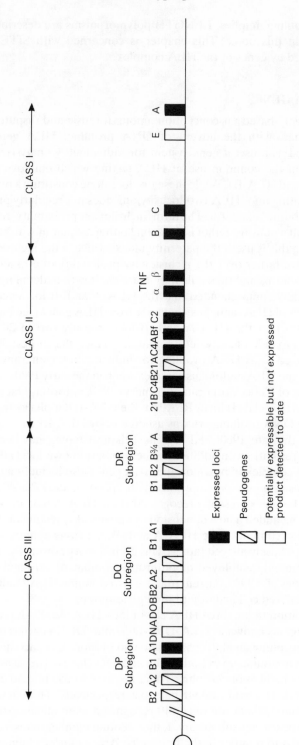

Fig. 7.1.

The biological function of the HLA gene complex is known. HLA genes are of central importance to the body's defence system for recognition of foreign ('non-self') from 'self' molecules. The HLA gene products that carry out this function are glycoproteins (proteins with sugar chains attached) that act like a biochemical fingerprint. These HLA products are located on the surface of nucleated cells and are the 'self' signal of the defence, or immune, system. 'Non-self' molecules are recognized by the immune system in association with one or more 'self' HLA molecules. HLA genes are important in diseases in which risk involves immunity genes. The diseases are very diverse, and include those in which the immune system attacks the individual's own cells (Autoimmune diseases: rheumatoid arthritis, insulin-dependent diabetes etc.), complications of infectious diseases, and the development and course of a range of cancers.

HLA genes are also crucial in acceptance or rejection of 'foreign' organ grafts (kidney, heart, liver, bone marrow, etc.). One of the main medical purposes of HLA gene (tissue) typing is to match potential organ donors with patients needing organ or tissue transplantation. HLA gene individuality is a major problem for organ donor identification. If the requirement was for matching all HLA genes, very few transplants would be performed because complete donor-recipient matches between unrelated individuals is uncommon. In current practice, matching is sought for only 3 of the major loci (HLA-A and -B loci at Class I; HLA-DR at Class II). While HLA gene differences between unrelated people are the main problem in transplant donor-recipient matching, these very differences contribute to the power of HLA gene typing for individuality identification in forensics and disputed paternity.

Immunogenetics is the name given to the science of the genetics of immunity. The HLA multilocus complex is at the core of immunogenetics. In 1987, several conferences were held to celebrate the 50th anniversary of immunogenetics. For the first 20 years or so, the field was confined to studies of genes in experimental animals corresponding to those of HLA in humans. The discovery of HLA genes dates back to 1958, so there is now comprehensive research knowledge as well as extensive clinical literature in the application of immunogenetic knowledge to humans.

Over this 30-year period, HLA gene typing has been carried out by a serum-based technique in which the HLA gene products ('antigens') are reacted with anti-HLA antibodies, resulting in the killing of those white blood cells (lymphocytes) bearing the corresponding HLA antigen (hence the name 'lymphocytotoxicity' for this serological technique). Hundreds of thousands of humans of virtually every ethnic type have been HLA typed, mainly by lymphocytotoxicity, but also by other laboratory techniques such as mixed lymphocyte culture reaction. In the present decade, sophisticated biochemical and DNA techniques have been added to the technical armamentarium. Without doubt, the HLA complex is the most studied of all human gene systems.

A schematic diagram of the fine genetic structure of the HLA complex is shown in Fig. 7.1. The complex is located on the short arm of chromosome 6. It comprises some 3 million bases. This number is approximately 1/1000th of the total genome's DNA content of 3000 million bases. The arrangement of the loci is such that the class I HLA-A locus is nearest to the tip of the small arm, while the class II DP region is nearest to the region where the two chromosomes of each pair are most closely associated (the centromere).

It can be seen that there is at least one alpha gene locus and at least two beta loci for each of the three class II regions. For HLA-DR, the number of beta loci varies between individuals, depending on which particular gene types are present. Thus, for gene types known as DR1, DR2 (DRw15, DRw16), DRw8, and DRw10, only the DR beta I locus is present. In types DR3 (DRw17, DRw18), DR5 (DRw11, DRw12), and DR6 (DRw13, DRw14), both DR beta I and beta III loci are present. Finally, in individuals who have the DR gene types DR4, DR7, or DR9, the DR beta IV locus is present with that of DR beta I. Only for the DR region does the number of loci vary between individuals. DR beta II is known as a pseudogene since it does not express a product. Similarly, at the DQ and DP regions, there is one alpha gene (DQA2 and DPA2) and one beta gene (DQB2 and DPB2) that are not expressed. There is an additional alpha locus (DNA), and a beta locus (DOB), situated between the DQ and DP regions which also do not transcribe any chemical message, and hence do not give rise to any HLA gene product detectable at the surface of nucleated cells. Located between the HLA-B and HLA-DR loci are some 20 genes, including those classified as class III because the chemical structure of their products is different from those of classes I and II. These class III loci mainly produce serum proteins involved in the classical and alternative complement system pathways in immunity function. Finally, it should be noted that there is space available for other genes to be discovered during the ongoing efforts to sequence the 3 million base span of the HLA complex.

A summary of the expressed and non-expressed alpha and beta class II loci is shown in Table 7.1. By definition, only the expressed genes encode the HLA antigens that are involved in immunity genetics, including tissue and organ transplantation. Therefore, for HLA tissue typing purposes, the only component of each expressed locus that is important is the DNA sequence variations responsible for allelic differences in the coding regions (exons). For DNA profiling, any polymorphic locus is informative in distinguishing between individuals, irrespective of whether the DNA sequence variants are sited in product-encoding exons, in the intervening sequences (introns) that separate exons, or in the exon-equivalent or intron regions of the non-expressed loci. Thus, typing HLA genes by DNA methods combines HLA typing and DNA profiling as a single procedure, resulting in a high degree of genetic individualization.

## 7.5   RFLP (RESTRICTION FRAGMENT LENGTH POLYMORPHISM)

The first generation of DNA testing for HLA typing employed analysis of RFLP patterns resulting from the use of DNA probes. DNA from the tested subject's genome (genomic DNA) is extracted from a convenient source of nucleated cells (usually white blood cells) and digested with endonuclease enzymes into fragments. Under electrophoresis the fragments spread out in a gel, the smaller fragments migrating the greatest distance, while the larger fragments remain nearer the 'origin' of the gel, where the digested genomic DNA test sample is loaded. The invisible smear of fragments is transferred to a membrane by a blotting process first described by Dr Southern (hence 'Southern blotting'). The membrane on to which the DNA has been transferred is then exposed to a DNA probe. Probes comprise the exons of each locus joined end-to-end as a result of a recombinant engineering procedure in

**Table 7.1** — HLA locus probes

|               | DRA | DRB      | DQA  | DQB  | DOB | DNA | DPA  | DPB  |
|---------------|-----|----------|------|------|-----|-----|------|------|
| Exon α chains | DRA |          | DQA1 |      |     |     | DPA1 |      |
| Exon β chains |     | DRBI     |      | DQB1 |     |     |      | DPB1 |
|               |     | DRBIII/IV |      |      |     |     |      |      |
| Not expressed |     |          | DQA2 | DQB2 | DOB | DNA | DPA2 | DPB2 |

which the introns that intervene between the exons are spliced out, leaving only chains of juxtaposed exons. The procedure results in a DNA, multiple-exon, sequence that is complementary to the genomic sequence, so the probe is known as a cDNA probe. The cDNA probes employed in RFLP identify genetic loci based on the specificity of the (complementary) sequence for target loci of interest. As mentioned earlier, when the cDNA probe combines with those fragments containing sequences from the locus of interest, then hybridization occurs. Hybridization can be detected by radioisotopic labelling of the cDNA (usually with radioactive phosphorus — 32P), or by non-isotopic enzyme — substrate colour change reactions.

## 7.6   HLA TYPING BY RFLP

For HLA typing, RFLP has an important advantage over the classical serological method. By lymphocytotoxicity, only those HLA gene products (antigens) can be detected for which reagent antibodies have been previously identified. New HLA genes, encoding antigens for which no reagent antibodies exist at the time of testing, cannot be detected. Such subjects will have a maximum of only one detectable antigen, so it is not possible to distinguish between homozygosity (two copies of the same allele), or heterozygosity, involving the detected gene and an as yet undetectable gene (so-called 'blank' antigen). Also, it is difficult to detect the occurrence of two alleles that are very closely related (in HLA tissue typing vernacular, subtypes of a single supertypic antigen) even when lymphocytoxicity antisera are available. By contrast, using RFLP for HLA typing, there are no 'blanks'. All the genomic DNA from the test subject exists between the origin and the lower end of each electrophoretic lane. Provided that enzymes are chosen which discriminate between all allelic variants at each locus, complete typing is possible. Furthermore, heterozygosity can be distinguished from homozygosity on the basis of the total number of observed fragments. Using computer programs [negative cluster for all allelism analysis; positive cluster tree dendrogram for allele assignment — (Simons *et al.* 1989 and Fig. 7.3], heterozygosity can be identified, new variants recognized, and the two alleles assigned.

## 7.7  LINKAGE DISEQUILIBRIUM

HLA DNA typing by RFLP is possible because of the correlation between fragment patterns and HLA gene types. To understand the basis of the correlation it is necessary to briefly consider a genetic phenomenon termed linkage disequilibrium. Consider two loci such as HLA-A and HLA-DQA1 (see Fig. 7.1). As already noted, there are some 20 alleles at the HLA-A locus. In Caucasians, 8 allelic sequence variants have been demonstrated at DQA1 (Horn *et al.* 1988). Independence means that there are no factors causing any pair of alleles to occur together with a frequency greater than that of chance. If the two loci were independent, then any of the 20 locus alleles would occur on one chromosome with any of the 8 DQA1 alleles with a frequency given by the multiple of the separate frequencies of each allele of the pair. By definition, pairs of alleles that do not exhibit linkage equilibrium are said to be in linkage disequilibrium. Aside from the presence and pair-wise patterns of 2-locus alleles existing in the founder breeding pool, there are a number of factors which favour the occurrence of linkage disequilibrium. Two of the main factors are the distance between the two loci, and whether there is any indication that certain combinations of alleles confer increased survival advantage.

*(1)  Distance between the two loci*
The significance of the distance between the two loci relates to the process of cell division that produces germ cells (sperm and ova). During division of germ cells (a process known as meiosis), cross-over occurs between (homologous) chromosomes, resulting in the exchange of segments of equal length. The precise position of the chromosomal break that is necessary for the cross-over to occur varies in different cell divisions. The genetic exchange occurring between pair members of each chromosome results in recombination between a segment of one chromosome and the remainder of the second chromosome of the pair. The closer together are any two loci, the greater is the chance that the loci will be transferred together during recombination. In other words, the chance of recombination or crossing-over occurring between the loci is smaller the closer together are two loci. Recombination is an important evolutionary process in that it is the major way in which gene-bearing chromosomal segments are 'shuffled' at each generation, giving rise to new combinations of genes in the population breeding pool.

*(2)  Natural selection*

One explanation of linkage disequilibrium between alleles is that certain allelic combinations co-occurring on the same chromosome as haplotypes confer survival advantage to individuals having that gene type. Since HLA genes are primarily concerned with recognition of foreignness, it is speculated that particular allelic haplotypes provide for superior immune responsiveness to foreign antigens relative to that conferred by other haplotypes. This notion is central to the Darwinian theory of natural selection. While intuitively reasonable, it is proving to be difficult to test the hypothesis, largely because HLA gene haplotypes evolved under very different historic environmental pressures from those that prevail in contemporary societies. The obvious approach is to examine HLA types in indigenous populations still subjected to the infectious disease agents that ravaged our ancestors. Most of these studies were performed before 'all' the HLA loci were discovered, and before 'all' allelic variations at these loci were known. Now, with the loci known, and with the availability of DNA techniques that can provide comprehensive locus and allele typing, it is timely to repeat such studies.

For the purposes of HLA typing, the occurrence of linkage disequilibrium indicates those combinations of alleles that are most likely to be present as haplotypes in the subjects under test. However, individuals may share the same HLA genes, but may not share the same haplotypes because the shared genes are distributed between the two chromosomes as different haplotypic arrangements. Despite HLA sharing, individuals with disparate haplotypes are more likely to have different genes at other, untyped, HLA loci. Desirably, if a potential organ donor and a recipient are matched for both haplotypes, other HLA genes that are not usually and/or not readily detected will be shared unless recombination has occurred.

Individuality testing by HLA DNA profiling utilizes knowledge of linkage disequilibrium in the selection of loci that are independent; i.e. in which paired combinations of alleles exhibit linkage equilibrium. Candidate pairs of loci in the HLA system are the distantly separated HLA-A and DPB1 loci, and each with the centrally positioned DQA1 locus.

## 7.8   HLA RFLP SCIENCE AND TECHNIQUE STANDARDIZATION

Between 1985 and 1987, the tenth in a series of international HLA genetic workshops was held (10th International Histocompatibility Workshop — 10IW). HLA typing by RFLP (Southern blot) was one technical component among several (serology, biochemistry, DNA sequencing) employed to test cells from over 100 individuals. The cells were chosen to provide the maximum understanding of HLA genetics. In the DNA RFLP study, over 70 laboratories world wide utilized 13 cDNA HLA probes to detect over 1100 fragments generated by digestion with 12 endonucleases. The 10IW HLA RFLP study has been reported in detail (Simons *et al.* 1989). This is by far the largest DNA RFLP study that has ever been conducted, and is probably the largest that will ever be undertaken. The current 11th International Workshop is focusing on second generation DNA polymerase chain reaction (PCR) gene amplification technology. Through participation in the 10IW, the world's leading HLA laboratories gained experience in HLA typing by RFLP. The important technical aspects were clarified, and standardization and quality control procedures established. The reliability of distinguishing between fragments differing in size by only a few tens of bases was affirmed by fragment cluster analysis wherein minimally distinguishable fragments were separable into different allele-associated clusters. Furthermore, hidden duplicates invariably had similarity indices of 100 for each locus (*vide infra*, Fig. 7.3), indicating that the fragment patterns were indistinguishable. Finally, confidence in both technical and interpretative aspects of HLA RFLP typing was provided by concordance of the data with the results obtained by using the other technologies (Dupont *et al.* 1989).

The experience gained from the 10IW by the international HLA scientific community, and the subsequent continuing use of RFLP by HLA scientists, meets court admissibility requirements for acceptability of HLA RFLP typing by the relevant scientific community, and for the existence of standardized procedures. The fulfilment of court requirements by HLA DNA genetics can be contrasted with current concerns about the extent of scientific community acceptance, and of the adequacy of standards in the performance of VNTR RFLP procedures for DNA profiling (Anon 1989, Lander 1989).

One major factor in achievement of standardization and performance reproducibility in HLA DNA profiling is that assignment in the presence of HLA genes is based on the recognition of multiple fragment patterns. By contrast, cDNA probes for single VNTR loci reveal only one fragment per allele. Instead of dependence on reproducible measurement of the size of single allele fragments, and on comparison of test fragments with database counterparts, the 'exact' size of HLA fragments is less critical than recognition of allele-associated multi-fragment patterns. This difference in RFLP test output analysis (multiple fragments per HLA allele versus single fragments per VNTR allele) is a fundamental difference between HLA and VNTR single locus RFLP typing. Furthermore, the occurrence of multiple fragments per HLA allele also provides for an internal quality control of test performance technical validity (see Fig. 7.3) that is possible only with multiple fragment per allele systems in which the relation between fragments and locus alleles is known. In the third category of polymorphism, that of multiple locus length polymorphisms such as those pioneered by Jeffreys *et al.* (1985), neither the particular alleles at any one locus, nor the fragment-locus allele relations, can be discerned from the DNA 'fingerprint'.

## 7.9   HLA DQA1 LOCUS RFLP TYPING

The DQA1 locus has been chosen to illustrate HLA RFLP because the first DNA profiling kit to utilize HLA genes is to be based on DQA1 allele typing. Cetus Corporation and Hoffman LaRoche have established a joint venture to develop PCR gene amplification-based diagnostics. The Cetus/Roche kit is scheduled to be released in early 1990. The use of DQA1 typing by oligonucleotide probe typing of PCR-amplified test DNA in forensics has already been described (Anon 1988, Higuchi *et al.* 1988), and forensic evidence utilizing PCR-enabling DQA1 typing has been admitted to courts in several states in the United States of America. Although the kit is based on second generation DNA technology (oligonucleotide probe typing of amplified genomic DNA) rather than on first generation RFLP, genetic and statistical considerations are similar in both.

Fig. 7.2 shows the RFLP patterns produced by 59 DQA1-associated fragments in 68 individuals. Each individual is identified by a 10IW number and by HLA- DR/DQ region types. The 59 columns depict fragments generated by 12 endonucleases as revealed by a DQA probe. The cells are grouped according to the eight recognized DQA1 sequence types, viz: 9005–9056, 9055–9009, 9011–9007, 9019–9088, 9021–9064, 9067–9071, 9047–9052, 9075–9106. While these eight major patterns are readily discernible, it can also be seen that some cells within each main group show differences associated with one or a few fragments. This reflects the fact that most RFLP polymorphisms are located in the introns, so that DQA1 allele-similar haplotypes can be further stratified by detection of intron polymorphic differences.

The same data are presented as a dendrogram in Fig. 7.3. RFLP dendrograms reflect all genetic events detectable as restriction sites occurring between defined sequences. This includes fragments arising from intra-exonic restriction sites that are subjected to selective pressures, and those associated with genetic rearrangements occurring outside of coding regions. The latter accumulate progressively since they play no part in gene product-mediated selective processes. Such dendrograms provide a measure of the genetic distance between the sequences, and thereby provide information on the evolutionary basis of haplotype sequence development. In addition to revealing evolutionary relationships between haplotypes currently existing among members of the human species, testing of DNA from primate and other species can reveal the phylogenetic basis of contemporarily observable human haplotypes. Thus dendrograms represent the evolutionary basis to individuality.

In Fig. 7.3, the cell order becomes rearranged according to RFLP pattern similarities. The similarity clustering of RFLP patterns of the cells is numerated as a similarity index (SI). Cell 9032 is the 'unknown' duplicate. It can be seen that the SI between the two 9032 samples was 100; i.e. the RFLP patterns were indistinguishable, indicating that technical procedures were satisfactory, in turn warranting acceptance of the test sample data as technically valid. Many other pairs of cells also had an SI of 100, indicating indistinguishability. The ability of RFLP typing to stratify HLA allele types into individual-distinguishable subtypes is illustrated by the SI values of the first 8 cells (9002–9003). These cells all have the DQA1 locus sequence allele, DQA1.1, and so would be HLA typed by an exon typing technique (e.g. oligonucleotide probing) as identical. However, cells 9002 and 9054, themselves indistinguishable, have an SI of only 75 in relation to the remaining DQA1.1 allele cells. Among those remaining six cells, three (9004, 9006 and 9057) are indistinguishable, with SIs of 100. Cell 9061 is most similar to these three (SI=96), followed by 9005 (SI=89), and finally by 9003 (SI=86). Thus, among the eight cells, there are a total of five distinguishable subtypes, or IdentiTypes (DQA1.1.1 — 9002, 9054; 1.1.2 — 9004, 9006, 9057; 1.1.3 — 9057; 1.1.4 — 9061; 1.1.5 — 9005). Similar HLA DQA1 allele haplotype stratification can be observed for the other seven sequence-defined alleles, providing for a total of 31 IdentiTypes among the eight alleles. The discriminatory probability ($P_D$) of the 8-allele DQA1 locus is approximately 0.96. Using DQA1 IdentiTypes, the $P_D$ is substantially increased (>0.99), the precise value being dependent upon population frequencies of the 31 types.

Similar information is available for the DPB1 locus (Simons and Erlich 1989). To date, 24 sequence alleles have been identified (H. A. Erlich, personal communication). Only eight of the 24 alleles occur with a frequency greater than 3%. The

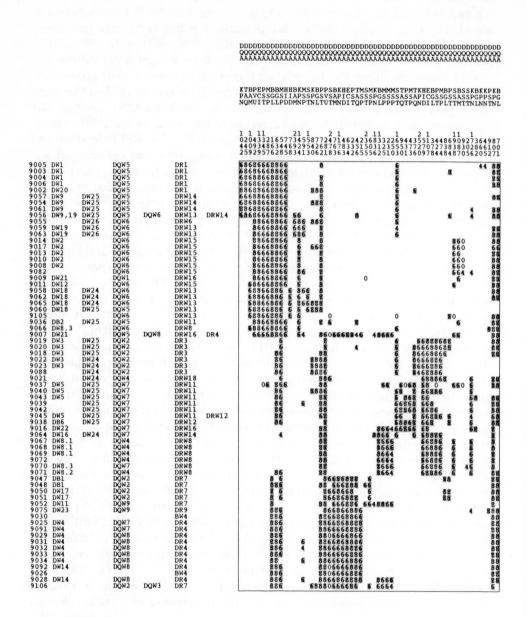

Fig. 7.2 — DQA1 locus RFLP fragment patterns and 10IW cells grouped according to DQA1 allele sequence type.

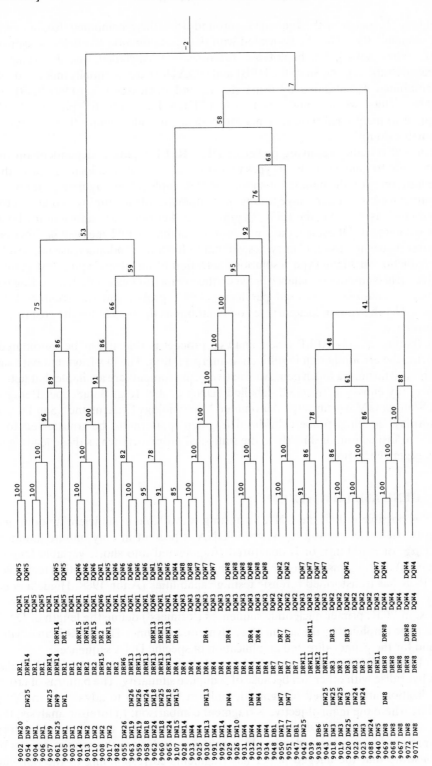

Fig. 7. 3 — Dendrogram of 101W cell relationships at the DQA1 locus.

remaining 16 occur with frequencies around 1%; their combined frequency is approximately 9%. The $P_D$ associated with the most common 12 alleles is approx. 0. 97. When sub-allelic, haplotypic differences are included, the $P_D$ is again increased to above 0.99. Since the DPB1 and DQA1 loci are essentially independent, the combined $P_D$ attained by using the 12 endonucleases is $>(0.99 \times 0.99)$, or $>0.9999$. Thus, when using only two loci, HLA DNA IdentiTyping is clearly adequate to meet legal requirements for evidence of individuality that is 'beyond reasonable doubt'.

The individuality resolving power of HLA RFLP typing is dependent on the number and frequency of IdentiTypes that are detectable at each locus. In turn, this depends largely on the number of endonucleases employed in fragment generation. In routine forensic or parentage testing, it is impracticable to employ as many as the 12 endonucleases used in the 10IW. In practice, 3–4 enzymes are sufficient for HLA allele assignment. Of course, the number of detectable IdentiTypes will be less than that observed when using 12 enzymes, so that reduction in endonuclease use results in a reduction in IdentiType resolution. Selection of an IdentiTyping test system involves achievement of a balance between the number of loci studied, including the number of endonucleases used per locus cDNA probe, and the combined $P_D$ conferred by the chosen loci/enzyme combinations as the benefit for the cost of test performance.

A feature of this RFLP result analysis process is that it can be automated, removing the error inherent in subjective interpretation. The raw fragment data can be captured through a touch pen. Alternatively, instruments are available that detect the beta ray emissions from 32P-labelled cDNA probes (e.g. BetaScope, Betagen Inc., Waltham, Massachusetts; Automated Microbiology Systems Inc., San Diego, California), enabling probe-hybridized fragment patterns to be transferred to a screen for inspection, or directly to the statistical programs such as those leading to dendogram generation.

## 7.10  GENE AMPLIFICATION

RFLP is possible only if the DNA for testing is available in sufficient amount and integrity. In those forensic cases where DNA is present in only minute amounts ($<0.1$ $\mu$g, or $<100$ ng), or is denatured (fragmented into short, variable length, sequences), testing was not possible until the advent of gene amplification technologies. PCR has transformed forensic testing capabilities (Anon 1988, Higuchi *et al.* 1988). Whereas in RFLP the loci of interest are delimited by locus-specific cDNA probes, in PCR, primer nucleotide sequences ('primers') define the length of DNA that is to be amplified by the action of a polymerase enzyme. Thus PCR is an *in vitro* method for the primer-directed amplification of specific DNA sequences.

In RFLP, cDNA probes not only define the 'primary' locus of interest, but also cross-hybridize with other loci because of sequence similarity. The patterns of cross-hybridization are now well recognized, and can be turned to advantage in DNA profiling where the main objective is fragment comparison. In forensic analysis, the crime scene and suspect DNA profiles must be identical; i.e. there is an obligatory requirement for genotypic identity. In parentage resolution, the requirement is to demonstrate that the alleged father has fragments corresponding to the obligate paternal haplotype. In HLA tissue typing, by contrast, the goal is to assign fragments to alleles of a particular locus.

The use of oligonucleotide probes with PCR-amplified DNA avoids the occurrence of cross-locus detection, since the primers define the exon within a locus of interest, and the oligomer probes hybridize with sequences such that the pattern of probe reactivity enables HLA alleles to be assigned. The essence of oligonucleotide probe typing is that probes should be of sufficient length to detect sequences that are unique within the exon (i.e. not present anywhere else in the genome), yet sufficiently short to be destabilized if they hybridize with any other sequences that have chemical base mismatches with the probe sequence. PCR is a revolutionary advance, not only to oligonucleotide probe typing, but to the wider span of molecular biology. For DNA profiling by HLA allele typing, PCR is a major development in that it is simple and rapid relative to RFLP. Nonethless, it is also demanding in its requirement for the selection and use of carefully controlled hybridization conditions, and for avoidance of contamination with extraneous DNA.

PCR has brought about a rapidly changing technological environment in forensic investigation. In addition to providing the means for assaying amounts of DNA too small and/or too degraded to be testable by RFLP, PCR eliminates the necessity for the intrusive procedure of venepuncture. Moreover, PCR not only avoids the destructive utilization of limited evidential material; it actually generates increased amounts of primer-defined sequences which can be used for confirmatory testing in a second laboratory.

The author has recently described an HLA typing method which combines the features of both PCR and RFLP while dispensing with the requirement for any form of HLA DNA probe. This method exploits the utility of PCR primers to define extended sequences which, when amplified, are then subjected to rapid RFLP fragment pattern analysis for HLA DNA IdentiTyping.

## 7.11  THE FUTURE

The objectives of simplified, rapid DNA testing are receiving widespread attention. DNA base sequencing and any other third generation procedure to emerge may supplement, or even supplant, RFLP and PCR oligonucleotide probe typing. In addition to scientific and technical considerations, non-research use of first and second generation DNA profiling systems is controlled by commercial considerations of technology ownership and licensing rights. The same commercial constraints are likely to apply to any new developments. It can therefore be expected that no one technology will come to predominate. Rather, commercial testing laboratories will use that method, or those methods, for which they have protected positions, either by patents or by licences. In evaluating DNA evidence, courts should recognize that the several types of DNA sequence polymorphic variation analysis will continue to be utilized. Accordingly, the type of DNA profiling system employed by any testing laboratory should first be scrutinized in each particular case, since this will influence the scientific, technical, and interpretive aspects of DNA data evaluation.

**REFERENCES**

Anon (editorial) (1989) Fingerprinting trials. *Nature* **339** 481–482.

Anon Research News (1988) Multiplying genes by leaps and bounds. *Science* **240** 1408–1410.

Bryant, M. J. (1980) *Disputed paternity. The value and application of blood tests* Pub. Brian & Decker, a Division of Threine-Statton Inc., New York.

Dupont, B., Simons, M. J., Wheeler, R., Ferguson, M., & Lalouel, J-M. (1989) A display of positive correlations obtained by serology, Southern blot analysis, T-lymphocyte clones, and two-dimensional gel analysis tested on the reference panel of B-lymphoblastoid cell lines for factors of the HLA system. In Dupont, B. (ed.): *Immunobiology of HLA*, Vol. 1: *Histocompatibility testing* 1987. New York: Springer-Verlag, 1035–1067.

Higuchi, R., von Beroldingen, C. H., Sensabaugh, G. F., & Erlich, H. A. (1988) DNA typing from single hairs. *Nature* **332**, 543–546.

Horn, G. T., Bugawan, T. L., Long, C. M., & Erlich, H. A. (1988) Allelic sequence variation of the HLA-DQ loci: Relationships to serology and to insulin-dependent diabetes susceptibility. *Proc. Nat. Acad. of Science* **85** 6012–6016.

Jeffreys, A. J., Wilson, V., & Thein, S. L. (1985) Individual-specific 'Fingerprints' of Human DNA. *Nature* **316** 76–79.

Lander, E. S. (1989) DNA fingerprinting on trial. *Nature* **339** 501–509.

Simons, M. J., Wheeler, R., Cohen, D., Lalouel, J-M., and Dupont, B. (1989) Restriction fragment length polymorphism of HLA genes. Summary of the Tenth international workshop Southern blot analysis. In: Dupont, B. (ed.) *Immunobiology of HLA*, Vol. 1: *Histocompatability testing* 1987. New York: Springer-Verlag, 959–1023.

Simons, M. J. & Erlich, H. A. (1989) RFLP — sequence interrelations at the DPA and DPB loci. In: Dupont, B. (ed.) *Immunobiology of HLA*, Vol. 1: *Histocompatibility testing* 1987. New York: Springer-Verlag, 952–959.

Stetler, D., Grumet, F. C., & Erlich, H. A. (1985) Polymorphic restriction endonuclease sites linked to the HLA-DR alpha gene: localization and use as genetic markers of insulin-dependent diabetes. *Proc. Nat. Acad. Science* **82** 8100.

# 8

# DNA analysis of paternity testing

**Dale Dykes**
Analytical Genetic Testing Center Inc., 7808 Cherry Creek South Drive, Suite 201, Denver, Colorado 80231 USA

## 8.1  INTRODUCTION

Until recently the selection of new genetic markers for use in cases of disputed parentage has depended upon methods which detected the by-products of the genetic code, namely HLA, red cell antigens, red cell enzymes, and serum proteins. These traditional techniques are well described by Bryant (1980). Recombinant DNA technology, however, has demonstrated a new set of highly variable genetic markers based upon DNA nucleotide sequence polymorphisms. The use of cloned DNA probes for detecting such polymorphisms has enabled geneticists to undertake extensive linkage mapping of the human genome. Although one of the main thrusts of such investigations is the identification of linkages to genetic diseases, it follows that these same polymorphisms have a variety of other applications. One such application is the individualization of human blood in cases of disputed parentage and blood stain analysis.

From a practical standpoint, the application of this technology to paternity testing provides greater versatility than conventional genetic marker systems, owing to the nature of the DNA target sequence to be identified. For example, unlike most genetic markers frequently tested, the identification of DNA sequence polymorphisms is independent of gene expression, post-translational variation, and age. Thus newborns, infants and aborted foetuses (8–10 weeks) from rape cases can all be reliably phenotyped. DNA extracts for testing are very stable and can be stored for years at $-20°C$ without a change in electrophoretic patterns. DNA polymorphisms detected by the ever increasing number of probes also offer the opportunity to select the loci, type of probe, and restriction enzyme. Furthermore, the allelic loci are codominant in nature, with heterozygotes often demonstrating two banding patterns of equal intensity. This eliminates some of the subjective problems related to cross-reactions and intensity variation that accompany certain conventional markers.

The methodologies used in the application of DNA probes to identify restriction fragment length polymorphisms (RFLPs), however, are relics of the research setting from which they were developed. Standardization, cost effectiveness, and speed of testing are currently drawbacks to routine use of this technology in the normal laboratory setting. In addition, until recently most probes of potential value in parentage testing were not commercially available to the public. Therefore, wide-spread application of this technology has been somewhat hindered.

The purpose of this chapter is to give an overview of the current state-of-the-art in the use of DNA RFLP analysis in parentage testing. Relative to many other documented genetic marker systems routinely used in parentage testing, the DNA tests are in their infancy. Currently available gene frequency data in this area are generally quite new or limited in nature, thus resulting in an overview which is part fact and part speculation. Indeed, by the time this book is printed we would expect that the general approach might be slightly different and the number of commercially available probes dramatically increased. The point which must be kept in mind is that DNA testing is new in this area of forensic science. The steps taken so far and those to be taken in the future must be carefully planned to assure reliable and reproducible results by means of standardization and rigid quality control measures.

## 8.2 STANDARDIZATION

Owing to the current state of DNA testing in paternity cases, beginning a discussion of standardization is rather difficult. The area of recombinant DNA is in a steady state of new scientific developments and discoveries, and many probes are not readily available to many of the laboratories currently concerned with disputed paternity testing. To deal with this dilemma it is perhaps best to begin with the recently adopted standards of the American Association of Blood Banks (AABB) Paternity Committee. These standards will serve as a framework for the remainder of this chapter.

The AABB standards for DNA testing were the first standards adopted by an organization to deal with the task of DNA phenotyping and reporting results in the area of forensic medicine. To be accredited by the AABB for DNA testing in 1989 a laboratory must meet the standards listed below. For the reader not familiar with standards, in general, it should be pointed out that standards are not intended to provide the details of a technique, but rather to provide an outline of general policies which should or must be followed to guarantee reliable results. Taken into consideration are potential problems with the genetic marker system(s) in question and how these problems should be dealt with by the average laboratory.

**AABB standards**

PARAGRAPH    P7.000    STANDARDS    FOR    DNA    POLYMORPHISM
TESTING

P7.100  DNA loci used in parentage testing shall meet the following criteria prior to
reporting results:

P7.110  DNA loci shall be validated by family studies to demonstrate that the loci
exhibit Mendelian Inheritance and low frequency of mutation and/or recombination, no greater than 0.2% (0.002).

P7.120  The chromosomal location of the polymorphic loci used for parentage testing shall be recorded in the Yale Gene Library or by the
International Human Gene Mapping Workshop.

P7.130  Polymorphic loci shall be documented in the literature stating the
restriction endonuclease and probes used to detect the polymorphism, the conditions of hybridization and size(s) of variable and
constant bands.

P7.140  The type of polymorphism detected shall be known (i.e., single
locus, multi-loci, simple diallelic, or hypervariable).

P7.200  A method shall be available to assure complete endonuclease digestion of
DNA for testing.

P7.300  Size markers with discrete fragments of known size shall span and flank the
entire range of the DNA loci being tested.

P7.400  A human DNA control of known size shall be used on each electrophoretic
run.

P7.500  Autoradiographs or membranes shall be read independently by two or more
individuals.

P7.600  DNA reports shall contain at the minimum:

P7.610  Name of the DNA loci tested as defined by the Nomenclature
Committee of the International Human Gene Workshop.

P7.620  Probe used to detect the polymorphism.

P7.630  Restriction enzyme used to cut DNA.

P7.640  Reported allelic fragments shall be listed by size or allelic description
(alpha numeric).

P7.700  Confirmatory testing by an independent laboratory shall be possible for all
DNA loci. These laboratories shall meet AABB standards for parentage
testing using DNA loci.

It should be apparent at this point that some of the standards are very precise,
whereas others seem to show an absence of direction. Consider, for example, the
requirement that the chromosomal location of a specific polymorphism be documented (P7.120). On the other hand, a laboratory should simply have some method
available to assure complete digestion of DNA with a specific restriction endonuclease (P7.200). Given that there is no tried and true method(s) available which will
work for all probes, loci, and restriction enzymes, we are faced with a dilemma. Lot-
to-lot differences in the quality of some restriction enzymes, occasional contamination and inappropriate reaction buffers, to name a few, have the potential of causing
partial digests or changing the restriction sites. Faced with such a problem, an
appropriate question might be whether anyone can adequately standardize an area

which lacks any recognized rules? Also, is it not presumptuous to require two individuals to interpret results, when in fact the method of interpretation, set of size controls, and assignment of allele and/or band size and population data bases are completely non-standardized?

Hedging a bit on an answer, we might state that the standards provide a guide for acceptability. As we become more aware of the problems and how to solve them, our approaches and the standards themselves must evolve in a positive direction. If, as stated above, they are used to provide a framework for the remainder of this chapter, I suspect we shall better appreciate where we stand and where we intend to go with RFLP analysis in parentage testing.

## 8.3  PROBES AND LOCI

The dual purpose of any paternity test is to identify the falsely accused father, and if not excluded, then to provide a likelihood that this subject is the biological father. To accomplish those goals with DNA analysis, we must have two essential items. Firstly, we need a probe to detect the target DNA, and secondly we need to know the chromosomal location of the target locus so that we can determine if it is sex-linked. If not, then determine whether it is closely linked to other genetic markers being tested.

Until recently, recombinant DNA technology has been primarily a method found in the research setting. With the tremendous profit potential of this technology it has been rather common to find that potential probes were difficult or impossible to obtain. Licensed use for commercial purposes has been sorely missing. The consequence to the public sector has been slow acquisition, practical application and data collection for routine use of the probes on specific loci, with various restriction endonucleases. Table 8.1 lists DNA probes which have recently appeared on the market, most of which will become valuable tools for parentage testing, in the short term, as population data are accumulated.

Major categories of polymorphisms can be classified as single locus, multi-loci, simple diallelic, or hypervariable, depending upon the type of probe and restriction endonuclease used. In a practical sense, the easiest and most reproducible form is the single locus probe. Stringency conditions are generally less critical, and population data can be readily obtained for differentiating population specific groups. Allele and band frequencies for specific loci have been reported, using such informative probes as pS194, L336, pAW 101, pLM0.8, pa3'HVR, p79-2-23, pAC061, pAC225, Sli103, pAC256, and pAC299 (Allen et al. 1989, Baird et al. 1986, Balazs et al. 1989, Dykes 1988). Most of these probes identify variable number tandem repeat [VNTR] sites (Nakamura et al. 1987) with 20 or more alleles, which make them good candidates for parentage testing because of high exclusion probabilities ($>0.8$–$0.9$). Since homozygotes have a single band and heterozygotes have two, an exclusion can be based upon a single band in the child not found in the mother or alleged father. Mutation rates are also negligible ($<0.1\%$), thus limiting the chance of a maternal exclusion or false paternal exclusion.

The multi-locus probes, such as Jeffreys 33.15 and 33.6 (Jeffreys et al. a,b, 1986), however, detect many fragments at different loci owing to partial homology with the repeat sequence of the probe. Reproducibility of the banding patterns requires

**Table 8.1** — DNA probes commercially available

| Probe | Locus | Enzyme | Hetero* | Bands (kb) | Source |
|-------|-------|--------|---------|------------|--------|
| pS194 | D7S107 | Pst I | 0.85 | 5.21–12.42 | CR |
|       |        | Taq I | 0.80 | 7.9–14 |    |
| pL336 | D1S47 | Pst I | 0.90 | 2–12 | CR |
|       |       | Rsa I | 0.88 | 4–12 |    |
| 3′HVR | D16S85 | Pst I | 0.90 | 0.5–6 | CR |
|       |        | Hae III | 0.90 | 0.5–5 |    |
|       |        | Pvu II | 0.93 | 0.5–8 |    |
| pL427–4 | D21S112 | Pst I | 0.94 | 1.4–3.4 | CR |
|         |         | Alu I | 0.94 | 0.5–2.5 |    |
| pL355–8 | D20S15 | Pst I | 0.66 | 6–8 | CR |
|         |        | Hae III | 0.83 | 0.8–2.3 |    |
| pL365–1 | D11S129 | Pst I | 0.66 | 1.5–3 | CR |
|         |         | Hae III | 0.66 | 0.8–2.6 |    |
|         |         | Alu I | 0.66 | 0.5–2.5 |    |
| pL159–1 | D18S17 | Pst I | 0.74 | 5–7 | CR |
| L45 | D5S61 | Msp I | 0.76 | 2.8–7.4 | CR |
| L892 | D3S17 | Taq I | 0.71 | 4.1–9.5 | CR |
| MS1 | D1S7 | Hinf I | 0.99 | 2–22 | CM |
| MS43 | D12S11 | Hinf I | 0.97 | 3.5–16 | CM |
| MS31 | D7S21 | Hinf I | 0.98 | 3.5–13 | CM |
| q3 | D7S22 | Hinf I | 0.98 | 1.5–22 | CM |
| pYNH24 | D2S44 | Hae III | 0.97 | 0.6–5.0 | PM |
| pCMM101 | D14S13 | Hae III | 0.95 | 1.0–3.5 | PM |
| pCMM86 | D17S74 | Hae III | 0.93 | no data | PM |
| pCMM6 | D20S74 | Hae III | 0.90 | no data | PM |
| pAC061 | D14S1 | Pst I | 0.95 | 3–19 | LC |
| pAC225 | DXYS14 | Pst I | 0.98 | 1–10 | LC |
| Sli103 | D2S44 | Pst I | 0.90 | 6.5–17 | LC |
| pAC256 | D17S79 | Pst I | 0.85 | 2.5–6 | LC |
| pAC229 | D14S13 | Pst I | 0.95 | 2–18 | LC |
| pAC404 | D18S27 | Pst I | 0.95 | 2–8 | LC |

Sources: CR=Collaborative Research, Inc.; CM=Cellmark Diagnostics; PM=Promega Corporation; LC=Lifecodes Corporation
Bands (kb): band sizes observed with the specified enzyme. Hetero: frequency of heterozygotes identified for probe and enzyme. Enzyme: restriction endonuclease.

highly standardized protocols which make them less acceptable for interlaboratory comparisons. Often, 20–30 readable bands are compared between the mother–child –alleged father. An exclusion is based upon the presence of a band(s) in the child not seen in the mother or alleged father. Since the probes listed above identify some highly mutable chromosomal regions, an exclusion cannot be based upon a single band mismatch. Indeed, a single band mismatch occurs in 10% of true trios i.e. mother, father, and child (Cellmark, personal communication). The question which has not been adequately addressed with such probes is, at what point (number of mismatches) does one feel confident with an exclusion? Although in most exclusion cases 8–15 bands are identified in the child, which cannot be attributed to either the mother or alleged father, we are unsure of a reasonable cut off. For example, are four bands enough? For all practical purposes this implies that exclusions become probability statements, a concept which is contrary to the general method of defining an exclusion.

In some cases, such as with 3'HVR, (Higgs *et al.* 1986, 1989) a probe can be made to look like a multi-locus or single locus probe by simply changing the stringency conditions (Gill *et al.* 1987, Werrett *et al.* 1988). The alpha-globin 3'HVR probe is a tandem repeat sequence consisting of a core sequence array of 17 base pairs. Under less stringent conditions multiple banding patterns will be observed, whereas low salt and high temperature post-hybridization conditions will demonstrate a single locus polymorphism with a heterozygosity of 89% (Allen *et al.* 1989). This provides the opportunity to easily utilize a minisatellite VNTR as a single locus probe and subsequently provide the opportunity for interlaboratory comparisons.

### 8.4 DIGESTION OF GENOMIC DNA WITH RESTRICTION ENDONUCLEASES

The choice of restriction endonucleases to be used to detect a specific locus is limited by the probe used, the degree of polymorphism observed, and the size of the fragments detected. With many probes several different restriction endonucleases can be used; however, the size fragments generated may differ considerably, Table 8.1. In the case of VNTRs, the proximity of the restriction endonuclease cut site to the core sequence polymorphism may often move the RFLPs over a range of 1–5 kilobases. For example, with the probe pS194, restriction with Taq I produces RFLPs which are approximately 2700 base pairs larger than fragments generated with Pst I (Dykes 1988). Fig. 8.1 shows a paternity case using both restriction enzymes.

This phenomenon provides two opportunities. First, it may be observed that when smaller fragments are generated the resolving power in the lower kb range will permit the identification of additional polymorphisms. For example, we found a 10–15% increase in polymorphism with probe pS194 when we changed from Taq I to Pst I. The result was a 5% increase in the exclusion probability. Second, with the opportunity to change the position of the bands on a gel, one can often choose two probes which do not detect overlapping bands. This enables the laboratory to simultaneously hybridize a single membrane with multiple probes. In our laboratory we hybridize with pS194 and pL427-4, resulting in a cumulative exclusion probability of 97–98%. Additional combinations have been pL365-1 with pS194, pL365-1 with pL159-1 and pL427-4 with p144-D6 and pS194. Fig. 8.2 shows several types of multiple hybridization.

One potential problem inherent in the use of restriction endonucleases is the matter of incomplete restrictions. A method of monitoring the digestion to determine when it is complete is necessary. Generally, it is easy to detect complete

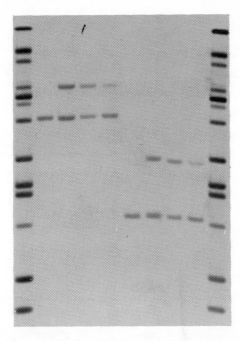

Fig. 8.1 — Two sets of samples restricted with Taq I and Pst I followed by hybridization to pL194. Size markers are in the right and left hand lanes. From the left lanes 2–5 are Taq I restrictions. Lanes 6–9 are the same individuals restricted with Pst I.

digestion by running a minigel of the restricted samples with a known digested control. By staining with ethidium bromide, a completely restricted sample will show an even band width throughout the lane. Partial restrictions will demonstrate a spiked high molecular weight region and smaller fragments which look similar to patterns often observed in rocket electrophoresis (Fig. 8.3).

Attempts to hybridize partial restrictions may yield the RFLP polymorphisms of interest and an array of larger fragments. Depending upon the degree of digestion, the larger fragments can be of the same intensity as the true polymorphisms, thus causing a possible error in phenotyping. Not all probes, however, seem to be equally affected by a partial digest. Depending upon the concentration of restriction sites in the area of the polymorphism and the proximity of the polymorphism to the end of the chromosome, one probe might detect the partial digestion pattern more readily than others. For example, we have noted that if genomic DNA is not completely restricted, probe pL336, which detects a site at the proximal end of chromosome 1, will show both the true polymorphisms and smaller fragments of varying intensities. However, when hybridizing the same sample with pS194, which detects a chromosomal region at position D7S107, the partial digests will go unnoticed. To determine how a locus is affected by a specific enzyme, it is good practice to intentionally create partial digests and hybridize the resulting bands. It is also good practice to test each new lot of enzyme by digesting a human control and lambda bacteriophage to determine if it will generate the correct number of bands. If intending to do

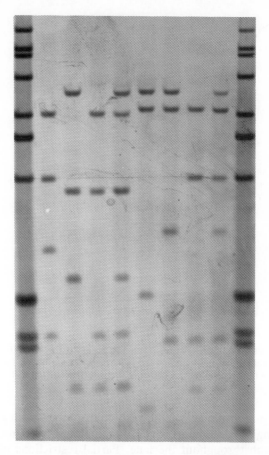

Fig. 8.2 — Simultaneous hybridization of Pst I genomic digests with p144-D6 and pL427-4. The
top series of bands are representing the p144-D6 hybrids, whereas the smaller bands are the
pL427-4 hybrids.

simultaneous probing of a membrane, it is important to select two probes which will
be equally affected by a partial digest in order to eliminate the chance of band
overlapping.

At present, data sets for different probes using various restriction endonucleases
are greatly lacking. Although adequate population data may be available for one
particular enzyme, comparable data are absent for other restriction endonucleases
which demonstrate a similar degree of polymorphism. Since band frequencies are
utilized in calculating inclusion probabilities, switching to another enzyme requires
the accumulation of additional data sets for various populations. This is imperative
because the resolving power of the gels in the lower kilobase (kb) range is greater
than that observed in the higher range. Simply trying to convert the band frequencies
identified with one RE to that of another, particularly with VNTRs, will give
erroneous data sets. Our experience has often been that larger fragments (8–15 kb)
will sometimes split into 2–3 bands if the alternative restriction endonuclease creates

Fig. 8.3 — Ethidium bromide staining of genomic samples restricted with Pst I. The lanes with uniform thickness are complete digests. The lanes with a thick upper region and streaming are partial digests.

fragments of 2–5 kb smaller. Table 8.2 shows the results of locus D7S107 hybridized with pS194 after digestion with Taq I and Pst I. Band 8.5 detected with Taq I split into bands 5.88, 5.73, and 5.65 when DNA was digested with Pst I. Occasionally some bands will show unequal shifts, which compounds the problem of making a simple size conversion.

## 8.5   DETERMINING BAND SIZES FOR CALCULATING PLAUSIBILITY OF PATERNITY [*W*] OR PATERNITY INDEX [*PI*]

A number of terms can be calculated to estimate the likelihood of paternity for the non-excluded alleged father. *W* and *PI* are two of these. The calculation of these is described in Bryant (1980).

For single locus probes which only identify several alleles at a specific locus the nomenclature can be either band size or alpha numeric. If band size is the method of choice, then one usually takes multiple readings of control samples and averages the band sizes. The result might be 5.1, 4.8, and 3.2 kb. For all practical purposes calling the bands 1, 2, or 3 is sufficient.

The task of dealing with VNTRs is complicated by the fact that many of the VNTR probes demonstrate a continuous allele distrubution. The 3′HVR probe described earlier consists of a 17 base pair core which identifies a locus found on chromosome 16, approximately 8 kb from the 3′ alpha haemoglobin gene complex. Polymorphism is by insertion, deletion, or unequal crossing over, resulting in allelic forms which can differ by only 17 base pairs (bp). The resolving power and reproducibility of the agarose gel electrophoretic technique used in separating the

**Table 8.2** — Allele size comparisons of D7S107 with restriction endonucleases Taq I, Pst 1

| No. tested 742 (Taq I) | | No. tested 348 (Pst I) | |
|---|---|---|---|
| Size (kb) | Frequency | Size (kb) | Frequency |
| 14 | 0.027 | 10.9 | 0.007 |
| 12.3 | 0.001 | 8.41 | 0.003 |
| 11.1 | 0.005 | 8.17 | 0.012 |
| 10.7 | 0.017 | 7.91 | 0.016 |
| 10.5 | 0.038 | 7.74 | 0.003 |
| 10.3 | 0.043 | 7.61 | 0.007 |
| 10.2 | 0.031 | 7.48 | 0.068 |
| 10.1 | 0.053 | 7.43 | 0.047 |
| 10.0 | 0.016 | 7.37 | 0.032 |
| 9.8 | 0.087 | 7.24 | 0.015 |
| 9.7 | 0.079 | 7.15 | 0.028 |
| 9.6 | 0.120 | 7.06 | 0.096 |
| 9.4 | 0.110 | 6.96 | 0.078 |
| 9.2 | 0.014 | 6.88 | 0.079 |
| 9.1 | 0.016 | 6.79 | 0.010 |
| 8.9 | 0.023 | 6.69 | 0.131 |
| 8.5 | 0.310 | 6.55 | 0.018 |
| 8.4 | 0.007 | 6.38 | 0.022 |
| 8.0 | 0.002 | 6.25 | 0.007 |
| 7.9 | 0.001 | 6.11 | 0.004 |
| | | 5.88 | 0.043 |
| | | 5.73 | 0.235 |
| | | 5.65 | 0.032 |
| | | 5.40 | 0.002 |
| | | 5.31 | 0.003 |
| | | 5.21 | 0.002 |

This white population sample was probed with pS194 which identifies D7S107. 0.7 g% agarose gels were run for 48 h at 1.3 U/cm. Membranes were detected with non-isotopic methods using biotinylated probes.

fragments, however, is incapable of differentiating separate alleles based upon a single tandem repeat. The consequence is that discrete alleles cannot be assigned and are defined as different only if they can be coelectrophoresed and clearly separated on the gel. Indistinguishability (lumping together of non-distinguished but separate alleles) will create an array of band readings in a population base which represent a best estimate of the degree of heterogeneity. Using a video scanner to identify bands (D7S107 with Pst I) after hybridization with pS194, in a population of 953 whites, we recorded the observed bands on a computer and rounded (binned) off the readings to the closest 10 bp. A total of 243 bands were observed. Table 8.3 shows only those bands observed from 5.97 to 5.60. As one might expect, several alleles probably exist within this size range, but we cannot clearly separate them owing to overlapping.

**Table 8.3** — Band size distribution of D7S107 with restriction endonuclease Pst I

| Size | No. observed | Frequency | Size | No. observed | Frequency |
|------|--------------|-----------|------|--------------|-----------|
| 5.97 | 1 | 0.0005 | 5.74 | 64 | 0.0335 |
| 5.89 | 1 | 0.0005 | 5.73 | 52 | 0.0272 |
| 5.87 | 2 | 0.0010 | 5.72 | 53 | 0.0278 |
| 5.86 | 1 | 0.0005 | 5.71 | 52 | 0.0272 |
| 5.85 | 1 | 0.0005 | 5.70 | 53 | 0.0278 |
| 5.84 | 1 | 0.0005 | 5.69 | 53 | 0.0278 |
| 5.82 | 3 | 0.0015 | 5.68 | 33 | 0.0173 |
| 5.81 | 4 | 0.0021 | 5.67 | 18 | 0.0094 |
| 5.80 | 6 | 0.0031 | 5.66 | 18 | 0.0094 |
| 5.79 | 3 | 0.0015 | 5.65 | 19 | 0.0099 |
| 5.78 | 18 | 0.0094 | 5.64 | 16 | 0.0085 |
| 5.77 | 14 | 0.0073 | 5.63 | 9 | 0.0047 |
| 5.76 | 32 | 0.0168 | 5.62 | 6 | 0.0031 |
| 5.75 | 57 | 0.0299 | 5.60 | 2 | 0.0010 |

This table represents a sampling of band frequencies observed for D7S107 using Pst 1 restriction enzyme and biotinylated probe pS 194.

Retesting of the same population on a separate series of gels would in all likelihood demonstrate a slight shift in band frequencies due to electrophoretic variation. Changing the electrophoretic parameters or comparing data on the same probe between different laboratories would also be expected to change the frequency of the separate band arrays.

Baird *et al.* (1986) determined that the error in measuring the polymorphisms of D14S1 and HRAS-1, using probes pAW101 and pLMO.8 respectively, resulted in a standard deviation which equalled 0.6% of the observed band size. This meant that if calculating the chance that random man could have contributed the same band as the alleged father one had to add all band frequencies ±0.6% from the observed obligatory band. For example, if the obligatory band was 6000 bp, then you must sum the obligatory band frequency and all band frequencies ±36 base pairs. The result is a more conservative PI owing to the error of the measurement. Allen *et al* (1989) observed a 0.6–0.8% variation, whereas Chimera (Roche Biomedical, personal communication) suggested a more conservative estimate of 1.2%. We measured the bands detected with pS194 and pL336 on a video scanner and found the error closer to 1.5 standard deviations or 1% of the observed band size. Table 8.4 gives an example of the observed PI values in a fictitious paternity case with assigned allele frequencies (Table 8.2) and binned band frequencies (Table 8.3) using a ±1% summation of all bands relative to the obligatory allele (5.73 kb). The result was an expected decrease, yet a more conservative estimate of the PI.

The chance, however, exists that the paternal contribution of a true father might fall outside the standard error of the measurement on a specific run if he is not run on the same gel as the child. One common practice to minimize this potential problem is to run the child and alleged father beside each other and include a mixture of the

**Table 8.4** — *PI* values using allele sizes and binning

| C | M | AF | C/AF | *PI* alleles | *PI* binning |
|---|---|---|------|------------|------------|
| 7.6,<br>5.73 | 7.60,<br>5.52 | 6.99,<br>5.73 | 7.60,<br>6.99,<br>5.73 | 2.13 | 1.92 |

*PI* alleles: *PI* values are based upon available allele frequency data.
*PI* binding: *PI* values are based upon ±1% of all bands from the obligatory bands.
C : child M : mother AF : alleged father C/AF : child alleged father mix.

child and father to assure that the obligatory allele is similar and not different due to lane to lane variation (see Fig. 8.4).

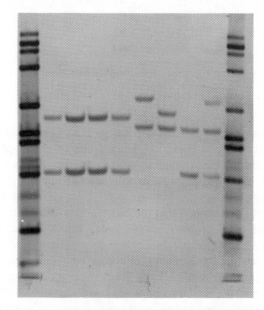

Fig. 8.4 — Two paternity cases restricted with Pst I and hybridized with pL194. From the left lanes 2, 3, 4 and 5 are child, mother, alleged father and C/AF mix. Lanes 6, 7, 8, and 9 are from a separate paternity case in the same order.

## 8.6   RELIABILITY OF PROBES

To determine the reliability and effectiveness of a probe in parentage testing the most practical approach is to use the probe in conjunction with conventional genetic marker systems. The intention is to detect unexpected maternal or paternal exclusions (indicating unacceptable mutation rates), to determine if the degree of polymorphism will effectively provide a satisfactory exclusion probability, and finally to identify the value of the probe at increasing the *PI* or *W* in cases of true fathers. Theoretically the statistical potential of a probe should match the observed results with a sufficiently large data comparison.

One method we have employed is to first test a parentage case with 12–16 red blood cell antigens, red blood cell enzymes and serum proteins (cumulative probability of exclusion CPE=0.98). Probes pS194 and pL336, which detect VNTR regions, and various 2 to 4 allele probes were subsequently used to see if the anticipated rate of exclusion fitted the observed results. We also wanted to see how valuable the probes were at increasing the *PI* and *W* values in nonexcluded cases. Table 8.5 shows the results of using pS194 with DNA samples restricted with Taq I

**Table 8.5** — Exclusion results of D7S107 using restriction endonucleases Taq I and Pst I

|                          | Taq I | Pst I |
|--------------------------|-------|-------|
| Not excluded             | 187   | 372   |
| Exclusions               |       |       |
|   Other markers only     | 18    | 37    |
|   Others plus DNA        | 57    | 107   |
|   DNA only               | 4     | 8     |
| Observed exclusion rate  | 0.073 | 0.076 |
| Expected exclusion rate  | 0.073 | 0.080 |

DNA only exclusions were observed in paternity cases with residual *PI* values. Expected exclusion rate was based upon band frequency data of Table 8.2.

and PstI. In general the observed rates of exclusion were similar to the theoretical probability of exclusion. The exclusions observed with only DNA were detected in cases which had low inclusion estimates with the other battery of tests. Allen *et al* (1989) performed a similar exercise with pa3′HVR on 100 paternity cases and identified 27 exclusions, compared with 30 identified with a battery of conventional marker systems. One DNA exclusion was identified which was not observed with the other test systems.

When comparing the *PI* values for non-excluded alleged fathers we found that 80% of the non-excluded fathers with *PI* values <19, before hybridization with pS194 had a *PI*>100 after probing. The average cumulative *PI* in these cases was 2540. Higher *PI* values were observed when we utilized probes pL336 and pL427-4 (data not included). The implication is that the use of highly polymorphic loci can have a dramatic effect upon inclusionary estimates, resulting in the resolution of borderline cases.

Such groundwork must be layed before reporting out results in true paternity cases. The ability to provide documentation for the reliability and accuracy of a claim for exclusion or inclusion will be required by the courts which demand to know the loci, probe, restriction enzyme, and accuracy of band interpretation. Permitting other laboratories to share probes and collaborate in the collection of data bases can only help the cause of providing another method of analysis to enter the arena of parentage testing.

## 8.7 SUMMARY

Parentage testing has gone through a variety of stages over the years, beginning with the use of ABO and followed by the application of other RBC antigens, RBC enzymes, serum proteins, and HLA. Each additional set of markers was intended to increase the probability of exclusion and further include the non-excluded alleged father. The recent application of DNA was intended to do the same. However, its direct application does require considerable standardization because of the idiosyncrasies of the methodology. Laboratories reporting results must be required to document the probe used to detect specific loci and the restriction enzyme utilized in digesting the DNA for the accumulation of the data base. Data sharing between laboratories and independent confirmatory testing of the same probes must become a reality rather than the exception in order to increase its acceptability. With the proper utilization of this new genetic tool we will come closer than ever before to excluding 100% of the falsely accused fathers and at the same time dramatically increase our certainty of fatherhood in the case of the non-excluded alleged father.

## REFERENCES

Allen, R., Bliss, B., & Pearson, A. (1989) Characteristics of a DNA probe (pa3′HVR) when used for paternity testing, *Transfusion* **29** 477–485.

Baird, M., Balazs, I., Giusti, A., Miyazaki, L., Nicholas, L., Wexler, K., Kanter, E., Glassberg, J., Allen, S., Rubenstein, P., & Sussman, L. (1986) Allele frequency distribution of two highly polymorphic DNA sequences in three ethnic groups and its application in the determination of paternity, *Am. J. Human Genet.* **39** 489–501.

Balazs, I., Baird, M., Clyne, M., & Meade, E. (1989) Human population genetic studies of five hypervariable DNA loci, *Am. J. Hum. Genet.* **44** 182–190.

Bryant, N. J. (1980) *Disputed paternity. The value and application of blood tests.* Brian C. Decker, a Division of Thienne-Stratton Inc. New York.

Dykes, D. (1988) The use of biotinylated DNA probes in parentage testing: Non-isotopic labeling and non-toxic extraction, *Electrophoresis* **9** 359–368.

Gill, P., Lygo, J., Fowler, S., & Werrett, D. (1987) An evaluation of DNA fingerprinting for forensic purposes, *Electrophoresis* **8** 38–44.

Higgs, D., Wainscoat, J., Flint, J., *et al*. (1986) Analysis of the human alpha-globin gene cluster reveals a highly informative genetic locus, *Proc. Nat. Acad. Sci. USA* **83** 5165–5169.

Higgs, D., Goodbourn, S., Wainscoat, J., Clegg, J., & Weatherall, D. (1989) Highly variable regions of DNA Flank the human alpha-globin genes, *Nucl. Acids Res.* **9** 4213–4224.

Jarmen, A., Nicholls, R., Weatherall, D., Clegg, J., & Higgs, D. (1986) Molecular characterisation of a hypervariable region downstream of the human alpha-globin gene cluster, *EMBO J.* **5** 1857–1863.

Jeffreys, A., Wilson, V., & Thein, S. (1985a) Hypervariable 'minisatellite' regions in human DNA, *Nature* **314** 67–73.

Jeffreys, A., Wilson, V., & Thein, S. (1985b) Individual-specific 'fingerprints' of human DNA, *Nature* **316** 76–79.

Jeffreys, A., Wilson, V., & Thein, S. (1986) DNA 'fingerprints' and segregation analysis of multiple markers in human pedigrees, *Am. J. Hum. Genet.* **39** 11–24.

Nakamura, Y., Leppert, M., O'Connell, P., *et al.* (1987) Variable number of tandem repeat (VNTR) markers for human gene mapping, *Science* **235** 1616–1622.

Werrett, D., Gill, P., Lygo, J., & Fowler, S. (1988) DNA polymorphisms: practical use, *Adv. Forens. Haemogenet.* **2** 320–338.

# 9

# DNA profiling — a legal perspective

**Ian Freckelton†**
Owen Dixon Chambers, 205 William Street, Melbourne, Vic, 3000 Australia

## 9.1 INTRODUCTION

DNA technology offers to crime investigators and to the courts an opportunity for an unparalleled degree of certainty in determining whether body samples collected in different sites have the same source. If properly presented by its developers, DNA profiling is likely to be enthusiastically accepted by a criminal justice system hungry for the benefits to proof that technology can bring. Happily, its contribution comes in fields that have long posed difficulties — sexual assault evidence, paternity testing, and all areas where body-tissue matching is relevant to proof of an important issue in dispute.

It has become a matter of considerable concern that judges and juries are increasingly being subjected to barrages of conflicting expert evidence with which they are in no position to deal competently. There is a danger that jurors especially will ignore relevant considerations and in their stead pay overmuch heed to irrelevant factors. These may range from the appearance, superficial impressiveness, and articulateness of the expert, to the time of day that he or she testifies and the kind of visual aids that are employed during delivery of testimony.

In Australia these fears became all too real in the 1980s with the Chamberlain and Splatt cases resulting in Royal Commissions and the release from custody, after some years, of persons convicted of murder as a result of in part flawed scientific evidence.

In Britain, too, the credibility of forensic science was set back by the scandal surrounding the testing procedures of Dr Clift who inclined toward the prosecuting authorities and failed to convey the full import of his results. In the United States, the

† The author acknowledges the assistance and helpful suggestions of S. Gutowski, Victorian State Forensic Science Laboratory, A. Ross and J. Robertson, South Australian Forensic Science Centre, L. Burgoyne, Flinders University, South Australia, M. J. Simons of Simons Genetype Diagnostics and H Selby, solicitor. However, all views offered and errors made are the responsibility of the author alone.

over-abundance of psychiatrists and psychologists willing to supply evidence relating to the state of mind of a series of notorious individuals accused of murder led to a critical change to Rule 704 of the Federal Rules of Evidence, limiting the nature of the testimony that they could give in Federal courts.

There have, of course, been other problems. In 1987 the director of a forensic toxicology laboratory operated by the Federal Aviation Administration in the United States pleaded guilty in an Oklahoma City Federal District Court to having falsified results of drug tests, when in fact they had never taken place at all. This, however, was a case of outright dishonesty, rather than one of inadequate procedures.

In all three countries, attempts have been made to move toward reducing the incidence of unreliable evidence being placed before judges and juries. In the United States debate has intensified about the proper criteria for admitting evidence of novel techniques and theories. In Britain proposals have been advanced for decreasing the role of juries where they are likely to be confronted with complex, conflicting, and esoteric evidence. In Australia the Law Reform Commission has drafted new rules of evidence that will, if adopted, have a substantial impact on the range of scientific evidence coming before the courts (Aust. Law Ref. Comm. 1987). As well, a series of Supreme Court decisions around Australia has edged toward adopting criteria for the reception of new forms of scientific evidence.

The arrival of DNA evidence comes for the most part as a refreshing contrast to other areas of scientific endeavour that have been characterized by disputation inside and outside the courtroom. Nonetheless, it arrives at the doors of the courts in the context of an adverse legal climate. Too many high profile problems have characterized forensic science in recent years in a number of jurisdictions. These problems have reinforced the pre-existing judicial mistrust of scientists and what they have to offer to the trial process. The direct effect of this judicial cynicism is that the onus is on scientists to demonstrate the reliability, accuracy, and relevance of a technique such as DNA profiling in such a way that there is no exaggeration of its utility or potential and so that what they are saying is easily and adequately comprehensible to judges and juries.

It is not the purpose of this chapter to consider in detail the best approach to DNA analysis. Other chapters in this book deal with the various approaches. Rather, this chapter outlines the contribution that DNA technology can make and has already made to legal processes. It examines the reception likely to be accorded to DNA evidence in the current legal climate, highlights possible controversies, and focuses upon how the benefits of DNA technology can be utilized most effectively in the courts.

## 9.2  ALTERNATIVE APPROACHES TO DNA ANALYSIS

(1)   The application of DNA analysis to forensic problems came about from the collaboration between a university-based scientist, Alec Jeffreys, and workers in the UK Home Office forensic laboratory system (Jeffreys *et al.* 1985; 1986). The term 'DNA fingerprint' was coined to describe the technique, which came to be marketed in the United States by Cellmark, because it provides a very high level of identifying information. The technique employs 'minisatellite probes' which detect numerous

genes in different locations throughout the 23 pairs of chromosomes, including the two sex chromosomes, which comprise the human genome. The result is a complex bar code-like pattern with a series of stripes of the kind found on grocery and other retail items. The complete 'bar code' which results from the analysis is unique to every individual except for identical twins. Two DNA tests from the same individual will always be identical except where a mutation has arisen in the interval between the two samplings. This is so rare as barely to merit mention. In those cases one bar of the code will be dissimilar, but an examination of another part of the DNA chain will reveal a perfect match. (DNA fingerprinting 1987).

(2)   The other predominantly used test, that employed by Lifecodes Corporation, uses a single-locus probe, in contrast to the Cellmark 'minisatellite' multi-locus probe. It is said to produce a print. At each single locus, variation that characterizes one person from another results from variable numbers of 'tandem repeats' of DNA stretches. Simons describes the process well:

> Variable number tandem repeat (VNTR) probes generate very simple patterns of only two fragments in each electrophoretic lane for each individual. However, the size of the two fragments varies greatly between individuals, reflecting inherited differences in the number of tandem repeats of the probe DNA sequence. (Simons 1989)

Because the VNTR test uses probes which are specific to non related loci a higher order of individuality may be achieved than when the loci are related as in minisatellites. The degree of probability of unrelated individuals matching for all loci is a multiple of the probabilities for matching at each locus. The VNTR technique achieves a high level of individuality and a high level of protection against false positive results by its separate treatment of loci.

(3)   The third of the current forms of testing employs the HLA system of testing that has been used for disputed parentage testing during the 1970s and 1980s. It uses probes for genes that occur at a single region of one chromosome but where the genes occur in multiple, close locations as a multi-gene complex (Simons 1989). The problem with the traditional HLA typing technique is that phenotyping of detectable gene products does not reveal the presence of a double dose of the same gene (homozygosity) while such a double dose cannot be distinguished from a single dose of a known HLA gene and the existence of an as yet undiscoverd gene. Conversely, RFLP (restricted fragment length polymorphism) patterns, derived by this third form of testing, reveal all the genes in the individual whose DNA is being tested. There are no blank or missing genes, and double doses of the same gene are readily identifiable. Simons (1989) points to the advantage of this procedure as 'achieving both a DNA fingerprint and an HLA gene tissue type as a single procedure'.

DNA typing using RFLP can be carried out where fresh samples are available, but where only small, or denatured, or degraded samples are available, RFLP is unsuitable. The gene amplification technique developed by the Cetus corporation in California can to a significant degree solve the problem. The process, called polymerase chain reaction (PCR), converts the small amount of DNA to a workable amount. Currently the amplified product is probed with sequence specific DNA probes producing a pattern of dots from which the individual's gene type can be determined. It gives the advantage of allowing tests on as few as 40 sperm heads or a single hair root. A lower level of information is achieved but with the benefit that a result of at least some significance may be presented in court.

Thus, it can be seen that a number of quite different DNA derived techniques exist. With the exception of PCR analysis they all share the laboratory procedure of RFLP analysis, involving enzyme digestion of DNA, size separation of DNA fragments by electrophoresis, Southern blot transfer to a membrane, and probing of the membrane with labelled DNA sequences. So as not to focus excessively on any of the three techniques described above, this chapter employs the all-embracing term 'DNA profiling'.

## 9.3   THE APPLICATION OF DNA PROFILING TO THE LAW

Because of the capacity of DNA profiling to introduce an element close to certainty in identifying two human tissues as having the same source, it is of enormous utility both to crime investigators and to legal counsel. In the legal context, it has the potential to reduce the issues in dispute in criminal trials by indicating definitively in an accusation of rape, for example, with whom sexual intercourse took place. It has the potential to match a suspect to body samples found at the scene of a crime. It is hoped that the introduction of such clarity may serve to increase the reporting rate in low-reported crimes such as sexual assault and the conviction rate in some instances where basic scientific evidence in the past was inconclusive or ambiguous.

Moreover, DNA profiling has application to a number of civil disputes involving paternity. These range from maintenance and immigration applications to inheritance disputes. If such matters can be resolved without the expense and fallibility of formal legal hearings, the cost of DNA testing will be well worthwhile.

*Sexual Offences*
DNA profiling offers forensic examiners an unprecedented opportunity to obtain and present to the courts highly relevant evidence from semen specimens in relation to sexual assaults. Moreover, the presence of spermatozoa on vaginal swabs will provide the opportunity for a male-specific DNA profile free from contamination of vaginal material. Thus the evidence obtained will be devoid of the confusion that in recent times led to a miscarriage of justice in the Helen Will case in England. In this case the forensic scientist failed to disclose to the court that both the victim and the accused were A group secretors, meaning that it was impossible in the circumstances to determine whether the groupings obtained came from her own body fluids or from semen. (Freckelton 1987, Pereira 1981, Phillips & Bowen 1985.)

The critical advantage of DNA profiling over more traditional serological tests is that the profile obtained from a vaginal swab or a sample of blood will be able to be traced to the victim or to another person tested with near certainty. It will be much more specific than traditional tests for typing blood, such as ABO typing, HLA (human leukocyte antigen) typing, or typing of red cell enzymes and serum proteins. With DNA analysis, where a mixture of vaginal and seminal material is present, it can usually be seen and can be interpreted as a mixture in the vast majority of cases. The seminal component of a swab can be separated from the vaginal component to a large degree, and the vaginal interference minimized. This has the potential to have a significant effect upon conviction rates for sexual assault crimes. This contrasts with previous typing methods in which, for example, Group A or B vaginal secretions will effectively mask Group O in the semen (O secretor = 33%) and where the PGM system is informative in only around 60% of possible subtype combinations. The difficulty remains that victims must be encouraged to submit to forensic medical examinations within a relatively short time after the commission of the offence (Pol. Compl. Auth. Vic. 1988).

*Other crimes*
Whenever an assailant is injured or leaves any form of body sample at the scene of a crime (such as hairs, torn nails, saliva, etc.), the DNA profile has the potential to identify positively the person from his or her own deposit of biological evidence. Similarly traces of the victim upon the assailant's clothing may provide extremely probative evidence. Note that as hairs and nails are composed of dead keratinised tissues little if any DNA will be present. It seems likely that success with these tissues will require the application of PCR technology.

Using the DNA profile, scientists also now have a good start at identifying victims of anonymous crimes, such as hit–run accidents. They may even have some chance of matching the victim's DNA with DNA recovered from blood or tissue found on a suspect's car. This could be of significant circumstantial, probative value in a trial.

*Investigating series of crimes*
DNA profiling will be useful in providing to investigators evidence of whether the same assailant is responsible for a series of crimes. This is particularly so in the case of serial rapes in which it is suspected that there is a single offender (Gill & Werrett 1987).

*Reopening unsolved cases*
As DNA frequently maintains a useful degree of integrity in dried specimens for extended periods, the DNA profile can be used to reevaluate old evidence that has not as yet, with the use of other techniques, been able to yield determinative or even useful evidence.

*Missing person and victim identification*
Government agencies in the United States estimate that up to 1.5 million people are reported missing each year, a significant percentage of these for extended periods. In addition increasing numbers of unidentified dead children are buried per year. All too often dental and X-ray records do not yield sufficient information to ascertain identity. The DNA profile allows scientists to compare DNA patterns of unidentified people with those of their parents and to determine their identity definitively. Lifecodes Corporation have also pointed out that this process may assist in identify-

ing the remains of soldiers missing in action in recent arenas of conflict. (Lifecodes Corp. 1987).

*Paternity determination*
In a number of contexts paternity is an issue of concern to the community (Simons 1989). These range from the perspective of the payment of social security benefits to issues of inheritance. Lifecodes Corporation has claimed that their profile will play a critical role in settling the more than 200 000 paternity suits filed in the United States each year and 'may eventually replace all other currently used procedures for confirming or disproving paternity' (Dodd 1985, Diamond 1987, Lifecodes Corp. 1987). DNA technology is capable of resolving the uncertainty about a child's paternity prenatally. This may be of major significance to sexual assault victims, women with multiple sexual partners, and husbands suspicious of their wives' adultery. DNA profiling has been included as a parentage test that can be ordered by the Australian Family Court (Aust. Fam. Law, 1988).

*Immigration decision making*
In Britain, the DNA test is now being regularly employed to screen immigrants requesting rights of residence on the basis of their familial relationship to a current British citizen (Jeffreys *et al.* 1986). By the end of 1986, 15 000 applicants from the Indian sub-continent were awaiting a decision from British authorities, and already the waiting time for such decisions has been cut significantly. It is likely that the technique will be employed more frequently in Australia in the near future, given the government's commitment to continuation of its 'family reunion' immigration policy. It was first used in 1988 before the Administrative Appeals Tribunal when DNA testing showed conclusively that a young man seeking to migrate to Australia was in fact the son of a refugee already living in Victoria.

## 9.4  LIMITATIONS OF DNA PROFILING

*No panacea*
DNA profiling has much to offer, but its contribution to the criminal and civil justice systems should not be overstated. It provides an opportunity for innocent people wrongly suspected to prove their innocence. Predominantly, though, it furnishes an enormously useful investigative tool to police forces, being able to resolve certain critical issues in criminal investigations. However, in a rape trial, for instance, the existence of sexual intercourse is only one of the issues. Frequently the victim and the alleged assailant are able to agree that intercourse took place. The aspect most problematic for the prosecution is disproof of consent on the part of the complainant. Similarly, even though blood belonging to the victim is found on the jacket of the accused some days after a violent altercation, the accused person may still have a plethora of arguments and defences open which remain unaffected by DNA profiling.

DNA profiling should have an impact upon arrest and conviction rates, but it will not be statistically dramatic. The tried and traditional techniques covered a considerable percentage of the field now to be taken over by DNA typing. What DNA contributes is refinement, improvement, and greater certainty. The potential for error is appreciably diminished, and this is to the advantage of investigators, prosecutors, and defence teams alike.

*Tissue sampling powers*

A significant impediment in many jurisdictions to the employment of DNA techno-logy is the lack of police powers to compel suspects to provide a body tissue sample (usually blood) for analysis. In England the Police and Criminal Evidence Act 1984 provides that 'intimate samples', which include blood and semen, etc., may be taken from a person in police detention only if a police officer of at least the rank of superintendent permits it and the suspect gives a consent in writing. The officer can give such authorization if he or she has reasonable grounds for suspecting the involvement of the person in a serious arrestable offence and for believing that the sample will tend to confirm or disprove the suspect's involvement. Where consent is refused 'without good cause', the court in committal proceedings or the trial proper

> ...may draw such inferences from the refusal as appear proper; and the refusal may, on the basis of such inferences, be treated as, or as capable of amounting to, corroboration of any evidence against the person in relation to which the refusal is material.

This is clearly intended to provide an incentive to suspects to provide such samples and to be a *quid pro quo* for their retention of the right to refuse invasive procedures such as intimate body sampling. If the sample to be taken is other than saliva or urine, it must be taken by a registered medical practitioner. (Pol. & Crim. Evid. Act 1984). Under the English legislation non-intimate samples include 'a sample of hair other than pubic hair' or a swab from any part of a person's body other than a body orifice. These may be taken without the person's consent if the person is in police detention or in the custody of the police on the authority of a court and an officer of at least the rank of superintendent authorizes it. That can be done if the officer has reasonable grounds for suspecting the involvement of the person from whom the sample is to be taken in a serious arrestable offence; and for believing that the sample will tend to confirm or disprove the suspect's involvement. Ironically, the difference between intimate and non-intimate sampling for the purpose of DNA sampling is already becoming outdated. Ten hair roots are sufficient as of 1989 for conventional DNA testing; only one is enough if Cetus amplification procedures are employed. It can confidently be expected that standard techniques (without the assistance of amplifi-cation procedures) will soon require smaller quantities of sample. That may entail that the traditionally invasive procedures, such as extraction of blood, will not be required for DNA testing. This will mean that English police will much more often be able to obtain samples for testing even if it is in relation to matters other than those for which the suspect is being held in custody.

For the present, though, English police are subject to substantial restrictions in relation to those whom they can compel against their will to provide samples for DNA testing. In fact, they are thrown upon their ability to 'persuade' suspects in custody that it is 'in their best interest' that they provide DNA samples rather than suffer the suspicion of judges and juries over why they refused to cooperate.

In Australia the Victoria† Police Force is alone in having no power to compel the provision of body samples. By contrast, in New South Wales s353A(2) of the Crimes Act 1900 provides that when a person is in lawful custody for any crime or offence and reasonable grounds exist for believing that a medical examination will afford evidence as to the commission of the crime or offence, a medical practitioner or any person acting in good faith in his aid and under his direction may conduct an examination at the request of an officer of or above the rank of sergeant. The use of force is not mentioned. In Queensland, Western Australia, and South Australia the provisions are similar but provide for the use of such force as is reasonably necessary.‡ The Tasmanian legislation differentiates between intimate sampling in relation to the offence with which the person is charged and is in lawful custody and in relation to other offences with which the police suspect him or her to have been involved.§ With respect to the former the legislation is similar to that in New South Wales but with respect to the latter the consent of a magistrate is required.¶

With the exception of Tasmania and the Northern Territory, in those jurisdictions where the police do have a right to take body samples, their reason for doing so must be related to proof of *the* offence with which the person is in lawful custody. Thus, the police cannot take people into custody for the purpose of procuring DNA profiles, and cannot insist that people in the community provide samples when they have not been arrested for the offence into which the police are inquiring. Nor can they arrest a person for one offence and take samples to show that they are guilty of another. This is a most important practical restriction on the investigator's capacity to employ DNA technology when investigation has yielded only circumstantial evidence and a range of suspects who, without more evidence, cannot be arrested and charged with commission of the offence.

In those jurisdictions where the police do not have the rights that they wish to take fingerprints and photographs and compel participation in identification parades, a tendency has been recognized for them to rely upon their skills to 'persuade' a suspect to comply with their wish to do what strictly he or she is not obliged to do. On occasions they overstep proper limits. This produces many complaints against police procedures (Freckelton & Selby 1989) and is likely to produce more as police become aware of the benefits tantalizingly offered by DNA technology. In many jurisdictions where they do not possess the technology to be able to compel those in custody to provide body samples for DNA testing, police are vigorously campaigning for extensions to their powers. Aside from the fundamental issue of whether suspects should in any further circumstances be compelled to 'assist'

---

† In Victoria the opposition Liberal Party introduced a bill in 1987 that included for compulsory provision of body samples by persons in lawful custody on a charge of committing 'an offence' — Police (Powers of Investigation) Bill 1987 (Vic), cl 15.
‡ The Criminal Code 1899 (Qld), s 259; Criminal Code 1899 (WA), s 236; Police Offences Act 1953 (SA), s 81(2). See also *R v Franklin* (19) 22 SASR 101.
§ The Criminal Process (Identification and Search Procedures) Act 1976 (Tas), ss 6 & 7.
¶ This was the approach adopted by the Criminal Investigation Bill 1981 (Cth). The powers extended by the Northern Territory Police Administration Act 1979, s 145, are the widest in Australia. They permit a police member to arrange for 'an examination' (broadly defined to include the taking of various forms of samples) if he has reasonable grounds for believing that it may provide evidence of an offence punishable by imprisonment. If a consent in writing is not given by the person under arrest, the process must be approved by a magistrate who 'may approve' it if he is satisfied that the member of the police force has 'reasonable grounds' for his belief. Reasonable force may be used.

the prosecution by providing intimate body samples, the issue of whether we should give far-ranging and invasive new powers must be confronted. In many places concerns have been expressed that the police are abusing the powers that they already have to an unacceptable degree, and that they are not adequately policing themselves (Fed. Comm. Leg. Cen. 1987, Freckelton & Selby 1989, Freckelton 1990, Selby 1988). It has been claimed in Australia that there are few effective external checks on police misconduct. If this is so, it is inappropriate that police should be given any additional powers, never mind ones that have the potential for such serious abuse as the right to insist upon the provision of intimate body samples.

Civil libertarians will be uneasy with the granting of such powers to the police. It is fundamental to the common law systems of justice that suspects are not compelled to incriminate themselves. For an analysis of the principles behind the privilege see Freckelton, 1985. However, this is not an invariable rule, and there are a number of jurisdictions where motorists suspected of driving with an excessive drug or alcohol content are compelled to provide breath and blood samples. As well, those involved in accidents requiring hospitalization are required to submit to a blood test in some jurisdictions. Defences involving alibi evidence have to be communicated to the prosecution ahead of the trial proper under rules of procedure in a number of states and countries. Police often have been accorded powers by the legislature to take fingerprints against a person's will.

It is arguable that to go any further may be to erode a fundamental and longstanding right to refrain from being the author of one's own downfall, from being 'hoist by one's own petard'. While there may be a time and cost saving, it may be that the delicate balance of the criminal justice system between the prosecution and defence may be irretrievably disturbed by giving the prosecution the power to compel the giving of potentially critical evidence by the defendant in serious criminal proceedings.

These are issues with which our legislatures must grapple during the 1990s. It is significant that DNA testing may require even less invasive procedures than the provision of blood within the next few years. But this may not affect the ultimate question — whether an individual suspected of a potentially serious crime should be compelled to incriminate him or herself.

*Cost*

DNA testing is not cheap. In 1987 ICI in England were charging £105 plus VAT for each sample tested, and testing tends to be multiple, particularly in the parternity area. It has been estimated that the average is four tests per case, meaning that costs amount to £420 plus VAT per case (Anon. 1987a, 1987b). Law centres have also encountered difficulties in obtaining legal aid for tests in the early stages in Britain with the government being slow to grant ICI 'registered tester' status under the Family Law Reform Act 1969. An early English investigation in which hundreds of people were DNA typed for this reason is unlikely to be frequently repeated, and only in the most heinous and otherwise insoluble of cases. In Australia too sampling is expensive, costing for application of the Lifecodes System is $A100–$150 on average per item without computing the man hours involved in the extensive processing of the samples. This was the figure supplied in January 1989 by S. Gutowski of the Victorian State Forensic Science Laboratory. The Collaborative

Research System being investigated by the South Australian Laboratory is cheaper. In the United States it has been estimated that testing samples to determine paternity, costs approximately $400 per person (Anon 1987).

The consequence of the comparatively high cost of utilization of the technique is that its employment will have to be regulated and prioritized so that only the most needy of cases take advantage of what it has to offer. Inevitably this will mean that major crime investigators will enjoy its advantages more than other areas of policing and law enforcement and probably ahead of immigration and adoption authorities. In the short term it is unlikely that financial stringencies will permit DNA testing to be employed as readily as those who could utilize its fruits may wish.

*Quantity of samples*
Current DNA technology of the first two forms described in this chapter requires 1 to 10 $\mu$g of DNA for a single analysis. Blood contains between 5000 and 10000 nucleated cells per microlitre, this corresponding to 25 to 50 $\mu$g of DNA/mL. Thus bloodstains need to contain at least 50 $\mu$L of blood to be amenable to analysis (Sensabaugh 1986). The corresponding limit for semen is about 10 $\mu$L which is approximately one tenth of the fluid held by a vaginal swab (Gill *et al.* 1987). However, though a swab may hold, for example, 100 $\mu$l, not all of that 100 $\mu$l will be semen. Ten to twenty hairs are necessary for DNA probing, unless gene amplification technology is employed, in which case as little as one hair root may be sufficient. Sensabaugh (1986) comments that:

> These threshold values are not very encouraging since tests for many of the currently used genetic markers are more sensitive. However, the DNA technology is advancing rapidly and improvements in sensitivity can be expected.

Until the techniques become more sensitive, therefore, one of the limitations upon the use of DNA technology is its need for amounts of sample larger than are required by some longer established testing procedures. The development of the polymerase chain reaction (PCR) with its ability to amplify minute quantities of DNA to typable levels offers great promise in this regard.

*Age and state of samples*
DNA fragments have been reported as recovered from mummy tissue and from 100 year old dried skin (Miller). In 1987 it was reported that blood and semen stains kept at room temperature for longer than 4 years had not been successfully typed (Gill *et al.* 1987). The same study demonstrated a steady decline in the success rate for typing sperm DNA from vaginal swabs up to 20 hours after the act of intercourse. Donors varied, with one donor showing a high success rate (10 out of 12) up to 25 hours after intercourse. One swab was successful at 36 hours, and a combination of two swabs was successful at 48 hours. Lack of success was due to loss of sperm from the vagina over time and resulted in fewer bands being detected for comparison against a blood stain extract, where it existed. Gene amplification technology can be expected to have a significant impact in the 1990s on the quality of DNA testing on denatured and degraded samples.

*Time required for testing*
DNA testing is not a quick exercise. The following are standard steps and time periods

| | | |
|---|---|---|
| (1) | Sample extraction: | 2–4 days |
| (2) | DNA digestion: | 1–2 days |
| (3) | DNA fragment separation: | 3 days |
| (4) | Blotting and hybridization: | 2 days |
| (5) | Visualization: | 2 hours–7 days |
| | TOTAL: | 10 days–18 days |

These estimates were provided by S. Gutowski of the Victorian State Forensic Science Laboratory in an address to the Australian and New Zealand Forensic Science Society (Victorian Branch), Melbourne, August 1988. It was suggested to me in April 1989 that 7–11 days is a time-frame expected by some laboratories.

A series of steps in every case must be pursued, and few short cuts are possible. Further development of techniques undoubtedly will reduce the time factor, but as of March 1990 DNA testing is a slow and comparatively highly labour intensive procedure.

*Potential for error*
As recently as 12 March 1988, Alec Jeffreys and co-writers penned an article in *The Lancet* in which they acknowledged that, although DNA printing as developed by Jeffreys requires only simple manipulations, the process is labour-intensive and interpretation of bands in the final autoradiographs requires experience (Helminen *et al.* 1988).

Similarly, it was suggested in *Policing London* (1987) that claims of an error risk of only one in 1200 million

> take no account of the probability of human error and doubt about the accuracy of these tests must remain.

Von Beroldingen and Sensabaugh gave vent to a similar concern recently:

> The procedure itself is somewhat tricky. Bands may appear or disappear, depending upon the hybridization conditions. The pattern of bands is complex and may be difficult to interpret (in Thompson & Ford 1988).

DNA testing is a complex process requiring considerable expertise (Newmark 1986) and no small investment of time and money. There can be no denying that some potential exists for human error in its application. However, DNA typing is unusual in the contributions made by science to criminal investigation and the legal process in that its potential for error is remarkably low. One of its very positive characteristics is that most errors in the laboratory will simply produce uninterpretable results or miss finding matches between samples and a common source.

A recent study has estimated that analysis of paternity cases with the DNA probes pAC061, pAC222, pAC255, and pAC256, each probe recognizing an independent single locus, 'is expected to exclude approximately 99.5% of falsely accused males' (Baird *et al.* 1989). Lifecodes Corporation maintains that if two patterns match, 'investigators can conclude with 99.9% certainty that the biological specimens are from the same individual' (Lifecodes 1987). Controversy continues about the claims of accuracy for the various DNA profiling procedures. Thompson & Ford (1988), for example, point out that the probability of two people having the same DNA profile under unimpeachable laboratory conditions etc. is not the meaningful statistic it may appear. They counsel having greater regard to the probability that DNA profiles of two different people will be mistaken for one another under the conditions in which the test procedure is actually performed. They also note the pecuniary and marketing aspects of some of the claims made by the different companies with an interest in the development of DNA profiling systems.

However, to most intents and purposes, if the band patterns, as elicited by the single locus or multi-locus tests, do not match, it can be assumed from the DNA evidence that the suspect, for example, is not the perpetrator. However, while no two people have identical DNAs, except for identical twins, two unrelated people may have identical DNA test readouts because they happen to have polymorphic DNA segments of the same length (Thompson & Ford 1988). If gene amplification technology of the kind developed by Cetus Corporation is used, the critical element is the set of dots produced indicating whether specific DNA characteristics are present or absent in a sample. Under this test, two unrelated people may 'have identical results ... because they happen to have the same alleles'. Thompson & Ford (1988) have summed up the situation well:

> The probability that two unrelated people will have matching DNA prints depends, in part, on the type of probe used. Such a coincidence is unlikely where a multi-locus probe is used, because each of the approximately 15 bands on the 2 DNA fingerprints would have to match by chance. Such a coincidence is more likely where a single-locus probe is used, however, because only two bands would need to match. Further, ... bands in certain positions are quite common.

They go on to point out that a misidentification may occur because two different DNA types are mistaken for one another: 'similar but not identical DNA prints may, as a practical matter, be indistinguishable because within certain ranges, electrophoresis gels have "poor resolution" '. This results from the presence of DNA bands larger than the resolution range of the gel which then tend to run together as one band. A similar situation exists with very small bands of DNA. There is now technology for separating either very large bands — pulsed field electrophoresis — or very small bands — acrylamide gel electrophoresis — but these are not normally used unless the investigator expects this problem to arise.

Thompson & Ford also raise the concern that if a specimen from the scene of a crime is contaminated by a suspect's DNA, that specimen may produce an artifactual DNA type matching the suspect's. They claim that such an error can occur even when each specimen is analyzed separately because minute quantities of DNA from one sample occasionally will accidentally contaminate reagents and materials used in analyzing a number of samples. They suggest that the danger is highest when the laboratory is analyzing small specimens with limited amounts of DNA and where polymerase chain reaction is used to 'amplify' DNA (Thompson & Ford 1988).

DNA technology in its forensic applications is still in its early stages. Many different variations on the original Jeffreys probe are being developed by researchers in different laboratories. Some rely on detection of high molecular weight DNA, like the Cellmark System; others, like the Cetus system, have application to very low molecular weight DNA and are less affected by degradation of samples. DNA testing is now a major industry of scientific endeavour, and the process is at this stage fluid and dynamic. New techniques and forms of probes are being developed all the time, and assessment of the advantages of DNA testing can be done only in the context of the particular testing process involved and those responsible for it.

Much remains to be learned. It is not as yet known, for example, whether there will be particular characteristics common to Australian Aboriginals' DNA different from those that have been discovered in relation to non-Caucasians elsewhere in the world. Particularly unusual distorting factors of the test continue to absorb the energies of its developers. However, by 1989 it is evident that the applications for forensic purposes of DNA technology are extensive and that its error potential and biasing factors are for the most part acceptably low. This is not to say that cross-examining trial lawyers will not and should not ask penetrating questions about the circumstances and procedures of particular instances of DNA profiling.

## 9.5   EQUAL AVAILABILITY OF THE TECHNIQUE FOR THE DEFENCE

Some techniques of DNA testing are constrained by the patents held over their processes by the corporations owning them. This means in the case of testing by Cellmark, for example, that it is difficult for the defence to assess the results of testing adequately. ICI, the owners of Cellmark, currently do not supply autoradiographs or photographs of the results of DNA testing. This means that the defence is not in an adequate position to cross-check the testing process and to have equal access to the new technology. Justice Morling in the Australian Royal Commission into the Conviction of Lindy Chamberlain (Royal Comm. 1987) was extremely critical of testing in the Chamberlain investigations which denied the defence access to the testing processes employed by the investigating scientists. It is likely that the courts in Australia at least would not react kindly to testing processes in relation to DNA profiling which did not allow the defence, or the prosecution for that matter at a proper time, to evaluate the initial profiling results in a full and fair manner.

## 9.6   EARLY APPLICATION OF DNA TECHNOLOGY

*United States*
The introduction of DNA technology into the United States legal system occurred in a curious way in a Pennsylvania murder case (Anon 1987c). The accused funeral director and his wife were charged with the murder of a 92 year old retired coal miner, Joseph Kly, who had been under their protection. An autopsy showed the old man to have been severely malnourished and to have died from starvation. Nonethe-

less, Mr Pestinakis, the funeral director, was granted permission to bury the old man's remains and the burial took place in due course uneventfully. Some time later suspicions of macabre foul play surfaced and the Scranton prosecutor obtained an order for the old man's exhumation and for a re-autopsy. The suspicions became more concrete when sutures on Kly's remains different to the autopsist's wont, were discovered. Then re-examination of Kly's remains yielded food particles and faecal matter not found by the autopsist during the course of the first autopsy. The prosecutor suspected that the funeral director had interfered with Kly's remains for the purpose of confounding the real reason for the old man's death.

In the course of further testing it was discovered that ABO bloodtyping was disrupted by the formaldehyde used in the embalming process. DNA typing was undertaken by digestion of the tissue specimens, extraction of DNA from them, purification of the DNA, amplification of the DNA fragments, and hybridization probe analysis with allele specific oligonucleotides with a dot blot assay. The testing proved disappointing to the prosecutor as the DNA was found to be 'severely broken with an average fragment length of 50 to 75 bp (base pairs)'. Amplification was conducted with some success: only the 1,1 type allele was discovered in all the tissues examined, a type found in about 10% of the Caucasian population. The expert, accordingly, reported that the tests failed to disclose a genetic difference between any of the tissues examined. This did not assist the prosecutor's tissue insertion thesis, and so he was not minded to introduce the evidence. The defence objected, requiring the DNA findings to be introduced over the wishes of the prosecutor. Experts were not called by the prosecution to dispute the admissibility of the DNA evidence.

### Britain

In January 1987 a disabled woman was the victim of a particularly serious sexual assault in her own home near Bristol in England. She was unable to identify her assailant but samples of his body fluids, as recovered from the victim, were sent for DNA testing at the Home Office Forensic Science Laboratory at Chepstow and then to the Central Research Establishment at Aldermaston. A suspect was prevailed upon to give a blood sample, and testing revealed that the samples came from the same individual, the possibility of misidentification being 1 in 4 million of the male population. Confronted with the evidence to be used against him, the accused changed his plea to guilty and was sentenced to 8 years' imprisonment (Phillips 1988).

DNA profile evidence in 1986 led to the discharge of a young man who had been held in custody for some months after being charged with the murder and rape of a schoolgirl in July. The accused was suspected of having committed a similar crime in November 1983. Conventional ABO and PGM tests revealed that both crimes could have been committed by the same man, but the frequency of occurrence of the relevant groups meant that the semen could have come from at least 10% of the male population. DNA profiling was then carried out at the Central Research Establishment from a whole blood sample and a blood stain from the suspect. It conclusively excluded him as the rapist as the pattern obtained did not match the sperm DNA extracted from swabs and clothing attributed to the two victims. Furthermore, the sperm DNA patterns from the semen found on the two victims matched, meaning that the same man had had intercourse with the victims shortly before/after their death. The youth who had been held in custody was released. (Gill and Werrett 1987).

Phillips (1988) also reports the 1983 case of British immigration authorities refusing to accept that a boy was the son of a woman who possessed residency rights. Conventional tests left the issue in doubt, but DNA testing established the woman's maternity of the boy as a matter of overwhelming probability, and showed that the alternative relationship of aunt and nephew existed at odds of 500 000 to one. At the door of the appeal tribunal the immigration authorities withdrew their objection to the boy's entry.

In 1987 ICI offered the services of its DNA testing to Diego Maradona, one of the world's best known soccer players. He was in the throes of a paternity dispute with a woman who claimed to have had a relationship with him. The woman claimed that Maradona had fathered her child and had won a legal battle in Italy to take the case to a full trial. By December 1987 ICI's laboratory at Abingdon had dealt with approximately 600 disputed paternity cases. It is not known whether Mr Maradona took advantage of ICI's entrepreneurial offer.

*Australia*

The South Australian Forensic Science Centre and the Victorian State Forensic Science Laboratory have conducted developmental and experimental work on DNA testing. Both expect to introduce DNA testing on a limited basis during 1989. At the time of writing only one case involving DNA testing has come before an Australian court or tribunal — the Federal Administrative Appeals Tribunal in an immigration dispute concerning paternity. However, the technique has been the subject of considerable press interest. Most recently, *The Age* (20 February 1989) has reported that the first Australian criminal trial involving 'genetic fingerprinting' is expected to take place soon in the Tasmanian Supreme Court. It has been reported that blood samples were obtained by police from more than 20 people during investigations into the fatal stabbing of a Tasmanian woman.

**Admissibility of scientific evidence: general principles**

Scientists are governed by the same rules as apply to all other witnesses when they give evidence of what they have said, seen, or heard. However, in certain circumstances they are allowed the privilege of giving evidence in the form of opinions — a right not generally accorded to lay witnesses. In England and Australia they must, however, convince the court that their contribution to proceedings is not restricted to matters of 'common knowledge' and that it does not trespass upon the 'ultimate issue' (Freckelton 1989, Gillies 1986) in the case. These limitations are unlikely to prove a barrier to testimony by scientists because of the esoteric nature of the evidence usually to be provided, and so long as the scientist does not employ legal terminology in relation to matters at the centre of the forensic dispute to explain his or her opinions.

On occasions the 'expertness' of scientists is attacked on the basis of their lack of practical experience in the area on which they seek to give expert opinions. As in all other areas of scientific endeavour, it is critical that scientists called to testify about DNA technology be both thoroughly familiar with the latest theoretical developments in their area and in a position to outline their practical acquaintance with the technique (Freckelton & Selby 1989).

In the United States the principal hurdle for scientific evidence to overcome is embodied in Rule 702 of the Federal Rules which stipulates that scientific, technical or other specialised knowledge must 'assist the trier of fact'. In addition, Rule 403 permits the trial judge to exclude evidence if it would be unduly misleading, confusing, or time-consuming. This provides a useful means of keeping away from a jury, material which is not capable of adequate comprehension or resolution as between different versions by a lay tribunal.

## 9.7   THE *FRYE* TEST

British and Australian courts have not had occasion as yet to determine definitively what should be the criteria for receiving evidence of new scientific techniques or theories. The approach has generally been a *laissez-faire* one, allowing the evidence to be put before the tribunal of fact, so long as it is relevant and does not offend one of the long cherished rules of evidence.† This has left the responsibility with the judge or jury to decide how much weight should be given to the expert testimony to which they have been exposed.

However, there are increasingly strong indications that the 1923 United States decision of *Frye v United States*‡ is at the least being absorbed into the law of Australia. It was held in that case that:

> Just when a principle crosses the line between the experimental and the demonstrable stages is difficult to define. Somewhere in this twilight zone, the evidential force of the principle must be recognised, and while the courts will go a long way in admitting expert testimony deduced from a well recognised scientific principle or discovery, the thing from which the deduction is made must be sufficiently established to have gained general acceptance in the particular field in which it belongs.

In 1977 the New South Wales Court of Appeal in *R v Gilmore*§ went some way toward introducing into Australia the *Frye* test, citing the United States case, adopting its language of 'field of expertise', and using it in the context of voice identification evidence. *Gilmore* was followed in 1983 by the same court in *R v McHardie and Danielson*.¶ A hint of a similar approach had come in 1976 in Queensland when the Full Court of the Queensland Supreme Court had confronted difficulties in relation to the expertness of a witness called to testify as an expert upon the effect of wearing seat-belts. Justice Dunn focused on the need for the judge to find as a fact that 'there exists relevant technical or scientific knowledge' not possessed by the fact-finder and a need for that knowledge. He held that:

† In *R v Murray* (1982) 7 A Crim R 48, for example, expert evidence in relation to polygraph examinations was ruled inadmissible by a District Court Judge because the evidence was hearsay and self-serving.
‡ 293 F 1013, 1014 (1923).
§ [1977] 2 NSWLR 935.
¶ [1983] 2 NSWLR 733, at 753.

The state of the evidence was such that, in my opinion, whilst there may be some room for difference of opinion upon the matter, it has not been shown that the learned trial judge was wrong in the relevant sense in his conclusion that "the study of seat-belts" has become a recognised field of specialist knowledge.†

In November 1985 the Queensland Court of Criminal Appeal rejected expert odontology evidence upon the identity of bite marks found on the body of a victim. Justice Kneipp held that there was . . .

a body of eminent opinion which holds that valid identifications cannot be made by reference only to bruise marks or they should be referred to only for the purpose of excluding suspects and not from [sic] positive identification.‡

Similar evidence relating to bite marks upon a victim and their similarity to the dentition of the accused person fell to be considered by the Northern Territory Court of Criminal Appeal in 1987 in the case of *Lewis*.§ Justice Maurice specifically referred to the previous Queensland odontology case and the passage cited above. Neither he nor his brother judges dissented from it. However, they stopped short of explicitly adopting the *Frye* test. Justice Maurice held that . . .

the jury should [not] have been permitted to place any reliance on the dentists' opinions. It really matters not whether that conclusion is supported by saying the evidence was strictly inadmissible, or its prejudicial effect far outweighed any probative value it may have had, or simply that it would be unwise to place any reliance on it.¶

Justice Muirhead noted pointedly that there was 'no established universal view' as to the reliability of the technique in identifying, as opposed to excluding, a suspect.

It is unclear, therefore, whether a superior court in Britain or Australia, if pressed, will unequivocally adopt the *Frye* criteria for determining whether a technique such as DNA profiling should be admitted into the courtroom. It does appear likely, though, at the very least that in formulating such criteria, judges may well borrow *Frye* language and focus upon the degree of dissension about any new technique within the scientific community.

Within the United States, the *Frye* test has been subjected to considerable and at times stringent criticism. It has been said that it is unduly difficult to determine what constitutes 'general acceptance' within the scientific community, what the relevant scientific community should be regarded as being at any one time, and how one determines the 'scienticity' of a theory or technique in the first place. Some judges have departed absolutely from the *Frye* test, the court in *United States v Williams* for example, asserting that . . .

---

† Id, at 320.
‡ *Carroll* (1985) 19 A Crim R 410.
§ (1987) 29 A Crim R 267.
¶ At p. 274.
‖ 583 F 2d 1194, 1198 (1978).

the established considerations applicable to admissibility of evidence come into play and the probativeness, materiality, and reliability of the evidence on the one side, and any tendency to mislead, prejudice, or confuse the jury on the other, must be the focal points of inquiry.

The court identified five indicators of reliability:

(1) potential rate of error in use of the technique;
(2) existence and maintenance of standards among its users;
(3) care with which the technique was employed in the case;
(4) analogy of the technique to others whose results are admissible; and
(5) presence of safeguards in the characteristics of the technique.

The *Kelly* court,† by contrast, adopted what has become the majority stance, and maintained that the essentially conservative standard of the *Frye* test shielded the jury from the unwarranted impact that a new scientific discovery could exert upon their otherwise reasoned considerations. In *Reed v State*‡ too, the Maryland Court of Appeals reasoned that judges and juries are not equipped to assess the reliability of scientific techniques when scientists are disagreeing on the issues, the danger being inconsistency of results. The court also voiced the fear that such a dispute over reliability could distract the jury from the real merits of the case. It held that the basis of the scientific opinion must be accepted as reliable within the expert's scientific field before the opinion will be admitted into evidence.

Generally speaking, the critics of the *Frye* test have maintained that it lacks clarity, is unduly rigid, sweeps too broadly, and is inconsistent with the traditional judicial perogative to decide the accuracy and reliability of expert testimony (McCormick 1987; Saltzurg 1975). The cases have evidenced patchy, but apparently increasing, application of the *Frye* test in the United States to determine whether, pursuant to Rule 702 of the Federal Rules of Evidence, expert scientific evidence would be 'helpful' to the tribunal of fact (Freckelton 1987).

During the 1980s United States courts strove to resolve some of the uncertainty surrounding the implementation of the *Frye* test. Thus in 1984 it was stressed that the *Frye* test applied only to novel scientific techniques and methodologies, as against opinion testimony which, while controversial in its conclusions, is based on 'well-founded methodologies'.§ Even in the case of novel scientific evidence, the opinion expressed need not be generally accepted, but the methods by which it was reached must be methods upon which other scientists in the field would reasonably rely to reach their own conclusions, even though those may possibly be different.¶ The party offering the novel scientific evidence has the burden of demonstrating that it has been accepted as reliable among impartial and disinterested experts within the

---

† *People v Kelly*, 17 Cal 3d 24; 549 P 2d 1240; 130 Cal Rptr 144 (1976).
‡ 283 Md 374, 387–9, 391 A 2d 364, 371–2.
§ *Ferebee v Chevron Chemical Co*, 736 F 2d 1529, 1535 (1984).
¶ *Osburn v Anohor Laboratories*, 825 F 2d 908, 915 (1987).

scientific community.† Such impartial experts' livelihood must not be intimately connected with the new technique.‡

## 9.8  IMPLICATIONS OF *FRYE* FOR DNA EVIDENCE

As a result of traditional judicial mistrust of scientific evidence,§ concern within the legal fraternity about the reliability of novel scientific evidence in the wake of the concerning cases, and the moves toward greater use of the *Frye* test in Australia, there is reason to expect that DNA evidence will be scrutinized particularly carefully at first by the courts. Judges are likely to focus upon the parameters of its claimed accuracy, the possibility of human error during its testing processes, and any likelihood of bias in its reliability factors as a result of racial differences. Because of its probative value, the technique has high prejudical potential should any of the claims made on its behalf be flawed. Thus, the onus will be on the prosecution to satisfy the courts that the likelihood of error in employing DNA technology is so minimal as not to represent any significant danger of false correlation of samples.

An early question that must be answered is whether the courts will classify DNA print techniques as 'novel'. In this they have little guidance by way of precedent outside the United States. However, because of DNA profiling's reliance upon techniques with which courts are for the most part as yet unfamiliar, it is likely that DNA profile evidence will be regarded as novel. This established, it is probable that the *Frye* test will be applied. However, it should be recognized that many constitutent parts of some of the techniques are known and recognized by the courts. HLA testing and electrophoresis, for example, are not novel. As well, bar-code-like patterns have been employed for decades in analysis of electrophoretic patterns of serum protein and enzyme polymorphisms. Where these 'classical' approaches employed protein stains, DNA profiling employs enzyme-substrate colour change systems or autoradiography if radiolabelled probes are utilised. It can cogently be contended that the practice of pattern analysis of step-ladder like fragments is little different from longstanding protein polymorphism analysis.

Arguably, the third of the techniques described in this chapter could be said to be based on processes already accepted as sufficiently reliable by the courts. On the other hand, their combination and the new application of these processes may be said to constitute a novel technique. The courts will have to make the final determination on this issue.

Assuming the *Frye* test to apply, attention will focus on determining whether scientists within the relevant scientific community regard the methodology by which the DNA experts express their opinions as reliable. Experts will need to be sought

---

† *Kluck v Borland*, 413 NW 2d 90, 91 (1984) (thermography evidence).
‡ *People v Young*, 418 Mich 1; 340 NW 2d 805 (1983) (electrophoresis of evidentiary blood stains).
§ Best in 1911 noted:

> There can be no doubt that testimony is daily received in our courts as "scientific evidence" to which it is almost profanation to apply the term; as being revolting to common sense, and inconsistent with the commonest honesty on the part of those by whom it is given.

(Best, see also *Whitehouse v Jordan* [1981] 1 All ER 267 at 281, 284; *Lord Abinger v Ashton* (1873) 17 LR Eq 358 at 374; *Thorn v Worthing Skating Rink Co* (1877) 6 Ch D 415.

whose livelihood does not depend intimately upon DNA technology. They will need to be prepared to depose that the methodology is well-known and regarded as dependable, accurate, and mainstream by most scientists with acquaintance of it.

Evidence will then need to be given by experts concerned with the testing procedure about its different stages, the possibilities of contamination of the sample, and the likelihood of false results being reached. Because the testing process is a long and complex one, trial judges will wish to be satisfied that the scope for human error has been minimized by adherence to appropriate protocols and adherence to standard laboratory procedures to safeguard against confusion of samples. Finally, the continuity of the evidence in the particular case must be able to be guaranteed by reference to careful logging of the processes undergone by specimens at all relevant times.

## 9.9   CONCLUSIONS

DNA techniques have made their first foray into the courts and tribunals of the United States, Britain, and Australia. They have not yet been the subject of substantial objection by either defence or prosecution counsel. It can confidently be expected that they soon will be.

While trial judges will not extend open arms to DNA profiling technology, there is no reason to suppose that it will not be classed as an admissible form of evidence. It should satisfy the criteria of the *Frye* test, so long as the procedures adhered to by laboratories using it are standardized and scientifically stringent. Ensuring that clear procedures are uniformly followed, that cross-checks are done, and that possibilities of contamination and human error are guarded against, are major contributions that scientists can make toward securing prompt legal acceptance of the technique.

The testing procedure in all probability will be classed as methodologically sound, and it is unlikely that there will be significant disagreement among those called upon to give their expert opinions on the basis of the tests that they have conducted. Further than this, the acceptability of the technology will depend upon the articulateness of those testifying about it and their effectiveness as communicators. This entails preparation for presentation of its steps in the courtroom by overheads, graphics, and diagrams, where appropriate, and preparedness on the part of the experts to make only those claims for DNA technology of which they can be completely confident (Malone 1988).

However, there are enough aspects of DNA profiling that remain controversial and subject to human error and misinterpretation for trial lawyers to have a responsibility to test DNA evidence in the courtroom. It is likely that they will focus upon laboratory conditions and procedures and upon the propriety of investigative steps followed in each particular case. The well-prepared forensic scientist from a well-functioning laboratory should be able to meet such questions more than adequately with straightforward explanations.

DNA technology promises to provide a form of evidence to judges and juries upon whose accuracy and reliability they will be able to rely with a confidence that they can rarely experience. It has an already demonstrated potential to result in increased conviction of the guilty and less charging and conviction of the innocent.

At present, though, the utility of DNA profiling in the criminal context is dependent upon the success of the police in 'persuading' suspects to provide intimate body samples. The challenge facing our legislators, assisted by those whose responsibility it is to draft proposals for law reform, is to determine the powers that should be given to our investigative agencies to demand intimate body samples. Then they must assess the impact that such a power given to the prosecution would have on the delicate balance of the criminal justice system.

## REFERENCES

Australian Family Lawyer, Regulation 21B, August 1988.

Australian Law Reform Commission (1987) *Evidence*, ALRC Report NO 38, Govt Printer, Sydney.

Baird, M., Wexler, K., Clyne, M., Meade, E., Ratzladd, L., Smalls, G., Benn, P., Glassberg, J., & Balzs, I. (1987) The application of DNA-print for the estimation of paternity. *Advances in Forensic Haemogenetics* **2** 354–358.

Best, W. M. (1911) *Principles of the law of evidence*, 11th edn, London.

Byrne, D. & Heydon, J. D. (1986) *Cross on evidence*, 3rd Aust edn, Butterworths, Sydney.

Cherfas, J. (28 March 1985) Geneticists develop DNA fingerprinting *New Scientist* **21**.

Diamond, J. M. (1987) Abducted orphans identified by grandpaternity testing. *Nature* **327** 552.

DNA fingerprinting (Sept 1987) **1** (19) *BNA Criminal Practice Manual* **1**.

DNA testing (Dec 1987) *Policing London* **5** 41.

DNA fingerprinting at a price at ICI's UK laboratory (1987) *Nature* **327** 548.

DNA typing draws first blood in Pennsylvania (1987) *Forensic Science in Criminal Law* **11(3)** 1.

Dodd, B. E. (1985) DNA fingerprinting in matters of family and crime *Nature* **318** 506.

Federation of Community Legal Centres (1987) The investigation of complaints made against the police. Melbourne.

Fowler, J. C. S., Harding, H. W. J., & Burgoyne, L. (1987) A Protocol Using an Alkali Blotting Procedure for the Analysis of Restriction Length Fragments of Human DNA, paper presented at the *12th International Congress of the Society for Forensic Haemogenetics*, Vienna.

Freckelton, I. (1985) Witnesses and the privilege against self-incrimination. *Australian Law Journal* **59** 204.

Freckelton, I. (1987) *The trial of the expert*, Oxford University Press, Melbourne.

Freckelton, I. (1987) Novel scientific evidence: the challenge of tomorrow. *Australian Bar Review* **3(3)** 243.

Freckelton, I. (1989) DNA Profiling: Optimism and Realism. *Law Institute Journal*.

Freckelton, I. (1990) On political pragmatism and police obstructionism. In: Goldsmith, A. (ed) *Complaints against the police*, Oxford University Press, Oxford (forthcoming).

Freckelton, I. & Selby, H. (1989) The use and abuse of expert witnesses. *Law*

Institute Journal **63(1)** 31.

Freckelton, I. & Selby, H. (1989) Piercing the blue veil, In: Wilson, P. & Chappell, D. *Australian Policing*, Butterworths, Sydney.

Freckelton, I. & Selby, H. (1988) (ed), *Police in our society*, Butterworths, Sydney.

Gianelli, P. C., (1980) The admissibility of novel scientific evidence: *Frye v United States*, a half century later. *Columbia Law Review* **80** 1197.

Gill, P. & Werrett, D. J. (1987) Exclusion of a man charged with murder by DNA fingerprinting. *Forensic Science International* **35** 145.

Gill, P., Lygo, J. E., Fowler, S. J., & Werrett, D. J. (1987) An evaluation of DNA fingerprinting for forensic purposes. *Electrophoresis* **8** 38.

Gillies, P. (1986) Opinion Evidence. *Australian Law Journal* **60** 597.

Goldsmith, A. (ed) *Complaints against the police*, Oxford University Press, Oxford (forthcoming).

Gutowski, S. (1988) DNA profiling, paper presented to the *Australian and New Zealand Forensic Science Society*, Melbourne, August.

Helminen, P., Ehnholm, C., Lokki, M., Jeffreys, A., & Peltonen, L. (1988) Application of DNA 'fingerprints' to paternity determinations. *The Lancet* 574.

Jeffreys, A., Brookfield, J., & Semeonoff, R. (1986) DNA fingerprint analysis in immigration test cases (1986) *Nature* **322** 290.

Jeffreys, A. J., Wilson, V., & Thein, S. L. (1985) Individual-specific 'fingerprints' of human DNA. *Nature* **316** 76.

Lifecodes Corporation (1987) *Background information — DNA print: new genetic identification test*, Sydney.

Malone, D. M. (1988) Direct examination of experts. *Trial* **24(4)** 42.

McCormick, M. (1981) Scientific evidence: defining a new approach to admissibility. *Iowa Law Review* **67** 879.

Miller, J. A. Mummy DNA intact after 2400 years. *Science News* **127** 262.

Newmark, P. (1986) DNA fingerprints go commercial. *Nature* 104.

Odds of grandparenthood. *Science News* **125** 376.

Pereira, M. (1981) How a forensic scientist fell foul of the law. *New Scientist* **91** 575.

Phillips, J. H. & Bowen, J. K. (1985) *Forensic science and the expert witness*, Law Book Co, Melbourne.

Phillips, J. H. (1988) Genetic fingerprinting. *Australian Law Journal* **62** 550.

Police and Criminal Evidence Act, Sections 62 and 63 (1984).

Police Complaints Authority of Victoria (1988) *Sexual assault victims and the police*, PCA DP1, Govt Printer, Melbourne.

Police Complaints Authority of Victoria (1987) *Interim Report*, Victorian Govt Printer, Melbourne.

Royal Commission of Inquiry into the Chamberlain Convictions (1987) *Report*, Govt Printer, Darwin (*Morling Report*).

Royal Commission Concerning the Conviction of Edward Charles Splatt (1984) *Report*, Govt. Printer, Adelaide (*Splatt Report*).

Saltzburg, S. A. (1975) Standards of proof and preliminary questions of fact. *Staford Law Review* **27** 271.

Selby, H. (1988) Chapter 19, pp 229. Too little too late, In: Freckelton, I. & Selby, H. (eds), *Police in our society*, Butterworths, Sydney.

Sensabaugh, G. F. (1986) Forensic biology — is recombinant DNA technology in its future?. *Journal of Forensic Sciences* **31** 393.

Simons, M. J. (1989) DNA gene typing in disputed paternity resolution. *Australian Family Lawyer* (forthcoming).

Thompson, W. G. & Ford, S. (1988) DNA typing *Trial* **56** 24.

Wilson, P. & Chappell, D. (1989) (ed), *Australian policing*, Butterworths, Sydney.

# Glossary

**Acrylamide; acrylamide electrophoresis:** Acrylamide is a low molecular weight, water soluble, organic chemical that, when in dilute solution with suitable catalysts and cross-linking agents, can be polymerized into a covalently linked molecular network, a pseudo-solid gel that may contain as little as 2.5% of the polymerized acrylamide; the rest being a conductive aqueous solution that is a suitable medium for electrophoresis. (*See* electrophoresis). (Warning — unpolymerised acrylamide is extrmely toxic.)

**Agarose; agarose gel electrophoresis:** Agarose is a very high molecular weight, uncharged, water soluble, carbohydrate of marine origin. It can be dissolved in aqueous solutions on heating and when these solutions are cooled, the physical association of the agarose molecules may cause the solution to become a pseudo-solid, i.e. 'gel'. As little as 0.65% agarose in a solution may cause the remaining 99.35% of volume to be transformed from a mobile liquid into a conveniently pseudo-solid gel. Agarose gels of conductive aqueous solutions are suitable media for gel electrophoresis. *See* electrophoresis.

**Alleles:** Genes or any other sections of DNA that behave as alternatives in inheritance. Most commonly genes that are physically located in the corresponding positions on a pair of homologous chromosomes. The meaning of the term 'allele' is widening with usage while the meaning of the closely related term 'gene' is becoming more narrow with usage. *See* gene.

**Alphoid satellite; alphoid DNA; alphoid satellite DNA:** A class of repetitive DNA that commonly has a sequence of approximately 170 base pairs that is repeated tandemly many hundreds or thousands of times with only slight variations from the theme. This family or class of DNA sequences is very commonly associated with centromeres.

**ALU:** An acronym used interchangeably for both a particular restriction endonuclease and also for a particular class of repetitive DNA distinguished by having a characteristic sensitivity to this restriction endonuclease. The context of its usage determines which meaning applies.

**Antibody:** An immunological term that refers to those proteins, commonly serum proteins, that identify foreign cells or foreign proteins and then bind to them. This is usually the first step in the destruction of the foreign material. The target of an antibody, whatever it may be, is conventionally called the 'antigen'. (*See* antigen.)

**Antigen:** An immunological term that refers to any substance that is recognised and bound by antibodies. (*See* antibody). However, such substances are most commonly proteins or the complex carbohydrates on glycoproteins and glycolipids. Commonly, cellular antigens are the proteins which are exposed on the outer membranes of the cells.

**Autosome:** An ordinary, non-sex, chromosome. All human chromosomes, excepting the X and the Y chromosome are autosomes.

**Alpha globin:** *See* globins.

**Base:** In DNA structure, the word base commonly refers to one of four heterocyclic structures, adenine, thymine, guanine, and cytosine. The order of usage of these four structures along the DNA determines the information that the DNA carries. It should be noted that RNA commonly uses a structure related to thymine called uracil, instead of the base thymine.

**Base sequence:** *See* sequence.

**Biotinylated; biotin:** The vitamin biotin can be attached to DNA in various ways. The DNA is then said to be labelled with biotin or is said to be biotinylated. Biotin has a very high affinity to the egg protein avidin and there are various techniques for using this affinity to cause the development of a visible colour wherever the biotinylated DNA may be.

**Beta globin:** *See* globins.

**BP: Base pairs;** one of the common ways of measuring distances along DNA. (*See also* KB kilobases).

**C-DNA:** Literally, complementary DNA. This is a term used as a common abbreviation and the 'complementary', the 'C' before the DNA, has a meaning that depends on the context of usage. However, the 'C' always implies that the DNA is complementary to some other nucleic acid that is important in the discussion. Commonly, a C-DNA probe may be said to be used when a mobile radioactive DNA sequence is used to probe for the complementary sequence that may be bound to a membrane. In another context, the term C-DNA is also commonly used to describe the DNA that is made whenever reverse transcriptase copies RNA to make a DNA copy.

**Centric:** Found in the centromere; *see* 'centromere'.

**Centromere:** The section of a chromosome that is responsible for its attachment to the apparatus that moves the chromosome in cell division. An attachment point that is responsible for the correct assortment of chromosomes in cell division.

**Centromeric:** Some feature of a chromosome, e.g. a particular sequence of DNA of heterochromatin that is found in the centromere.

**Chelating agents; chelation:** Agents, usually complex anions, that very tightly bind polyvalent metals into tight complexes. EDTA and EGTA are examples of commonly used chelating agents.

EDTA=ethylene diamine tetra acetate.

EGTA=ethylene glycol-bis-(2-aminoethyl ether)-$N,N'$-tetraacetic acid.

In molecular biology, these are commonly used to make the metals Calcium and Magnesium unavailable for enzymes, e.g. make them unavailable for enzymes that hydrolyse DNA and thus protect the DNA.

**Chromatids:** A pair of daughter chromosomes that have newly arisen from the replication of a pre-existing single chromosome. Conventional photographs of 'chromosomes' at metaphase of mitosis or meiosis are usually photographs of pairs of chromatids that have not yet separated. There is no real difference between mature chromatids and chromosomes, it's mainly a semantic difference; a convention of terminology.

**Chromatin:** The complex of DNA and proteins that makes up the chromosomes and the nucleus. *See* chromosomes.

**Chromosomes:** (Literally 'coloured bodies') Microscopic structures formed by DNA molecules in eukaryotic cells. The carriers of the genes. The cell nucleus is composed of them but they can usually only be seen as separate entities at cell division. i.e. Mitosis or meiosis. Chromosomes are composed of approximately 50% by weight DNA and 50% protein. This substance is called chromatin. (*see* chromatin). Chromosomes are actually quite colourless but stain intensely with both basic and acidic dyes, hence the name 'chromosomes'.

**Complement:** When this word is used as a noun it commonly refers to a family of serum proteins that cause the cell membranes of 'foreign' cells to become leaky after they have been identified and marked by antibody. Thus complement proteins commonly lyse and kill the invading cells.

**Complementary:** An adjective commonly used in molecular biology to describe the situation when two molecules bind together because they have 'matching' structures in some way, e.g. when two DNA sequences are complementary they will bind to each other and form a double helix.

**Condense; condensed:** With respect to chromosomal material, the word condense implies that the coiled or folded mass of chromatin is being forced to coil or fold into an even smaller volume than before. It thus becomes much more optically dense and much more intensely stainable. Strongly condensed chromosomes, that is to say, very compact structured chromosomes, have a much more clearly defined morphology than weakly condensed chromosomes.

**Cytokinesis:** The division of the cytoplasm of the cell. This usually (but not always) occurs straight after mitotic division of the nucleus.

**Deoxyribonucleic acid:** *See* DNA.

**Deoxyribonucleotides:** The monomers of DNA. A class of nucleotides that are based on the pentose sugar, deoxyribose. (*See* 'nucleotides').

**Disequilibrium in linkage:** *See* linkage equilibrium.

**Domain:** A term that has different meanings in different contexts. A domain generally implies some region of the genome that has some common feature about it that makes it a relative of other domains but it also has some peculiar features that distinguish it from its relatives. For example, it may refer to particular patches of satellite DNA that are somehow, distinguishable from other patches of similar satellite material elsewhere in the genome. In this case the differences between the 'domains' may have grown up due to their isolation from each other and random drift, and thus divergence, over the period of isolation. Thus the same basic, ancestral sequence could give rise to many clearly related but clearly distinguishable sub patches or domains of this family.

**DNA; deoxyribonucleic acid:** The genetic material of higher organisms. An unbranched, linear, heteropolymer of subunits called nucleotides (strictly deoxyribonucleotides), DNA is usually double stranded. Each nucleotide consisting of a deoxyribose-phosphate and a base, (adenine, thymine, cytosine, or guanine) and each deoxyribose being attached to the next by a phosphodiester linkage through the 3′ and 5′ hydroxyls. DNA commonly occurs as a helix of two complementary strands of the linear polymer that are then bound together by hydrogen and hydrophobic bonds. The two strands are complementary so they contain the same information. The deoxyribose phosphate is responsible for the molecule's linear integrity and is non-informational, the informational content, the code, comes from the order of the bases along the molecule. (*See also sequence*).

**DNA sequence:** *See* sequence.

**Electrophoresis:** Any process of using an electric field to move charged molecules through a conductive aqueous solvent. Commonly in order to separate the moving molecules from each other for the purposes of analysis. In a mixture of molecules, the relative mobility of each molecule will be principally determined by its charge, its molecular weight and its shape. Thus the technique is very suitable for distinguishing a very wide variety of charged water soluble molecules from each other. Electrophoresis can be carried out on molecules in free solution but this is almost never done. More usually the solution carrying the electric field and its ionic current is immobilised by being held as wet paper or as a 'gel'. Gels are particularly useful for the separation of very large molecules such as the various size classes of DNA from each other. They are also useful for separating proteins from each other and RNA species from each other. Gels are usually created from an inert, uncharged, water absorbent substance that will form a three-dimensional network in an aqueous solvent. Such a network or gel allows the aqueous solution to be handled in a more convenient form as pseudo-solid slabs. The network also contributes strongly to the separation properties of the gel as the average 'mesh-size' of the molecular work network retards molecules moving through it according to the molecular size of the moving molecules. For gels *see* acrylamide and agarose.

**Enhancers; enhancer sequences:** Sequences of DNA that are found in the vicinity of genes and functionally associated with the genes they are near. They often have a strongly stimulatory effect on the gene that they are near and they are thought to be 'control elements' or sequences, that, when bound to their corresponding control proteins, modulate the activity of the gene they are associated with. Enhancers appear to be the elements on DNA that allow the developmental programs and tissue-determining programs to turn on and off the genes that are appropriate to each tissue or developmental stage a cell is in. A typical enhancer might be approximately 70 bp long and be located approximately 1 kilobase from a gene. Their position, with respect to the gene that they affect, is highly variable.

**Eukaryotes:** All those organisms with a well defined nucleus and chromosomes of the type that are complexed with histones are call eukaryotes, e.g. mammals, flowering plants, birds, reptiles, fish, yeast and other fungi, but not the typical bacteria, the prokaryotes.

**Exons:** Those parts of the eukaryotic gene that code for a definite amino acid sequence that can be ultimately translated into a section of a protein. In the typical eukaryote gene, exons alternate with introns.

**Field inversion gel electrophoresis:** A method of electrophoresis of DNA in agarose gels in which the electric field is periodically reversed so that there is a nett foward motion of the DNA but the DNA reverses the direction of its motion at a frequency determined by some programmed switch. This enhances the separation of large DNA molecules (above approx. 10 KB) and the actual period of these reversals determines which size classes of DNA will have their separation most enhanced. *See* electrophoresis.

**FIGE:** *see* field inversion gel electrophoresis.

**Gel electrophoresis:** *See* under electrophoresis.

**Gene:** The old usage of this term came from genetics and referred to any inherited determinant of characters. i.e. any sequence of DNA. This usage is still valid and often used. The more modern usage of the term is limited to those sections of DNA which are actually transcribed by RNA polymerase; i.e. genes are those sections of DNA which are expressed via a molecular copy made of RNA. It should be noted that this modern usage is a very limited definition of a gene that specifically excludes a large variety of other sequences found within DNA such as controlling sequences, that clearly have inherited effects, and under the old usage would have been called genes. However, increasingly, these other sequences are now being referred to by other names more appropriate to their mode of expression, or are just being referred to by more general terms such as the non-committal 'allele'. *See* allele.

**Genome:** A term for the whole of the DNA of the organism. The nuclear genome is the whole of the DNA in the nucleus, the mitochondrial genome is the whole of the DNA in the mitochondria.

**Globin(s):** The polypeptide chains that form haemoglobin together with Haem. They occur as two families of proteins and thus families of genes. The beta-globin cluster is a closely linked cluster of genes on chromosome 11 of the human being, which code for beta globin and the polypeptides most closely related to it. The alpha-globin cluster is on the human chromosome 16.

**Haplotype:** An abbreviation for the genetic term 'haploid phenotype'. In discussions of diploid organisms such as man, it refers to the genotype of one 'theoretical gamete' that is to say, a gene or a set of genes that might be expected to be found in one gamete after a theoretical (or actual) meiosis. In the simplest case it merely refers to one particular gene or mutant gene at one particular locus. (A heterozygous diploid genotype of Hbs/Hb would be said to have two possible haplotypes; Hbs and Hb. In this case it is really only another way of referring to a single, specific gene. However a diploid with more than one, say two heterozygous loci under consideration has many possible haplotypes (a maximum of four haplotypes for two loci, eight for three loci etc.) and in the general case it refers to all the possible combinations of genes that may be found in one gamete. Each haplotype being one possible combination.

**Heterochromatin:** A term used to describe anomolously staining zones on chromosomes. Many heterochromatin zones of chromosomes are being found to be loci of massive deposits of simple-sequence tandemly repeated DNA. *See* satellite DNA.

**Hexamer random priming:** Hexamer refers to a highly heterogenous mixture of hexanucleotides that are random in sequence. These are usually synthetic and are used for random priming methods of labelling nucleic acids. *See* random priming, priming, and probes.

**Histones:** A family of small protein molecules that are characterized by being rich in the basic (positively charged) amino acids Arginine and/or Lysine. They act as counter-ions and as packing proteins for the negatively charged DNA. They are characteristic of non-sperm chromatin and are replaced by protamines in sperm. (*See* protamines).

**HLA; HLA locus:** HLA is an abbreviation for 'human lymphocyte antigens'. The HLA locus is a zone of closely linked loci on chromosome 6 within the region known as the 'major histocompatibility complex'. The human lymphocyte antigens are proteins found in the outer membranes of many cell types beside lymphocytes. They are highly variable proteins that are responsible for the immunological individuality of each person. It is the variation of these proteins that largely determines the likelihood of heterograft rejection. These proteins are so variable that their locus, actually a cluster of linked loci, is a well studied and valuable source of genetic variation.

**Human lymphocyte antigens:** *See* HLA.

**Hybridization:** In the context of molecular genetics this term is used to describe the process of two nucleic acid strands first randomly coming together, then if they have complementary base sequences, the forming of a stable helix together. This process is thus a process of two strands recognising each other and binding together. Hybridization is generally carried out by placing the two single stranded nucleic acids together such that at least one of the strands is in free solution and mobile and under conditions of temperature and salt concentration such that the double helix that they will form is only just stable, i.e. is marginally stable. (*See* stringency.) So long as the base sequences are complementary it is then only a matter of time before they match up and form double helices. Hybrids may be formed between DNA strands from different sources, DNA strands and RNA strands, or even RNA and RNA strands. If the DNA strands are the same ones that were originally together in a double helix then the process is usually called 'renaturation' rather than hybridization.

**H-Ras:** A particular proto-oncogene. (*See* proto oncogene and oncogene).

**Introns:** These are non-coding sequences of DNA that are found inside the transcribed region of a gene, that is to say, the region that is used to produce an RNA copy. They are transcribed but are usually not translated. The RNA that corresponds to these regions is excised from the primary transcript before it can be used as a 'message' for translation into amino acid sequences. Introns are very common in the genes of the eukaryotes but uncommon in the prokaryotes. The functions of introns appear not to be critical in that their base sequences are not highly evolutionarily conserved. Introns of a gene alternate with the coding regions, the exons, and appear to divide the gene up so that each exon corresponds to one functional module of the protein it codes for. This implies a long-term function of introns in the evolution of new genes by the rearrangement of old genes.

**Isozymes:** When two or more structurally different enzymes catalyze the same chemical reaction, then these enzymes are isozymes. The various isozymes, within their group, may be derived from entirely different genes to each other and thus have quite different polypeptide chains even though they catalyze the same reaction. (However, sets of 'isozymes' may also arise as modified forms, all derived from one original enzyme).

**Kb** (*See* kilobases).

**Keratin(oid):** A general term to describe proteins that have their structure stabilized by many disulphide cross-links. Such proteins are extremely stable to denaturation unless subjected to reducing conditions. Examples are; hair, nail, cuticle, feathers. The chromatin of mammalian sperm heads, although a nucleoprotein rather than a protein, is also classified as a keratin-type nucleoprotein or keratinoid.

**Kilobases:** 1 kilobase (kb) is one thousand bases distance along a piece of DNA. One of the common methods of measuring distance along DNA.

**Leader sequences:** A term with a number of usages depending on context. In its most common usage it refers to the short stretch of base sequence that is located at the region of the gene or message RNA, just in front of the origin of translation. It is thus the sequence that occurs between the origin of transcription and the origin of translation. It is a sequence that contains the ribosomal binding and locating site.

**Linkage:** A genetic term that refers to the deviations from random assortment of genes or loci that is often found when two genes or loci are physically close together on a chromosome. The shorter the physical distance between the genes or loci, the closer the 'linkage' commonly is. However, the degree of statistical linkage of two genes or loci is also affected by factors other than the physical distance apart of the two sites; e.g. it is also strongly affected by the local susceptibility of breakage and rejunction (crossover) of the chromosome.

**Linkage equilibrium/disequilibrium:** Over a number of generations of sexual reproduction, two particular base sequences that are sited at linked loci, will slowly become separated from each other by the random effects of crossover occurring between them. If this proceeds in a random way, over many generations, eventually the probability of finding any particular sequences at the two linked loci will simply be determined by chance, i.e. by the simple product of the frequencies of the two sequences concerned. This end state is referred to as a state of 'linkage equilibrium' for the two sequences concerned.

If however, two particular sequences have not had time to be redistributed away from each other, or if there are selective forces that continually favour the survival and/or reproduction of one particular combination of sequences, then these overly probable combinations, that occur for whatever reason, are said to be in a state of 'linkage disequilibrium'.

**Locus;** (Loci, plural): Literally a place on a chromosome or within the genome. It refers to the place of location on a chromosome where the gene or mutant under consideration is located. A locus may be a sharply defined place such as a single base-pair at a particular point on a chromosome or it may be a zone many thousands of bases long. The context of usage will determine the exact meaning. A locus may be named by some interesting gene that is located there or it may be defined as a zone or site on a chromosome, e.g. 1q2 (The second zone on the large arm of chromosome 1). Conventionally the word locus is used in the singular when talking about two homologous genes (alleles) in a diploid organism, e.g. a pair of alleles are said to be at the same locus. The plural is used when discussing genes at different locations on chromosomes; e.g. the genes for sickle cell anaemia and for phenylketonuria are at different loci, whereas the genes for sickle cell anaemia and for its corresponding normal gene are at the same locus.

**Lyse; lysis:** Refers to the dissolution of a complex structure such as a sperm head, or a cell, so that some or all of the components of the structure go into free solution, e.g. ionic detergents such as sodium dodecyl sulphate will usually cause complete solubilization (lysis) of all the components of an erythrocyte. Osmotic shock together with the enzyme lysozyme may cause the dissolution and solubilization of many bacterial cells.

**Macrosatellite; macrosatellite DNA:** (*See* minisatellite and satellite DNA).

**MHC locus:** (*See* major histocompatibility locus).

**Major histocompatibility (MHC) locus:** A large zone of DNA on chromosome 6 that has three functional subzones. Two of these are the two main clusters of HLA loci (*see* HLA) and the other is a cluster of genes mainly coding for the proteins that lyse immunologically foreign cells. The complement genes.

**Maternal inheritance:** Genes may be carried in such a way that they are passed only from mother to progeny (male and female), i.e. the genes are only transferred via the egg. The male, the sperm, does not transfer these characters to any of the progeny. The genes on the mitochondrial DNA are usually maternally inherited.

**Meiosis: Sexual cell division.** The process that occurs to a cell in the production of gametes (sperm or eggs), meiosis consists of two divisions of the cellular chromosomes with the first division separating the homologous chromosomes from each other. Just before this first division, the chromosomes duplicate themselves to give double the chromosomal complement in the form of paired chromatids, the homologous chromosome-pairs then intimately bind to each other, (synapse) and then break and rejoin in such a way that the homologous chromosomes exchange sections between themselves (genetic recombination). After this whole process is complete, there are the two divisions that usually result in four new cells, each cell having one half the chromosomes of the original parent cell.

**Message:** (*See* messenger RNA).

**Messenger RNA:** The final RNA copy of the gene that contains the translatable code free of introns and properly processed in all other ways. Processing refers to the variety of modifications that the primary transcript may undergo on the way to becoming the message. The message is read on the ribosome.

**Minisatellites; minisatellite DNA:** A class of repetitive DNA that is characterized by having a simple sequence, usually 4 to 12 bases long, that is found to occur in patches in which the basic, simple sequence is repeated, end to end, that is to say, in tandem, many times, perhaps hundreds or thousands of times. The difference between minisatellites and macrosatellites is principally in the amount of the species found in the nucleus. Their biological function is still speculative.

**Mitochondria:** A membranous organelle found outside of the nucleus, in the cytoplasm of a eukaryote cell. It is the organelle which is responsible for much of the aerobic oxidative biochemistry of the cell. Human mitochondria contain a small amount of DNA that is maternally inherited.

**Mitosis:** Asexual cellular division. This is a process that occurs in a cell just prior to the cell's division. During this process the newly duplicated chromosome pairs, conventionally called chromatids at this stage, are drawn apart such that one chromatid of each pair goes to opposite poles of the cell, thus ensuring that the duplicated chromosomes or chromatids are distributed exactly equally to each of the daughter cells.

**Nick translation:** A method of labelling DNA with radioactive or otherwise labelled nucleotides. A bacterial polymerase (Pol I from *E. coli*) is applied to double stranded DNA containing many randomly placed breaks in the deoxyribose phosphate backbone of the type that give 3′OH groups on the deoxyribose. The polymerase then attaches to these sites and hydrolyses one strand of the double strand while simultaneously replacing the hydrolysed strand with labelled nucleotides. This replacement process creates labelled DNA in the place of some of the old, unlabelled DNA. This process has NO relationship to the process of 'translation', i.e. protein synthesis.

**Nucleosome:** The lowest level of fold/coiling of chromatin. Packages approximately 200 base pairs of DNA per nucleosome, 140 of which are wrapped around a complex of eight histone molecules. The remainder of the 200 base pairs leads from one nucleosome to the other.

**Nucleotides:** The precursors or monomers of nucleic acids. They consist of an heterocyclic base such as adenine, thymine, cytosine, uracil, or guanine, attached to a sugar, usually a pentose such as ribose or deoxyribose which, in its turn, is esterified to at least one phosphate group. Commonly, there may be a chain of up to three phosphate groups attached to the 1′ position of the pentose sugar, the extra phosphate groups being attached to the first one by pyrophosphate bonds. These pyrophosphate groups are lost during the polymerization process and only the base, the pentose and one of the phosphates is incorporated into the nucleic acid polymer.

**Nucleotide sequence:** (*See* sequence).

**Oligo nucleotide:** A sequence of nucleotides only a few bases long. For example a piece of DNA that was single stranded and only 20 bases long would usually be called an oligonucleotide. Polynucleotides are sequences many bases long. The division between lengths a 'few' long and lengths 'many' long is not defined by any convention and is merely a matter of opinion.

**Oncogene:** Any section of DNA that can cause cancer. Dominant oncogenes almost always arise from molecular accidents or rearrangements of normal DNA that occur during an individual's life span. Recessive oncogenes may arise during an individual's life span but these may sometimes be inherited as an inborn predisposition to cancer. Those sections of normal DNA which, on rearrangement or mutation, give rise to an oncogene, are referred to as 'proto oncogenes.' (*See* proto oncogene).

**PCR:** Polymerase Chain Reaction. A technique where by a repetitious, cyclic program of heating and cooling together with a heat resistant DNA polymerase and two sequence specific DNA primers are used to selectively amplify one particular small region of a genome. The amplification process is exponential and thus may achieve very large values. PCR is typically used when only very small amounts of a particular sequence are available and it must be amplified (reproduced) a great many times in order for there to be enough of it to study.

**Peptide bond:** This is the type of bond that links the amino acids of proteins together. It is an amide bond formed between the alpha amino of one amino acid and the carboxyl amino of the adjacent amino acid. (Note the minor exception, in the case of the amino acid proline, the reacting nitrogen is from an imino group rather than an amino group).

**Pericentric:** Some feature of a chromosome, e.g. a piece of heterochromatin or some repetitive DNA sequence that is found on both sides of the centromere and near to it but not actually in the centromere.

**Phenotype:** The characteristics of an individual that can be observed or measured in some way; e.g. height or colour of a plant. Blood group or degree of colourblindness of a human being.

**Phosphodiester bond:** The linkage of sugar to sugar that joins the monomers that make up both DNA and RNA has the form sugar-O-PO2-O-sugar, where the sugars are deoxyribose or ribose. The phosphate group between them (O-PO2-O) is attached to the two of them by an ester bond. Hence the term phosphodiester.

**Plasmid:** A small, typically circular, piece of DNA that usually carries one or a few genes that can be moved between bacterial cells and multiplied within them. Under natural circumstances, plasmids carry drug resistance genes and other specialty-function genes through bacterial populations, in genetic engineering procedures. In the laboratory, plasmids are common vehicles used for the carrying of pieces of DNA that may need to be reproduced and studied.

**Polynucleotide:** A piece of a nucleic acid that is many bases long. (For comparison *see* oligonucleotide.

**Primary transcript:** The unmodified RNA transcript just as it was first copied off the gene. (*See* transcript).

**Priming:** A primer is a site to begin polynucleotide synthesis. In the context of nucleic acid synthesis, this refers to a 3'OH on a ribose or deoxyribose that is suitable as a nucleotide-acceptor site for a polymerase and thus acts as a place where nucleic acid synthesis can proceed from. Typically or commonly, a primer is a short stretch of nucleotides that has a free 3′OH at one end and is complementary to a stretch of the single stranded template polynucleotide. Synthesis proceeds from the primer 3′OH group so that the incoming nucleotides form a polynucleotide strand bound to the template and complementary to it.

**Probe:** A general term for any highly detectable molecule that will attach to some other, much more cryptic molecule, thus allowing the detection of the cryptic molecule. However, in DNA studies, a 'probe' is usually a piece of known DNA sequence that is either made radioactive or has some reporter molecule such as Avidin attached to it. The radioactivity or the reporter section is referred to as the 'label'. The labelled 'probe' sequence is then used to search for complimentary sequences in a particular individual's DNA, by being hybridized with the unlabelled DNA of interest. The probe binds to complimentary sequences in the unlabelled DNA so that the label now allows the detection of the previously undetectable sequence of interest. Commonly the probe sequence is in free solution and thus mobile while the target sequence to be detected is immobile and bound to a membrane.

**Prokaryotes:** Most of those cellular organisms have a simple circular chromosome with no histones on it and without internal respiratory organelles such as mitochondria. Respiration and photosynthesis are located in the external membrane of the organism, e.g. the common bacteria such as *E. coli* and *S. aureus*.

**Promoter:** This is a class of DNA sequences that are found next to the origin of transcription of a gene. Promoter sequences are the places on the DNA where the RNA polymerase first binds. These places are usually located just to the upstream side of the origin of transcription although some eukaryotic promoters are located on the downstream side of the origin of transcription.

**Protamines:** A family of small protein molecules that are characterized by being rich in arginine, a positively charged amino acid, and by being found in the sperm chromatin of the higher eukaryotes. The protamines of mammals are also rich in the amino acid cysteine.

**Protease; Proteinase:** This is a general name for a diverse class of enzymes that all depolymerize proteins by hydrolysing some or many of the peptide bonds of the protein. The products of such a hydrolysis are amino acids and/or shorter chained polypeptides. The actual spectrum of hydrolytic products is highly dependent on the specificity of the protease concerned.

**Proto oncogene:** A normal gene that on being mutated appropriately, or being rearranged by random breakage and rejunctions, is known to be capable of producing a gene that will cause the cell that contains it to become cancerous, or increase its likelihood of becoming cancerous. Many normal genes involved in cellular control are thus potential sources of oncogenes and are referred to as proto oncogenes.

**Pro-virions:** Some virions are capable of inserting themselves into the DNA of a genome in such a way that the virus may be reproduced as an integral part of the host genome but eventually re-emerge from the genome and resume its existence as a freely multiplying virus independent of any particular genome. When such a virus is laying dormant in the host genome then the form that is in the host's genome is the Pro-virus. (*See* virus).

**Pseudogene:** Literally, a false gene. These are sections of DNA that, on casual examination appear to code for some definite protein. However on close examination it becomes apparent that they are non-functional, in that they are unable to be transcribed and/or unable to be translated. They are thus non-functional as genes. They are common, inherited, and some are probably quite ancient. They appear to occur as relics of two quite different sorts of molecular accidents. The duplication of a gene with the inactivation of one of the duplicates by mutation accumulation, and by the reverse transcription of a messenger RNA with the insertion of its DNA-copy back into the genome. This latter type is referred to as 'processed pseudogenes'.

**Random priming:** This refers to a technique whereby nucleic acid synthesis is begun at many random points along a polynucleotide. The aim of this is usually to produce a labelled copy of the nucleic acid to use as a 'probe' (*see* probe). Random priming is obtained by applying a highly heterogenous mixture of short oligonucleotides, say six bases in length, of random sequence to the very long template sequence that is to be copied. (*See* priming).

**Repetitive DNA:** An old term used to describe all and any species of DNA sequence that exists in a genome in multiple copies, usually many copies (dozens to hundreds of thousands). The term covers an enormously wide range of unrelated phenomena, unrelated except in the one fact that they are all sequences that are repeated in the genome many times. Currently, the term is losing its usefulness as it is usually too broad to be of value. It is becoming more useful to refer, more specifically, to the subsets within it as these subsets have, at least some commonalities of sequence and for function within them. Examples of subsets of the general class of repetitive DNA are — simple tandem sequences, Satellite DNA of various types such as minisatellites, short interspersed repeats, long interspersed repeats, multiple copies of ribosomal genes, and others.

**Reporter molecule:** A molecule that is readily detected at very low concentrations. Reporter molecules are sometimes said to act as 'labels'. Most commonly, this may be due to the fact that it has a highly radioactive atom within it, (e.g. phosphorus-32 in phosphate) or a molecule with a very specific reactivity or affinity (e.g. biotin). Most DNA 'probes' that are used in detection of their complementary sequences have been 'labelled' with a reporter group or reporter molecule, in some way just before usage. Sometimes the two terms 'reporter molecule' and 'probe' are used loosely and interchangeably. (*See* probe).

**Restrict:** In the context of DNA technology this means to cut the DNA with a restriction endonuclease.

**Restriction endonuclease:** A class of enzymes of bacterial origin that have the biological function of protecting the bacterial cell from foreign, invasive, viral DNA. The name 'restriction' arises from the fact that it is these enzymes that restrict particular various from attacking some types of bacteria. In the absence of DNA methylation, restriction endonucleases will cut particular DNA sequences, commonly 4 to 6 bases long, at one specific sequence that is a specific target for that particular endonuclease. Thus they are used in DNA technology as a tool for cutting DNA at particular places. There are over 100 different restriction endonucleases known.

**Retrovirus:** A class of virus that has, as a part of its infection cycle, a stage when the viral RNA is copied into DNA by the enzyme reverse-transcriptase. Copies of this DNA may then be inserted in the genome to form pro-virions. *See* pro-virions.

**Reverse-transcriptase:** An enzyme that uses RNA as a template to make DNA. This is the reverse of the usual situation, hence the term 'reverse'-transcriptase. This enzyme is made by many retrovirions.

**RFLP:** Restriction fragment length polymorphism. A method of characterizing any zone of DNA that detects any gross differences, throughout the population, in the zone of sequence concerned. Restriction enzymes and sequence-specific probes are commonly used to break up and observe some particular region of DNA under study and if samples of this DNA region, taken from different individuals, give non-identical (variable) length sets of fragments then a 'polymorphism' exists; that is to say, an RFLP. Although RFLP sometimes arise from minor differences in DNA sequences, even as little as one base difference if it is within a restriction site, the technique is much more applicable to the detection of very large deletions and insertions into the sequences of interest.

**Ribose nucleic acid:** (*See* RNA).

**Ribosome:** Organelles found in the cytoplasm of cells that bind to the message RNA, read the message RNA and translate its message into an amino acid sequence. Ribosomes are complex multimers of a number of polypeptide chains together with a number of RNA molecules.

**RNA; Ribose nucleic acid:** An unbranched, linear, heteropolymer of subunits called nucleotides. (Strictly ribonucleotides.) RNA is usually, but not always, single stranded. (Unlike the closely related DNA.) Each nucleotide of RNA consists of a ribose-phosphate and a base (commonly adenine, uracil, cytosine, or guanine), and each ribose is attached to the next by a phosphodiester linkage through the 3′ and 5′ hydroxyls. The ribose phosphate is responsible for the molecule's linear integrity and is non-informational, the informational content, the code, comes from the order of the bases along the molecule. In human beings, almost all RNA is formed as copies of DNA sequences during the process of transcription.

**RNA polymerase:** The enzyme that copies DNA sequences into RNA. Transcriptase is an RNA polymerase. (*See* transcription).

**Satellite; satellite DNA:** The old and broad usage of this term is appropriate for any sequence of DNA that has been replicated such a large number of times within the genome that it appears as a distinct peak or sub class of DNA in a caesium density gradient. This broad usage of the term is slowly becoming narrowed and the term is being reserved for the most common class of DNA within this category, the highly repetitive, tandem repeats of simple sequences about 4 to 170 base pairs long that are repeated in a tandem fashion many hundreds or thousands of times. The largest masses of this tandemly repetitive DNA are often located near centromeres and telomeres of chromosomes and can be observed cytologically as 'Heterochromatin'. (For example *see* alphoid satellite and satellite III. Compare minisatellite and macrosatellite.)

**Satellite III; satellite three DNA:** The sequence 5'-TTCCA-3' with its complement, repeated many thousands of times in a tandem fashion. Characteristically found in the higher primates.

**Sequence:** In the context of DNA, this refers to the actual order of bases along the nucleic acid molecule. For example 5-'AATGC-3' implies that the order of bases along the DNA molecule being discussed is adenine, followed by another adenine, then thymine and then a guanine and then a cytosine. The 5' and 3' give the intrinsic 'direction' of the strand. There is an underlying direction to all sequences that is commonly not mentioned but is ALWAYS assumed. This direction arises from the structure of the deoxyribose, and the 5' and 3' refer to sites on the deoxyribose. (Refer to a diagram of DNA structure.) Conventionally, the assumed direction of sequences is always in the one standard direction, the 5' to 3'direction.

With respect to nucleic acid molecules being synthesized, this is the direction of both the DNA and RNA synthesis processes.

**Shearing of DNA:** This refers to the mechanical breakage of DNA molecules that occurs during their handling in solution. Shearing forces are the mechanical tearing of DNA that occurs when long, extended, DNA molecules are caught across regions of fluid flow with differential movement of adjacent layers of fluid. Some degree of shearing is unavoidable with free solutions as it occurs during pouring, pipetting or shaking any solution of DNA.

**Somatic; e.g. somatic chromatin:** 'Somatic' is an adjective used to describe materials from the 'normal' tissues as opposed to the materials from the 'germ-line' tissues. Eggs and sperm are examples of germ-line cells, liver, and brain tissues are examples of 'somatic' tissues.

**Southern Blot; Southern transfer** (synonyms): A technique whereby bands of DNA that have been migrating in an agarose gel are transferred by capillarity to some adsorbant membrane that will bind the DNA. Agarose gels are too unstable an environment for studying the DNA bands that they contain while retaining the positional information of the DNA. Thus, an adsorbant membrane is laid on the gel face and then fluid is supplied to the underside of the gel and drawn through the gel and membrane by the use of adsorbant tissues above the membrane so that the DNA bands exit the gel and adhere to the membrane in the same planar positions that they occupied within the gel. The aim of this technique is to form a replica 'image' of the contents of the agarose gel on the surface of the membrane by transferring the contents in a neatly rectilinear fashion. The DNA image may then be 'fixed' by various reactions that covalently bind it to the membrane. The DNA image is then positionally stable while being highly accessible to probes and other reagents, i.e. the DNA is reactive with the same positional information that it had in the original gel.

**Spindle apparatus:** This is a structure that forms up within the cell duting mitosis. It is composed of contractile threads of protein that attach to the centromeres of chromosomes and draw them to the poles of the cell after the centromeres have parted.

**Steric:** An adjective used by molecular scientists to describe how molecular shapes fit into each other or around each other when shape and the simple occupation of space is the main consideration, e.g. steric hindrance might be used to describe a situation when a reaction of some sort has been hindered because some unreactive but bulky part of a molecule has got in the way of a reactant's approach.

**Stringency:** Refers to how much the regime of salt concentration and temperature stabilizes the double helices being formed during the technique of hybridization of single stranded nucleic acids into double stranded helices. (*See* hybridization.) During the process of formation of nucleic acid hybrid molecules, conditions of temperature and salt concentration are usually chosen to just stabilize the helices formed by the complementary molecules. This is choosing the conditions of maximum stringency. However, conditions may be used that allow the formation of slightly imperfect, and thus, less stable double helices. These are called conditions of lesser stringency. Conditions of lesser stringency are commonly used when comparing populations of molecules with closely related but slightly different sequences.

**Superhelicity; superhelical tension:** The DNA helix can be torsionally stressed so that it forms massive 'writhe' loops or, alternatively, slightly changes the number of base pairs per turn of the helix, a change of 'twist'. Superhelicity can only be enforced on a DNA molecule when it is totally free of single strand breaks and/or its ends are prevented from rotating and releasing the tension-energy. Superhelicity is usually expressed as a simultaneous change in both twist and writhe. The relative degree to which it is expressed in both or either of these phenomena is a function of the DNA sequence and of various physical factors such as temperature and salt concentration around the molecule.

**Telomere:** The natural terminus of a chromosome. A stable chromatin terminus.

**Template:** In the context of nucleic acid synthesis, the template strand is the nucleic acid strand that is being copied. The template strand is thus not changing in length during the synthetic reactions copying it. The new strand, the strand that is being synthesized, is complementary to the 'copied' strand, not identical to it. The new strand has the active 3'OH group or priming end that is accepting the incoming nucleotides.

**Topoisomerase:** The general name for enzymes that change the degree of superhelical coiling or tension in a DNA molecule. Some are merely passive and relax the superhelical tensions (e.g. Topo I) some are active and use energy from adenosine triphosphate to put superhelical tension into a DNA molecule (e.g. Topo II).

**Trailer sequences:** A term with a number of usages depending on context. In its most common usage it refers to the short stretch of base sequence that is located at the region of the gene or message RNA, just after the site for the termination of translation. It may have a large section of poly A attached to it. It is thus the sequence that occurs between the termination of translation and the processed end of the message. Note; the termination of transcription, which might be thought to be the end of the message, is often not the end of the message because, after transcription, some of the end of the primary transcript may be processed off and is then often replaced with a section of poly A.

**Transcript:** The RNA that has been copied from the DNA gene by the enzyme RNA polymerase. The primary transcript is the unmodified RNA as it comes off the gene, before it has undergone any of the changes that are usually referred to as 'messenger processing'.

**Transcriptase:** Another name for the RNA polymerase that produces primary transcripts. (*See* transcription).

**Transcription:** Refers to the primary process in the sequence of processes that lead to gene expression. Transcription involves an enzyme called 'RNA-polymerase' or 'transcriptase'. This enzyme makes an RNA copy of that section of the DNA that is to be expressed. This RNA copy of the DNA gene is then further used to express the gene's information. This copying of DNA sequences into RNA sequences is referred to as Transcription. (*See* translation for the next step.)

**Transcriptionally active gene:** A gene that is being transcribed. (*See* transcription).

**Translation:** The term used to describe the process of reading an M-RNA and converting its nucleotide-sequence-information into a sequence of amino acids (not to be confused with 'nick-translation', where the word of translation has an entirely different usage and meaning.)

**Transpositional activity:** (*See* transposons).

**Transposons:** Base sequences within DNA that are notable for being able to reproduce themselves and insert copies of themselves in other sections of the same genome. Some of them are viewed as a sophisticated type of molecular parasite or symbiont. A sequence that has this ability to insert copies of itself elsewhere is said to have 'transpositional activity'.

**Virus:** An infective entity, conventionally regarded as having life when it is within a host and being regarded as non-living when outside of the host cell. When moving between hosts it typically consists of a core of genetic information in the form of DNA or RNA which is protected by a protein coat. This is the simplest case and there are many types of virus that are more complex. More complex virions have multiple coats and may have complex coats containing phospholipids as well as proteins. A true virus has no metabolism outside of its host's cell. Within the host cell, the viral genetic information overrules the host information and subjects the host cell to the task of reproducing the viral information and the appropriate coat proteins to protect the newly replicated viral information. The host cell may or may not die or become exhausted during this process of molecular exploitation.

**Virion:** The plural of virus.

**VNTR:** Variable number tandem repeats. A literal description of the internal arrangement of a class of repetitive DNA. The term strictly fits both the class that is commonly found as single loci and the class that is found at many loci, the so-called minisatellites. However, the term has commonly been used in the more restricted fashion, to refer to the variable number tandem repeats that occur at one locus only. The context of usage usually makes clear whether the general meaning or the restricted meaning is implied.

# Index